M Loose & Strict Seq.
Tu Selection
W Distribution
Th Match & Hybrid
F O/A review

Other Kaplan Books on Law School Admissions

LSAT 2006 Edition Premier Program

LSAT 2006 Edition Comprehensive Program

LSAT 180

Get into Law School: A Strategic Approach

Test Prep and Admissions

LSAT®
Logic Games
Workbook

Staff of Kaplan Test Prep and Admissions

Simon & Schuster

NEW YORK · LONDON · SYDNEY · TORONTO

Kaplan Publishing
Published by SIMON & SCHUSTER

Rockefeller Center
1230 Avenue of the Americas
New York, NY 10020

Contributing Editor: Ben Baron
Editorial Director: Jennifer Farthing
Project Editor: Eileen McDonnell
Production Manager: Michael Shevlin
Content Manager: Patrick Kennedy
Interior Page Layout: Dave Chipps
Cover Design: Mark Weaver

Manufactured in the United States of America.
Published simultaneously in Canada.

10 9 8 7 6 5 4 3 2 1

January 2006
ISBN-13: 978-0-7432-8424-0
ISBN-10:   0-7432-8424-0

For information regarding special discounts for bulk purchases, please contact Simon & Schuster Special Sales at 1-800-456-6798 or business@simonandschuster.com.

Table of Contents

How to Use This Book

Welcome to Kaplan's LSAT Logic Games Workbook. You have purchased the most comprehensive book on the market that focuses exclusively on the Logic Games section of the LSAT. Kaplan has prepared students to take standardized tests for over 60 years. Our team of researchers and editors knows more about preparing for the LSAT than anyone else, and you'll find their accumulated knowledge here.

This book is designed to benefit those who hope to significantly increase their LSAT scores by improving Logic Games performance. You may have already taken the LSAT, or at least one or more simulated LSATs, and you may be comfortable with your skills in Logical Reasoning and Reading Comprehension, but need to boost your Logic Game speed or accuracy in order to get into the school of your choice.

If you want a book that covers the entire LSAT, we recommend Kaplan's *LSAT 2006 Edition Premier Program* or *LSAT 2006 Edition Comprehensive Program*. If you're confident in all test sections, but want to get additional practice with the hardest questions in the hope of earning a perfect score, try Kaplan's *LSAT 180*.

PART ONE: GETTING STARTED

In Part One of this book, you'll find background information on the different sections of the test, what they cover, and how the test is scored. The first step to a higher score is to be sure you know exactly what you can expect. Next comes a brief introduction to the six types of Logic Games, the question types, how to recognize them, and the Kaplan Method for handling them, along with some basic strategies and principles. If you have already used one of Kaplan's *LSAT 2006* programs, this material will be familiar; we repeat it here for ease of reference and for those who have not had the benefit of those programs.

PART TWO: GAMES AND STRATEGIES

Once you have the big picture, it's time to focus on the specifics of the six different types of Logic Games—that's Part Two. We dedicate a chapter to each, examining its variations, how to set up your scratchwork, the question types you'll encounter on each, and exactly how to approach them. Everything is demonstrated using test-like sample games and questions.

PART THREE: PRACTICE LOGIC GAMES SECTIONS

When you are comfortable with the Kaplan Method and the many strategies offered for handling different game and question types, you'll want to try them out with more questions. The two practice test sections contained in Part Three are followed by detailed explanations. As you work through these, look for patterns—question types or game types that you tend to find easy or difficult, or tend to score well or badly on. Note your areas of strength, but focus the bulk of your study time on your areas of weakness. With sufficient practice, you'll be ready for anything that could appear on test day.

KAPLAN
Test Prep and Admissions

PART ONE

Logic Games Overview

Chapter 1: **Getting Started**

- The LSAT
- Logic Games
- Logic Game Types and Skills
- Question Types

The LSAT is unlike any other test, and Logic Games is the LSAT section test takers find the least familiar. Most tests you've encountered required you to know a certain body of facts, formulas, theorems, or other acquired knowledge. The LSAT Logic Games test data management and analytical thinking skills—all you'll be asked to do is think, thoroughly, quickly, and strategically.

You already have these skills, but you probably haven't acquired the know-how to use them to your best advantage in the rarified atmosphere of a standardized skills-based test.

That's where test preparation comes in. You can't study for a skills-based test, but you can and must prepare for it. Every strategy and method you'll learn and practice in this Workbook is designed to improve your timing, build your confidence, and save your energy on test day. Kaplan's LSAT program will teach you to tailor your existing deductive and analytical skills to the idiosyncratic tasks required by the LSAT.

THE LSAT

The LSAT consists of five multiple-choice sections: two Logical Reasoning sections, one Logic Games section, one Reading Comprehension section, and one unscored "experimental" section that will look exactly like one of the other multiple-choice sections. At the end of the test, there will be a Writing Sample section in which you'll have to write a short essay. Here's how the sections break down.

Section	Number of Questions	Minutes
Logical Reasoning	24–26	35
Logical Reasoning	24–26	35
Logic Games	23–24	35
Reading Comprehension	26–28	35
"Experimental"	24–28	35
Writing Sample	n/a	35

The five multiple-choice sections can appear in any order; the Writing Sample comes last. There's a 10 or 15 minute break between the third and fourth sections of the test.

For the most up-to-date information about the test, request the *LSAT/LSDAS Registration & Information Book* from LSAC by calling (215) 968-1001. You must register in advance, and the earlier you register, the better your chances of getting your first or second choice test center.

How the LSAT Is Scored

Logic Games accounts for just under 25 percent of your total LSAT score. You'll receive only one score for the test, ranging between 120 and 180. Here's how they'll calculate it.

There are roughly 101 scored multiple-choice questions on each exam:

- About 50 from the two Logical Reasoning sections
- About 24 from the Logic Games section
- About 27 from the Reading Comprehension section

Your **raw score**, the number of questions that you answer correctly, will be multiplied by a scoring formula (different for each test, to accommodate differences in difficulty level) to yield the **scaled score**—the one that will fall somewhere in that 120–180 range—which is reported to the schools.

Because the test is graded on a largely preset curve, the scaled score will always correspond to a certain percentile, which will also be given on your score report. A score of 160, for instance, corresponds roughly to the 80th percentile, meaning that 80 percent of test takers scored at or below your level.

All scored questions are worth the same amount—one raw point—and there's no penalty for guessing. That means that you should always fill in an answer for every question, whether you get to that question or not!

LOGIC GAMES

There are 23–24 questions in the Logic Games (a.k.a. Analytical Reasoning) section, almost always based on 4 games with 5–7 questions each. They require an ability to reason clearly and deductively from a given set of rules or restrictions, all under tight time restrictions. Games are highly susceptible to systematic technique and the proper use of scratchwork.

The section tests your command of detail, your formal deductive abilities, your understanding of how rules limit and order behavior, and your ability to cope with many pieces of data simultaneously to solve problems.

Here's a sample:

> Directions: Each group of questions is based on a set of conditions. You may wish to draw a rough sketch to help you answer some of the questions. Choose the best answer for each question and fill in the corresponding space on your answer sheet.

> Questions 2–3

> Five workers—Mona, Patrick, Renatta, Saffie, and Will—are scheduled to clean apartments on five days of a single week, Monday through Friday. There are three cleaning shifts available each day—a morning shift, an afternoon shift, and an evening shift. No more than one worker cleans on any given shift. Each worker works exactly two cleaning shifts during the week, but no one works more than one cleaning shift in a single day.

> Exactly two workers clean on each day of the week.

> Mona and Will clean on the same days of the week.

> Patrick does not clean on any afternoon or evening shifts during the week.

> Will does not clean on any morning or afternoon shifts during the week.

> Mona cleans on two consecutive days of the week.

> Saffie's second cleaning shift of the week occurs on an earlier day of the week than Mona's first cleaning shift

> 2. Which one of the following must be true?
>
> (A) Saffie cleans on Tuesday afternoon.
> (B) Patrick cleans on Monday morning.
> (C) Will cleans on Thursday evening.
> (D) Renatta cleans on Friday afternoon.
> (E) Mona cleans on Tuesday morning.

> 3. If Will does not clean on Friday, which one of the following could be false?
>
> (A) Renatta cleans on Friday.
> (B) Saffie cleans on Tuesday.
> (C) Mona cleans on Wednesday.
> (D) Saffie cleans on Monday.
> (E) Patrick cleans on Tuesday.

For question 2, the answer is (C); for 3 it's (E).

On the LSAT, you'll be answering roughly 125 multiple-choice questions (101 of which are scored) over the course of three intense hours. That's just a little over a minute per question, not counting the time required to read passages and set up games. Clearly, you have to move fast. But don't let yourself get careless. Taking control means increasing the speed only to the extent you can do so without sacrificing accuracy!

Because Logic Games is, for many students, the most time-sensitive section of the test, it's also the section in which you can improve your timing the most.

LOGIC GAME TYPES AND SKILLS

Although Logic Games can contain a wide variety of situations and scenarios, there are six common types:

- Relative Sequencing
- Strict Sequencing
- Selection
- Distribution
- Matching
- Hybrids

Certain skills are required again and again, with variations on the following being the most common:

Sequencing

Logic Games requiring **sequencing** skills—putting entities in order—have long been a test-makers' favorite. There are two types: **relative** (or "loose") sequencing and **strict** sequencing, each covered in its own chapter. In a typical sequencing game, you may be asked to arrange the cast of characters numerically from left to right, from top to bottom, in days of the week, in a circle, and so on. The sequence may be a matter of degree—say, ranking the eight smartest test takers from one to eight. Or it may be based on time, such as one that involves the order of shows broadcast on a radio station. Occasionally there are two or even three orderings to keep track of in a single game.

Grouping

Distribution and **selection** are two types of grouping games, each covered in its own chapter. In a pure **grouping** game, unlike sequencing, there's no call for putting the entities in order. Instead, you'll select a smaller group from the initial group or distribute the entities into more than one subgroup. You're not concerned with what order the entities are in, but rather who's in, who's out, and who can and cannot be with whom in various subgroups.

Matching

As the name implies, **matching** games ask you to match up various characteristics about a group of entities—often many characteristics at once. A game may involve three animals, each assigned a name, a color, and a particular size. It's no wonder test takers get bogged down in these types—there's a lot to keep track of. Some feel that these games bombard them with information. They don't know where to start. Organization is especially crucial. A table or grid can be helpful, but for some games you should rely on your instincts to organize the information efficiently based on the particulars of the game.

Distinguish each characteristic by using CAPS for one category, lowercase for another—and any other variants that work for you. If you do use a sketch, remember that thinking must always precede writing. A visual representation of a mental thought process can be invaluable; scribbling thoughtlessly for the sake of getting something down on the page is useless, even detrimental.

Hybrid and Other Games

Many games are hybrids, requiring you to combine sequencing, grouping, or matching skills. In hybrid games, expect to draw a separate sketch for each action, but consider whether you can combine the sketches. Keep in mind that it's not necessary to attach a strict name to every game you encounter. It really doesn't matter if you categorize a game as a sequencing game with a grouping element or as a grouping game with a sequencing element, as long as you're comfortable with both sets of skills.

Very rarely, other formats appear on a test. We'll discuss some of these in Part 2.

QUESTION TYPES

Within each game, only a few distinct question types will occur:

Acceptability Questions

If the question asks which choice would be "acceptable," one answer choice will satisfy all the rules; each wrong choice will violate at least one rule. These can be a good choice to answer if you're running out of time, since they can be answered without setting up the game first.

New "If" Questions

When the question adds a new "if" condition (a hypothetical), treat the "if" as a new rule and draw a new sketch if necessary.

Complete and Accurate List Questions

Answer the other questions first; their sketches will help you answer these. Use the choices to decide what possibilities you have to test.

Could vs. Must Questions

To answer, focus on the nature of the right and wrong answer choices:

IIf the question reads	The right answer will be
Which one of the following statements could be true?	a statement that could be true, and the four wrong choices will be statements that definitely cannot be true (that is, statements that must be false)
Which one of the following statements cannot be true?	a statement that cannot be true, and the four wrong choices will be statements that either must be true or merely could be true
Which one of the following statements must be true?	a statement that must be true, and the four wrong choices will be statements that either cannot be true or merely could be true
All of the following statements could be true EXCEPT…	a statement that cannot be true, and the four wrong choices will be statements that either could be true or even must be true
All of the following statements must be true EXCEPT…	a statement that either cannot be true, or merely could be true, and the four wrong choices will be statements that must be true
Which one of the following statements could be false?	a statement that cannot be true or could be true or false, and the four wrong choices will be statements that must be true
Which one of the following statements must be false?	a statement that cannot be true, and the four wrong choices will be statements that either must be true or merely could be true

Now that you know the basics and what you can expect, learn (or refresh your memory of) some basic principles that apply to all Logic Games and the Kaplan Method for handling them before moving on to Part Two.

Chapter 2:
Kaplan's Method and Strategies

- Kaplan's 5-Step Method
- Six Basic Logic Games Principles
- Two Essential Formal Logic Principles

Now that you have some Logic Games background, you're ready to marshal that knowledge into a systematic approach to games. Trial and error with the answer choices should be your last resort, not your first.

If you have already used Kaplan's *LSAT 2006 Edition* some of this material will be familiar; we summarize it here for those who have not—and for ease of reference.

KAPLAN'S 5-STEP METHOD FOR LOGIC GAMES

Step 1. Overview

Carefully read the game's introduction and rules to establish the situation, the entities involved, the action, and the number limits governing the game ("SEAL"). Make a mental picture of the situation, and let it guide you as you create a sketch or other scratchwork, to help you keep track of the rules and handle new information.

Step 2. Sketch

Developing good scratchwork will speed your performance on Logic Games. Although some games aren't amenable to scratchwork, for most games you'll find it helpful to create a master sketch that encapsulates the game's information in an easy-to-follow form. This helps to solidify in your mind the action of the game, the rules, and whatever deductions you made, and provides a quick reference.

Keep scratchwork simple—you get no points for elaborate, painstakingly drawn diagrams, and the less time you spend drawing the more time you'll have for thinking and answering questions.

Step 3. Rules

Not all rules are equal. Focus most on the concrete ones and the ones that involve the greatest number of the entities or otherwise have the greatest impact on the action. These are also the rules to turn to first whenever you're stuck on a question and don't know how to set off the chain of deduction. As you think through the meaning and implications of each rule, you have three choices. You can:

- Build it directly into your sketch
- Jot down the rule in shorthand
- Underline or circle rules that don't lend themselves to the first two techniques

Step 4. Deduction

Look for <u>common</u> elements among the rules; that's what will lead you to make deductions. Based on what you already know, what else *must* be true? Treat these deductions as additional rules, good for the whole game. If you can't make a single deduction by combining rules, you probably missed or misinterpreted something—check again. Be on the lookout for "blocks"—entities that must be in fixed relationships to each other—and "floaters"—entities not covered by any of the rules that can go in any open position.

Step 5. Questions

Skipping difficult questions is *strategic* (see chapter 3). Get the points you're sure of before spending time on others that may be less certain. Read the question stems carefully, taking special notice of words such as *must, could, cannot, not, impossible,* and *except.* Use hypotheticals to set off a new chain of deduction.

Don't worry about recalling all of this now, as long as you get the general idea. You'll be reviewing each step in every chapter of Part Two, with special focus on its application to each game type.

SIX BASIC LOGIC GAMES PRINCIPLES

For many students, Logic Games is the most time-sensitive section of the test. If you could spend hours methodically trying out every choice, you'd probably get everything right. On the LSAT, it's all about efficiency. And that brings you to the first, and somewhat paradoxical, Logic Games principle:

Slow Down To Go Faster

Spending a little extra time thinking through the stimulus, the action of the game, and the rules, helps you to recognize key issues and make important deductions that will save you time. Games are structured so that, in order to answer the questions quickly and correctly, you need to search out relevant pieces of information that combine to form valid new **deductions** (inferences). You can either do this once, up front, or you can piece together the same basic deductions for each question. That is the basis of the first four steps of Kaplan's Method.

Learn to Spot "Limited Options"

If a game breaks down into only two or three possible results, work out those results and you'll fly through the questions. Limited options can appear in any game type, wherever you see one entity or a bloc of entities that are restricted to one of two locations, or where arithmetic limitations force only two distinct possibilities. In these cases, it often makes sense to draw both options into the master sketch, and then see if the other rules fill in all or most of the blanks. New "if" questions may mean only one option can apply. You'll see examples in each chapter and practice test section.

No "Best" Choice

In Logical Reasoning and Reading Comprehension, the correct answer is the "best" choice, so you have to read all choices. The answers in Logic Games—like answers to math questions—are objectively correct or incorrect. So when you find an answer that's definitely right, have the confidence to circle it and move on, without checking the others. This is one way to improve your timing on the section.

Don't overcorrect yourself; just because an answer comes easily (when you know how to approach it) doesn't mean it's wrong.

Know What a Rule Means, Not Just What It Says

The LSAT measures critical thinking, and virtually every sentence in a Logic Game has to be filtered through some sort of analytical process to be of any use. So it's not enough just to copy a rule off the page (or shorthand it); it's imperative that you *understand* the rule thoroughly and think through any implications it might have. And don't limit this to the indented rules; statements in the stimulus are very often rules that warrant the same consideration.

Set Off New Chains of Deduction

When a question stem offers a **hypothetical**—an *if-clause* offering information pertaining only to that question—use it to set off a new chain of deductions. Only if you're entirely stuck should you resort to trial and error. Instead, incorporate the new piece of information into your view of the game, creating a new sketch if it helps. Apply the rules and any previous deductions to the new information in order to set off a new chain of deductions. Then follow through until you've taken the new information as far as it can go, just as you took the game and rules as far as you could before moving on to the questions.

Know the Question Types

You must have a solid command of the limited number of Logic Games question stems that were introduced in the first chapter and are reviewed throughout this Workbook: acceptability, new "if," complete and accurate list, and "could" vs. "must" questions. When you take a few seconds to think through what kind of statements would be the right and wrong answers to a particular question, your work becomes more efficient.

TWO ESSENTIAL FORMAL LOGIC PRINCIPLES

Two principals of formal logic are tested frequently in Logic Games, so it's best to get a solid handle on them before you start. Look at an example:

> Ian will go to the movies only when his wife is out of town. He'll go to a matinee alone, but will see a movie at night only if accompanied by Ezra and Mabel.

This scenario is made up of a couple of formal logic statements, each fraught with its own implications.

The Contrapositive

The contrapositive of any *if/then* statement is formed by reversing and negating the terms. The general model goes like this:

Original: If X, then Y.

Contrapositive: If not Y, then not X.

For any *if/then* statement the contrapositive will be equally valid. Now apply the contrapositive to the following statement:

> Ian will go to the movies only when his wife is out of town.

You can translate this into an if/then statement without changing its original meaning:

> If Ian goes to the movies, then his wife must be out of town.

If that statement is true, what statement must also be true? Its contrapositive:

> If Ian's wife is not out of town, then Ian does not go to the movies.

Warning 1: Wrong answers often result from either forgetting to switch around the terms before negating them, or negating only one of the terms. If Ian doesn't go to the movies, you can't infer anything about whether his wife is in or out of town. If Ian's wife is out of town, you can't tell whether Ian goes to the movies or not.

Warning 2: If one part of a formal logic statement contains a compound phrase, both parts of the phrase must be taken into account:

> Ian will see a movie at night only if accompanied by Ezra and Mabel.

If/then Translation: If Ian sees a movie at night, then he's accompanied by Ezra and Mabel.

Contrapositive: If Ian is not with Ezra *and* Mabel, then he does not see a movie at night.

Correct Interpretation: If either Ezra or Mabel is missing, then Ian doesn't see a night movie.

Warning 3: If one part of a formal logic statement is *already* negative, the same rules that apply to math apply to forming the contrapositive: negating a negative yields a positive. If the sun is shining, then Samantha does not wear green. What is the contrapositive?

Contrapositive: ~~If~~ *Samantha is wearing green, then the sun is not shining* [handwritten]

You should have written something along the lines of: If Samantha is wearing green (if she's not *not* wearing green), then the sun is not shining.

Necessary versus Sufficient Conditions

For success in formal logic, it's crucial that you distinguish clearly between necessary and sufficient conditions. Consider these two statements:

Contrapositive/sufficient [handwritten]

- If I yell loudly at my cat Adrian, he will run away.
- The TV will work only if it is plugged in.

My yelling loudly is a **sufficient** condition for Adrian to run away. It's all I need to do to get the cat to run; it's sufficient. But it's **not necessary**. My cat might run if I throw water at him, even if I don't yell loudly.

The TV's being plugged in, on the other hand, is a **necessary** condition for it to work. My TV won't work without it. But it's **not sufficient**. Other conditions must apply for the TV to work (for example, the electricity to the house must be on).

Adrian will not run away if I don't yell loudly at him [handwritten]

Recognizing these distinctions is vital to knowing what kinds of deductions you can and can't make. A <u>sufficient condition</u> is essentially an *if/then* statement, which means that the <u>contrapositive</u> can be used.

- If I yell loudly at my cat Adrian, he will run away.

If that statement is true, which one of the following must also be true?

• If I don't yell loudly at my cat Adrian, he will not run away.	valid ☐	not valid ☐
• If my cat Adrian has run away, then I yelled loudly at him.	valid ☐	not valid ☐
• If my cat Adrian has not run away, <u>then</u> I did not yell loudly at him.	valid ☒	not valid ☐

The third statement, the contrapositive, is the only one of the three that's valid based on the original. My yelling loudly is sufficient to make Adrian run away, but it's not necessary; it's not the only possible thing that will make him run. He might run if I squirt him with a water gun, so the first two statements are not valid.

Necessary conditions, on the other hand, are usually signaled by the words *only if* (or similar words or phrases like *only when)*:

- The TV will work only if it is plugged in.

If that statement is true, which of the following statements must also be true?

- If my TV is plugged in, it will work.   valid ☐   not valid ☐
- If my TV is not working, then it must not be plugged in.   valid ☐   not valid ☐
- If my TV is working, then it must be plugged in.   valid ☑   not valid ☐
- If my TV is not plugged in, then it won't work.   valid ☑   not valid ☐

The original statement means that it is *sufficient* that the TV is working to know that it *must* be plugged in—but not *vice versa*. The TV won't work without plugging it in, but plugging it in is not a guarantee that the TV will work. Maybe the picture tube is broken. So the first two statements are *not* valid based on the original statement, while the last two are.

You'll have a chance to see these major Logic Games principles in action when you review the explanations to the games in the following chapters and in the practice Logic Games sections at the back of this book.

Chapter 3: **Take Control of the Test**

Don't forget to practice general testing strategies while you focus on Logic Games. If you took a test in college and got a quarter of the questions wrong, you'd probably receive a pretty low grade. But on the LSAT, you can get a quarter of the questions wrong and still score higher than the 80th percentile. The test is geared so that only the very best test takers are able to finish every section. So don't let one bad game or passage ruin an entire section, and don't let what you consider a below-par performance on one section ruin your performance on the rest of the test.

If you feel you've done poorly on a section, it could be the experimental. And even if it's not, chances are it's just a difficult section—a factor that will already be figured into the scoring curve. Remain calm; do your best on each section and, once a section is over, forget about it and move on. Losing a few extra points won't do you in, but losing your head will.

TEST EXPERTISE

It's one thing to answer a Logic Games question correctly, and quite another to answer 24 of them correctly in 35 minutes. Time pressure affects virtually every test taker.

On most tests you take in school, you wouldn't dream of not making at least an attempt at every one of the questions. If a question seems particularly difficult, you spend significantly more time on it, since you'll probably earn more points for correctly answering a hard question.

Not so on the LSAT. Every LSAT question, no matter how hard, is worth a single point. And since there are so many questions to do in so little time, it's foolish to spend three minutes getting a point for a hard question and then not have time to get a couple of quick points from two easy questions later in the section.

Given this combination—limited time and all questions being equal in weight—you've got to develop a way of handling the test sections to make sure you get as many points as you can, as quickly and easily as you can. The following are the test strategies that will help you do that.

Answer Questions in the Order That's Best for You

Recognize and deal first with the questions, games, and passages that are easier and more familiar to you. Temporarily skip those that promise to be difficult and time consuming—come back to them at the end, and if you run out of time, you're much better off not getting to questions you may have had difficulty with, rather than missing easier ones. (Since there's no wrong-answer penalty, always fill in an answer to every question on the test, whether you get to it or not.)

Remember, LSAT questions, games, and passages are not presented in order of difficulty; in fact, the test makers scatter easy and difficult questions throughout the section, in effect rewarding those who get to the end. If you find sequencing games particularly easy, seek out the sequencing game on the Logic Games section and do it first.

Know That There Will Be Difficult Questions

It's imperative that you remain calm and composed while working through a section. Don't be rattled by one hard logic game or reading passage. Expect to find at least one difficult passage or game on every section; you won't be the only one to have trouble with it. The test is curved to take the tough material into account. Understand that part of the test maker's goal is to reward those who keep their composure.

Grid In Answers Efficiently

You not only have to pick the right answers, you also have to mark those right answers on the answer grid in an efficient and accurate way. It sounds simple, but it's extremely important: Don't make mistakes filling out your answer grid! When time is short, it's easy to get confused going back and forth between your test book and your grid. Here are a few methods for avoiding mistakes:

1. **Always Circle Answers You Choose:** Circle the correct answers in your test booklet, but don't transfer the answers to the grid right away. That wastes too much time, especially if you're doing a lot of skipping around. Circling your answers in the test book will also make it easier to check your grid against your book.

2. **Grid About Five Answers at Once:** Transfer your answers at the end of each Logic Game. You won't keep breaking your concentration, so you'll save time and improve accuracy.

3. **Always Circle Questions You Skip:** Put a big circle in your test book around the number of any question you skip (or circle the whole question). When you go back, it will be easy to locate them. And if you accidentally skip a box on the grid, you can more easily check your grid against your book to see where you went wrong.

4. **Save Time at the End for a Final Grid Check:** Take time at the end of every section to check your grid. Make sure you've got an oval filled in for each question in the section. Remember, a blank grid has no chance of earning a point.

LOGIC GAMES SECTION MANAGEMENT

Managing the Section

First, and most important, preview the section. Literally flip through the pages, having a glance at each game in order to decide which games look the easiest and most familiar to you. Previewing is not foolproof; a game that looks fairly straightforward at first glance could easily turn out to be daunting. But it works more often than not.

The goal is to tackle the games in order of difficulty, from easiest to hardest. But if you achieve nothing more than saving the hardest game for last, the strategy is a winner.

The best way to know which games may be difficult is to be familiar with the game types, and to have a sense of which types you're strongest in.

A game that doesn't look familiar at all could be an oddball game—a good candidate to postpone. But don't be scared off by games with a lot of rules; sometimes this works to your advantage. The more rules they give you, the more definite and concrete the game is, and the easier it will be to answer the questions. Games with few rules often turn out to be tough because they're inherently ambiguous.

Pacing

Four games in 35 minutes means roughly 8.75 minutes per game. Remember, this is an average—games that are harder or have more questions should take a little more time than others.

The last thing you want is to have time called on a section before you've gotten to half the questions. It's essential, therefore, that you pace yourself. Don't spend exactly one-and-one-quarter minutes on every question. But you should have a sense of the average time you have to do each question, so you know when you're exceeding the limit and should start to move faster.

Keeping track of time is also important for guessing. It pays to leave time at the end to guess on any questions you couldn't answer. For instance, let's say you never get a chance to do the last logic game in the section. If you leave the grids for those questions blank, you'll get no points for that entire game. If, on the other hand, you give yourself a little time at the end to fill in a guess for each of those questions, you'll have a very good chance of getting lucky on one or two questions.

Once you've mastered Kaplan's Method and strategies, build gradually to the point where you're ready to take full-length sections. First attempt one game in 8–9 minutes. Next, try two games in 16–18 minutes. When you're ready to move on, try three games in 24–27 minutes, until finally you can reliably handle a full four-game section in 35 minutes.

Finally, remember the way the test makers test efficiency. They're crafty—they'll sometimes throw an intentionally time-consuming question at the end of a game, possibly one involving a rule change that requires you to backtrack and set the game up all over again. When this happens, they may not be testing who's smart enough to get the right answer, but rather who's clever enough to skip the troublesome question in order to devote precious time to the next game, with a possible payoff of six or seven new points.

KAPLAN
Test Prep and Admissions

PART TWO

Game Types and Strategies

Chapter 4:
Relative Sequencing Games

As you saw in chapter 1, there are two types of sequencing games. The first type, the subject of this chapter, is the **relative** (sometimes called "loose") sequencing game, in which your job is to rank the entities only in relation to one another. The rules deal with the relationships between different entities, not between entities and specific slots.

GAME 1: THE METHOD

Game 1 offers a good example of the variety of question types and sequencing games issues you may encounter. Follow along, focusing on how Kaplan's 5-Step Method is applied. This will start your development of the organized, systematic approach that is the key to Logic Games success.

> <u>Questions 1-6</u>
> A survey of eight polka albums—F, H, J, L, N, P, S, and T—ranked them in order of popularity, the first being the most popular and the eighth being the least popular. There were no two albums that shared the same ranking. The order of popularity is consistent with the following:
>
> S and F are each less popular than T.
>
> S is more popular than J.
>
> L and N are each less popular than F.
>
> H and L are each less popular than J.
>
> P is less popular than L.
>
> P is not eighth.

Step 1: Overview

Read the game's introduction and rules carefully to establish SEAL (situation, entities, actions, and limits).

Situation: A survey of polka albums

Entities: Eight polka albums—F, H, J, L, N, P, T, and S

Action: To sequence the polka albums

Limitations: 8 albums, 8 positions, and no ties

Step 2: Sketch

Remember the first general principle of Logic Games: slow down to go fast. Let your overview guide you to create a sketch or other helpful scratchwork. When planning scratchwork for sequencing, consider whether the game is best drawn horizontally or vertically.

To sketch this game, think of the rankings in terms of top to bottom (with the top being the most popular album and the bottom being least popular), as they would appear in a magazine report, rather than left to right. (Left to right works too, but many students find it easier to envision activities like ranking as being more suited to vertical sketches.)

You may have started writing eight spaces, numbered 1 through 8. Looking at the rules, however, tells you those spaces won't help you. The rules are all "loose sequencing rules." As such, you won't be able to make use of this typical sequencing sketch.

Step 3: Rules

Know what each rule means, not just what it says, and remember that what a rule doesn't say can be as important as what it says.

The following is a list of the key issues in sequencing games, each followed by one or more corresponding rule formats.

Typical Selection Game Issues

Issue	Wording of Rule
Which entities are concretely placed in the ordering?	X is third.
Which entities are forbidden from a specific position in the ordering?	Y is not fourth.
Which entities are next to, adjacent to, or immediately preceding or following one another?	X and Y are consecutive. X is next to Y. No event comes between X and Y. X and Y are consecutive in the ordering.
Which entities cannot be next to, adjacent to, or immediately following one another?	X does not immediately precede or follow Z. X is not immediately before or after Z. At least one event comes between X and Z. X and Z are not consecutive in the sequence.
How far apart in the ordering are two particular entities?	Exactly two events come between X and Q.
What is the relative position of two entities in the ordering?	Q comes before T in the sequence. T comes after Q in the sequence.

Start by visualizing each rule. The first condition in Game 1 states that albums S and F are both less popular than album T. You aren't told anything about the amount of space between the entities, just the order. Visualize T above both S and F. Remember, you don't know anything about the relationship between S and F, just that they are both ranked below T:

The second condition states that S is more popular than J:

The next condition states that both L and N are less popular than F:

The next condition places both H and L below J:

The next to last condition states that P is less popular than L:

The last condition states that P is not eighth. Note this on your scratchwork, perhaps with "P ≠ 8" or "P not last."

Step 4: Deductions

Can you make any deductions? If you connected the S from rule 2 to the S in rule 1, this is exactly what you were doing! As long as you keep the given relationships intact, you can combine all of these parts into a sketch:

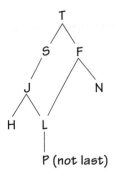

Which is higher, F or P? F is higher, and you know you can determine the relationship between them because you can travel from one to the other in one direction. Now look at F and H. Can you say that F is higher than H? No! To go from F to H, you would have to "travel" along the tree in more than one direction (up then down, or down then up); doing so means there is no definite relationship. F could be ranked higher than H, or H could be higher than F. Also note that all eight albums are bound to some condition or another, therefore there are no "floaters" or entities that are unrestricted. Now move on to the questions.

Step 5: Questions

When you've taken the scenario and rules as far as you can, you can move on to the questions. Before test day, be sure you have a solid command of the limited number of question types that will appear in the Logic Games section. Think through what kind of statements would be the right and wrong answers to a particular question, and your work becomes more efficient.

Here's the first question for Game 1. Take a few moments to consider how you would approach it.

1. Which of the following could be the order of the albums listed from most popular to least popular?

   (A) T, F, S, L, J, N, P, H
   (B) S, T, F, N, J, L, P, H
   (C) T, S, J, H, F, P, L, N
   (D) T, S, J, F, L, N, P, H
   (E) T, F, N, S, J, L, H, P

Complete and Accurate List Questions

To begin with, note that this could be viewed as a complete and accurate list question, since all entities are taken into account in each answer choice. If so, your strategy would be to save this question for last, since your work on the other questions could help.

Saving Time

But when—as may occur on your test—a question might be either of these two types, treating it as an acceptability question is the simpler approach.

Acceptability Questions

So, this is an acceptability question. All that is asked is which choice violates any of the rules. This type of question is the only exception to the general prohibition against looking back at the original rules. Use the rules as a checklist. Apply each individual condition to each choice and eliminate any that violates that condition. Choice (B) violates the first condition by making S more popular than T, therefore this choice must be incorrect. Rules 2 and 3 don't help eliminate any choices, but (A) violates the fourth rule by making L more popular than J, and is therefore incorrect. Choice (C) gives P a higher popularity rating than L, a violation of the fifth condition. Finally, (E) violates the sixth condition by giving P the eighth or lowest rating. The only acceptable order of popularity is (D).

New "If" Questions

When the question adds a new "if" condition (a hypothetical), treat it as a new rule and draw a new sketch if necessary. Do not add it to the original, which you will need for other questions.

2. If F is more popular than S and H is more popular than P, then which of the following must be true of the ranking of polka albums?

    (A) H is sixth.
    (B) L is sixth.
    (C) L is seventh.
    (D) N is eighth.
    (E) P is eighth.

This "if" question places two additional conditions on the order of popularity for this question alone. The first condition places F above S. The second condition places H above P. Re-draw your sketch to incorporate these new conditions:

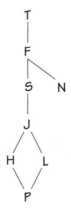

Since S must be more popular than four other entities (J, H, L, and P), and less popular than two (F and T), this leaves N to "float" somewhere below F's popularity. Now, since H and L (along with J, S, F, and T) are more popular than P, and since P CANNOT be the least popular album, this leaves only N to cover the least popular spot. Therefore, (D) is correct. Since both H and L could be in the sixth position, (A) and (B) don't have to be true. Also, if L were in the seventh position, then P would have to be in the last position, which is a violation of the last condition, and therefore both (C) and (E) are incorrect.

3. If J is more popular than F, then each of the following must be true EXCEPT

   (A) T is first.
   (B) H is fourth.
   (C) N is not fourth.
   (D) S is not third.
   (E) J is third.

This "if" question places J above F.

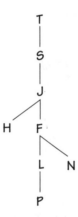

Therefore the top three albums must be T, S, and J, in that order. The question states that all the choices must be true EXCEPT one, which is the correct one. So you want to eliminate all choices that must be true. You already know that T is first and J is third, so eliminate (A) and (E). Since S is second, "S is not third" must be a true statement, so eliminate (D). Since N is less popular than F and F is less popular than J, (C)—"N is not fourth"—must be true, so eliminate (C). Choice (B), "H is fourth," is not necessarily true (and therefore is correct). H could be fourth, but it does not have to be. F could also be fourth.

Could vs. Must Questions

For these questions, start by focusing on the nature of the right and wrong answer choices. Refer back to the chart at the end of chapter 1 whenever you need to refresh your memory on the limited set of possibilities.

4. Which of the following albums CANNOT be ranked fourth?

   (A) N
   (B) L
   (C) J
   (D) F
   (E) S

For this question, you will need to refer to your original "tree" sketch. Since the question asks you for the one album that cannot be fourth, you will want to see if it is possible to place each choice in the fourth position. To be in fourth position, an entity must not have more than three entities above it, or more than four entities below it. For (A), N has only two entities above it, and none below it. N could be fourth, so it is the wrong choice. For (B), L has only one entity definitely below it, but it has four entities above it. There is no way that L could be fourth with four entities that all must precede it, and so (B) is correct. The remaining choices are possible to have in the fourth position: (C)'s J can come after T, S, and F; for (D), F can be placed after T, S, and J; and (E), S, can be placed after T, F, and N.

5. If N is more popular than J and S is less popular than F, then which one of the following could NOT be true of the ranking?

   (A) H is more popular than P.
   (B) N is the third most popular album.
   (C) S is more popular than N.
   (D) N is more popular than P.
   (E) F is the second most popular album.

This "if" question places two additional conditions on the order of popularity for this question alone. This alters the "tree" sketch only slightly. Since S is less popular than F, but F is still less popular than T, you now have a direct relationship of T...F...S in terms of popularity. Also, since N is now more popular than J, but still less popular than F, and S is still more popular than J, N and S both come between F and J.

The question asks for the one choice that must be false, so you can eliminate any choice that could be true. Since N is now placed somewhere after F but before J, the eighth position can only be taken up by H, since P cannot be eighth. Therefore H cannot be more popular than P, and (A) is correct. All remaining choices are possible.

GAME 2: PRACTICE

Game 1 provided a good review of Kaplan's 5-Step Method and of the question types you'll encounter. Applying Kaplan's Method, try the next game on your own, using the extra space provided for your scratchwork. Don't worry too much about your timing—yet.

Questions 1-6

Exactly seven students will be arranged in order from left to right for a photograph. The students will consist of three seniors—Robert, Susie, and Tom, and four juniors—Henry, Isabelle, Justin, and Kate. The following conditions apply:

> No senior can stand immediately next to another senior.
>
> Robert must be placed to the left of Justin.
>
> Justin and Isabelle must be separated from each other by exactly one student.
>
> Isabelle must be placed immediately to the left or to the right of Tom.
>
> Tom must be placed to the immediate right of Henry, unless Susie is placed to Henry's left.

1. Which of the following could be the order, from left to right, of the photograph?

    (A) Kate, Robert, Henry, Tom, Isabelle, Susie, Justin

    (B) Susie, Kate, Robert, Justin, Isabelle, Tom, Henry

    (C) Henry, Tom, Isabelle, Kate, Justin, Robert, Susie

    (D) Henry, Robert, Justin, Isabelle, Tom, Kate, Susie

    (E) Susie, Isabelle, Robert, Justin, Henry, Tom, Kate

2. If juniors cannot stand immediately next to other juniors, then which of the following must be true?

    (A) The first student on the left is Kate

    (B) A senior must stand in the middle

    (C) The fifth student from the left is Isabelle

    (D) The second student from the left is Robert

    (E) Two seniors must stand next to each other

3. If all students stand to the right of Henry, which of the following must be false?

    (A) Kate is sixth from the left

    (B) Susie is sixth from the left

    (C) Tom is second from the left

    (D) Robert stands immediately next to Justin

    (E) Justin is fourth from the left

4. If the third student from the left in the photograph is Isabelle, which one of the following could be the sixth student from the left?

    (A) Kate

    (B) Robert

    (C) Tom

    (D) Henry

    (E) Justin

5. If Susie is the fourth student from the left, which of the following could be the seventh student from the left?

    (A) Justin

    (B) Isabelle

    (C) Henry

    (D) Kate

    (E) Tom

6. Which of the following could NOT be the first student on the left?

    (A) Robert

    (B) Susie

    (C) Isabelle

    (D) Henry

    (E) Kate

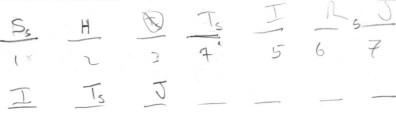

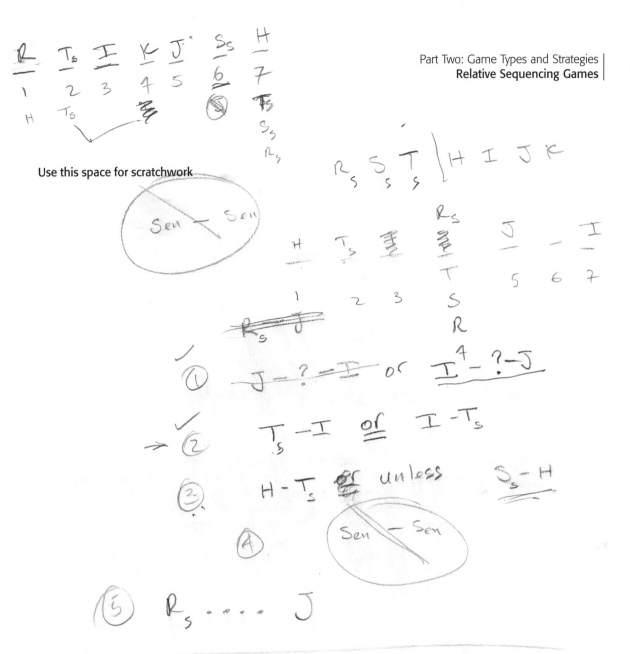

R	T_s	I	K	J	S_s	H
1	2	3	4	5	6	7
H	T_s				T_s	
					S_s	
					R_s	

Use this space for scratchwork

Sen — Sen

R_s S_s T_s | H I J K

H	T_s	I			J	I
1	2	3	T	S	5	6	7
			S	R		

R_s — J

① J - ? - I or I⁴ - ? - J

→ ② T_s - I or I - T_s

③ H - T_s or unless   S_s - H

④ Sen — Sen

⑤ R_s . . . . J

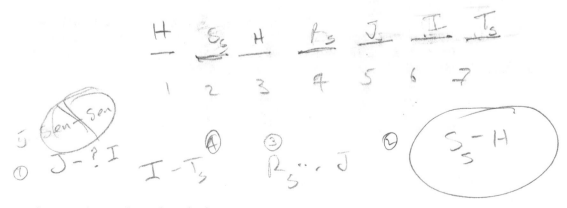

H	S_s	H	R_s	J	I	T_s
1	2	3	4	5	6	7

Sen — Sen

① J - ? I   ④ I - T_s   ③ R_s . . . J   ② S_s - H

Turn the page when you're ready to check your answers.

Game 2 Answers and Explanations

Step 1: Overview

Situation: Students taking a photograph

Entities: The students—Robert, Susie, and Tom are the seniors, and Henry, Isabelle, Justin, and Kate are the juniors

Action: Place the students in order, or sequence them, from left to right

Limitations: None—you just need to put the 7 students in 7 positions

Step 2: Sketch

You can sketch out seven places from left to right to denote the students' places, and list the entities involved in the game as well. You have both juniors and seniors, and you will need to differentiate between the two, so use ALL CAPS for seniors and lower case for juniors. Now go ahead and look at the conditions that limit the placements.

Step 3: Rules

The first rule says no senior can stand immediately next to another senior. Think through the implications of this rule: Robert and Susie cannot stand next to each other, Robert and Tom cannot stand next to each other, and Susie and Tom cannot stand next to each other. As to drawing it, a note next to your sketch reading something like "no sen sen" is probably sufficient. The second condition places Robert to the left of Justin. This means that Robert will be placed somewhere before Justin when reading the picture from left to right. You don't know the distance between the two, so "R...j" is a good way to draw it. The next condition places exactly one student between Justin and Isabelle. Note that there is no specific arrangement between Justin and Isabelle, so Justin could be to the right or left of Isabelle. "j/i ___ i/j " captures this nicely. Rule 4 says Isabelle is either to the immediate right or left of Tom. "iT or Ti" works well. The last condition is that Tom is placed to the immediate right of Henry, unless Susie is placed to the left of Henry. Be careful when you sketch this condition; "unless" conditionals can be tricky. This rule basically says that if Susie is *not* anywhere to the left of Henry (if she is to the right of him) then Tom is to the immediate right of Henry with Susie coming later. Also write down the contrapositive.

$$\text{If } h...S \rightarrow hT...S \text{ and If no } hT \rightarrow S...h$$

Saving Time

One more thing to note: nothing in these rules ties any of the entities to specific positions, so this is a fairly "loose" sequencing game. However, unlike some other loose sequencing games, you are given information about the relative distance between two different entities (there is one space between Justin and Isabelle). When you have information like this, a sketch with specific numbered blanks can come in handy.

Step 4: Deductions

Before you move on to the questions, take a look at the conditions one more time and see if you can make any deductions. Note that Kate has no conditions attached to her; this makes her a "floater." And note the interrelation between Robert, Tom, Justin, and Isabelle. Rules 2-4 tell you these four students are the major players; this will most likely play an important role in the questions. However, there is nothing else that MUST be true here, so you can move on to the questions.

___	___	___	___	___	___	___
1	2	3	4	5	6	7

jun: h, i, j, k   Sen: R, S, T

No sen sen

R ...j

j/i ___ i/j

iT or Ti

If h...S → hT...S

If no hT →S...h

Step 5: Questions

1. **A**

This is an acceptability question; apply each individual condition to each choice and eliminate those that violate that condition. Choice (C) has two seniors standing next to each other (rule 1). It also violates rule 2. (B) does not have exactly one student in between Justin and Isabelle (rule 3). (E) does not have Isabelle and Tom standing immediately next to each other, violating rule 4. And in (D), Henry is to the left of Susie, but Tom is not on Henry's immediate right. This violates the conditional rule, leaving (A) as the only order of the students that does not violate any of the conditions.

2. **B**

This "if" question stipulates that juniors can't be next to other juniors. Focus on the kind of information you are given; you don't need to figure out where individual students can stand, but only where seniors and juniors can stand. Since there are only seven spaces available, and no juniors can stand immediately next to one another, the juniors must be placed in every other position (1, 3, 5, 7). This leaves the seniors to occupy the spaces in between (2, 4, 6).

___	___	___	___	___	___	___
1	2	3	4	5	6	7
jun	sen	jun	sen	jun	sen	jun

Now, (B) becomes perfectly clear—a senior must stand in the middle. Notice that (A), (C), and (D) all mention specific students; you don't know anything specific about individual students here. (E) even goes so far as to break a rule, so that is definitely not the right answer.

3.   E

This "if" question stipulates that all students will stand to the right of Henry, which means Henry is the first student on the left—so there is no possible way that Susie can be to the left of Henry, therefore Tom must be to the immediate right of Henry. Tom is then in slot 2, so Isabelle must be to the right of Tom in slot 3, since Isabelle and Tom must stand immediately next to each other. This places Justin two spaces to the right of Isabelle, since there must be exactly one person in between Justin and Isabelle. Remember that Robert must be placed somewhere to the left of Justin, so Robert must be between Isabelle and Justin. This leaves Susie and Kate in the last two positions, with nothing left to tell you where they must go.

h	T	i	R	j		
1	2	3	4	5	6	7

Since the question asks for the choice that must be false, only (E) fits the bill. Justin cannot be the fourth from the left; he must be the fifth from left. Choices (A) and (B) discuss Kate and Susie; you don't know where they have to go; (C) and (D) have to be true.

4.   A

This "if" question places Isabelle in the third space from the left. Remember that there must be exactly one student in between Justin and Isabelle. This could potentially place Justin either first or fifth. Since Robert must be to the left of Justin, Justin cannot be the first on the left and therefore must be the fifth from the left. Tom must be immediately next to Isabelle, but he could be in either position 2 or 4. At this point, it might be a good idea to draw out both of these scenarios.

	T	i		j		
1	2	3	4	5	6	7

		i	T	j		
1	2	3	4	5	6	7

You can already rule out a few choices: (C) and (E) can't be correct, because both Tom and Justin have been placed, and neither one can go in the sixth slot from the left. You can also get rid of (B), because Robert must stand to the left of Justin. We're left with Kate and Henry—which one can be the sixth from the left?

Saving Time

If you were running out of time and had to guess, (A) would be a good bet. Kate is unlimited, so the odds are good that she can be the sixth from the left. But just to make sure, try Henry in this space. If Henry is in slot 6, you do *not* have "hT", so you must then have Susie coming to the left of Henry (according to our conditional). This means both Susie and Robert (from rule 2) must be in the two open slots to the left of Henry (slots 1 and 4 or 1 and 2, depending on where Tom is). But in either case, you will be forced to put two seniors next to each other. Either Robert and Susie are next to each other, or one of them is next to Tom. This violates rule 1, so Henry cannot be in slot 6. Therefore, (A) is correct. Kate is the only student listed who could be the sixth student from the left. (Susie could also be sixth, but she isn't one of the choices.)

5.   C

This "if" question places Susie right in the middle, in the fourth space from the left. At this point, you have two choices. You can try placing the entities further, starting with the most restrictive rules (here, the Isabelle-Justin rule). You can also test the choices, putting each one in the seventh, or last, slot. Choices (A) and (B) are Justin and Isabelle—you can test both together by putting this block in slots 5-7. If either one is in slot 7, then the other must be in slot 5, and Tom must be in slot 6, since Tom must be next to Isabelle (and slot 4 is already filled.)

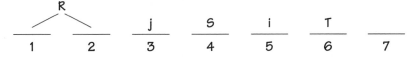

____	____	____	S	i/j	T	j/i
1	2	3	4	5	6	7

No matter where Henry goes, he will be to the left of Susie, triggering our conditional rule. However, the result ("hT...S") is impossible, so this scenario won't work. Neither (A) nor (B) is correct.

Now move on to (E), because Tom is also pretty restrictive. If Tom is last, Isabelle must be in slot 6, placing Justin in slot 4, which doesn't work. So we're left with Kate and Henry. But placing either one in the last slot won't tell you much. (If Henry is in the seventh slot, he will not be to Tom's left, so Susie must be to the left of Henry. So far, so good—rule number 5 holds. But what now?) You have to try placing the other entities, starting with the largest blocks.

Here, you have j/i ___ i/j. This can go in slots 1-3 or 3-5 (you already saw what happened when you put it in slots 5-7). Slots 1-3 don't work, because with Susie in slot 4, you won't have room to put Tom next to Isabelle and also to put Robert to Justin's left. So Justin and Isabelle must be the third and fifth students from the left with Susie between them. You now have:

____	____	i	S	j	____	____
1	2	3	4	5	6	7

____	____	j	S	i	____	____
1	2	3	4	5	6	7

But if Isabelle is in the third slot, Tom must be in the second slot, with Robert (who must be to Justin's left) in slot 1. But now Robert and Tom are next to each other, which violates rule 1. So Justin must be in the third space and Isabelle must be in the fifth, with Robert in the first or second space and Tom in the sixth.

R

____	____	j	S	i	T	____
1	2	3	4	5	6	7

Looking at our conditional, you definitely can't have hT, so Susie must be to the left of Henry, placing Henry in the seventh space—(C) is correct. (If Kate were in the seventh space, then Henry would be to the left of Susie, requiring that you have the hT block, which you can't have.)

6.   C

To find out which student could not be the first student on the left, first eliminate choices based on previous questions. From question 5, you know that Kate and Robert could both be the first on the left, so eliminate (A) and (E). Question 3 placed Henry in the first space on the left, so you can eliminate (D) as well. We're left with Susie and Isabelle. Isabelle is more limited, so look there first. From question 5, you figured out that Isabelle could never be first; Tom would have to be in the second space and Justin would have to be in the third space. But then Robert could not be somewhere on Justin's left. Therefore, the answer is (C).

GAME 3: PACING

Now you're ready for a more test-like question set on your own. Allow yourself no more than 12 minutes for the following game, keeping in mind that your goal is to average under 9 minutes per game on test day.

Especially when you are working on timing, it's important to be in a comfortable space where you can work without interruption for 15–20 minutes: 9 minutes for the game, and sufficient time to review the explanation thoroughly while the game is still clear in your mind.

Pushing yourself to stay within reasonable time limits is essential, even early in your practice. Always be looking for the way that gets you through quickest. There is no payoff in staying with a problem regardless of time, until you get every answer. Learning when to move on and not let a question bog you down is as much a part of the strategy for Logic Games as knowing how to work methodically. You must develop a sense of what 9 minutes feels like and the pace you have to maintain to achieve that goal.

Don't turn the page until your time is up or you have finished the game (whichever comes first).

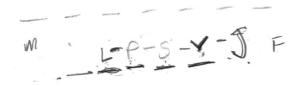

Contra negative

Questions 1-6

At an art exhibit, exactly seven paintings—F, J, L, M, P, S, and V—are to be arranged in one row horizontally along a wall. The painting on the extreme left is the first painting, followed by the second, third, etc., with the seventh painting all the way on the right. The order of their arrangement must satisfy the following conditions:

J is placed either first or fourth.

F is placed seventh.

M is placed somewhere to the left of S.

At least one painting is positioned between paintings J and S.

P is positioned either immediately to the left of V or immediately to the right of L.

At least two paintings are placed between paintings V and L.

1. Which of the following is an acceptable arrangement of paintings from left to right?

   (A) P, V, J, M, S, L, F
   (B) J, M, V, S, P, L, F
   (C) L, M, S, J, P, V, F
   (D) M, S, L, J, P, V, F
   (E) M, P, V, J, L, S, F

2. Painting V CANNOT be placed in which position?

   (A) second
   (B) third
   (C) fourth
   (D) fifth
   (E) sixth

3. If P is placed fifth and V is placed sixth, then S could be placed either

   (A) first or third
   (B) first or fourth
   (C) second or third
   (D) second or fourth
   (E) third or fourth

4. If S is placed immediately to the right of P, then V must be placed

   (A) second
   (B) third
   (C) fourth
   (D) fifth
   (E) sixth

5. Which of the following CANNOT be placed first?

   (A) J
   (B) L
   (C) M
   (D) P
   (E) V

6. Suppose it is no longer necessary to place at least two paintings between paintings L and V. Which of the following must be false?

   (A) V is in the fifth position.
   (B) S is in the second position.
   (C) M is in the fourth position.
   (D) L is placed to the immediate left of V.
   (E) S is placed to the immediate left of F.

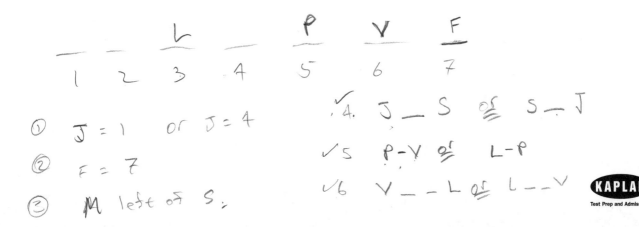

Game 3 Answers and Explanations

Step 1: Overview

Situation: An art exhibit
Entities: Seven paintings—F, J, L, M, P, S, and V
Action: Sequencing
Limitations: Seven positions, seven paintings, so one painting per position

Step 2: Sketch

You can start with seven blanks numbered from 1 through 7, and list the seven paintings. Now look at the rules.

Step 3: Rules

The first condition places painting J in the first or fourth space from the left, therefore you can mark J above or below the row, with lines connecting it to 1 and 4. You could also write "J—1 or 4." The next condition is straightforward: F must be in the seventh space. Write this directly in your sketch. Rule 3 states that M must be to the left of S. Write something like "M…S." The fourth condition places at least one painting in between paintings J and S. Note that there can be *more* than one painting in between paintings J and S; all you know is that there is *at least* one. You also don't know which comes first—J or S. Rule 5 says P must be immediately before (to the left of) V or immediately after (to the right of) L. Note this on your sketch with "PV or LP." The last condition places at least two paintings in between paintings V and L. This is similar to rule 4: you don't know the order of the two paintings, and you are only given a minimal distance.

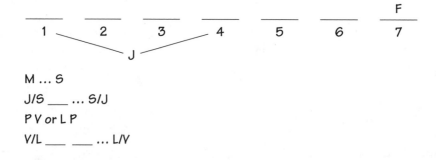

Step 4: Deductions

Note that all seven entities are mentioned in the rules. This means that each painting must conform to one or more conditions; there are no "floaters." Note that S, V, and L appear in multiple rules. While there isn't anything definite to be gleaned from these rules, it is often helpful to look for the most limited entities: these will always be the ones you'll want to deal with first. Unfortunately, that's about all you can do. Here, drawing out "limited options" based on rule 1 won't be helpful; placing J in either position doesn't tell you anything about any other entity. Now look at the questions.

Step 5: Questions

1. D

This is an acceptability question. Apply each individual condition to the choices and eliminate any that violates that condition. Choice (A) places painting J in the third position, violating rule 1. Rules 2 and 3 don't help eliminate any choices, but rule 4 is violated in (C), and (B) does not have P V or L P, violating rule 5. Finally, (E) places only one painting between paintings V and L, which violates the last condition. Only (D) is an acceptable arrangement.

2. C

This question asks for a limitation that was not stated in the set-up of the game; painting V cannot go somewhere. What do you know about V? It must be separated from L by at least two spaces. If V is second, L is fifth or sixth. If V is third, L is sixth. But if V is fourth, L cannot be seventh, so it must be first. And if L and V are in positions 1 and 4, where does J go? V cannot be fourth, so (C) is correct. Remember, if a question asks about an entity, first deal with the rules pertaining to that entity.

3. D

This "if" question places painting P in the fifth space and painting V in the sixth space. Since painting F must be in the seventh space, you have only four empty spaces. The question asks where S can go. The third condition states that painting M must be placed somewhere to the left of painting S, which means that painting S cannot be the first painting; eliminate (A) and (B). If S were placed third, then J must be placed first to comply with rule 4. This would place painting M in the second space since this is the only available space to the left of S. L is now the only painting left and must be in the fourth space, which places exactly one painting between painting L and V, violating rule 6. Therefore, S cannot be in the third space; eliminate (C) and (E). This leaves you with the one correct choice, (D).

Alternatively, you could have drawn two sketches based on rule 1: J is first or fourth. If J is first, S must be in either position 3 or 4. But as described above, if S is in 3, then M is in 2, leaving L in 4, which doesn't work. So if J is in 1, S is in 4, with M and L in positions 2 and 3. If J is in 4, then S must be in 2, so that there is room for M to be on its left.

J	M/L	L/M	S	P	V	F
1	2	3	4	5	6	7

M	S	L	J	P	V	F
1	2	3	4	5	6	7

4. E

This "if" question stipulates that painting S is to the right of painting P. According to rule 5, since you can't have P V, you must have L P, giving you the larger block "L P S." M also must come before this block, since M precedes S. Now turn to another specific rule: J is first or fourth. J must be first, because if J were fourth, there would be no room for our "block." So J is first, followed by M, with the "L P S" block starting in position 3 or 4. V is our remaining entity.

J	M	L	P	S	V	F
1	2	3	4	5	6	7

or

J	M/V	V/M	L	P	S	F
1	2	3	4	5	6	7

But when "L P S " is in positions 4, 5, and 6, L and V are too close together. Therefore, L must be in position 3, with V in position 6. Choice (E) is correct.

5. E

Since this question asks which painting cannot be placed first, look over your first four questions to determine which paintings have already been first. Go ahead and eliminate (A) and (C) based on questions 1 and 4. You need to test the remaining choices; if you test something in first, then painting J must be placed fourth. And if J is in 4, S must be in either 2 or 6, but in these three scenarios, it must be in 6. Placing S second wouldn't leave any room for M to come before it.

L			J		S	F
1	2	3	4	5	6	7

P			J		S	F
1	2	3	4	5	6	7

V			J		S	F
1	2	3	4	5	6	7

Now look at the L-V rule. If L is first, V must be fifth, and vice versa. If P is first, then L and V must be in positions 2 and 5.

L			J	V	S	F
1	2	3	4	5	6	7

P	V/L		J	L/V	S	F
1	2	3	4	5	6	7

V			J	L	S	F
1	2	3	4	5	6	7

Now with rule 5, if L is first, you can have the LP variation. If P is first, you can use the PV variation. But if V is first, rule 5 will have to be violated; you can't have LP or PV. So V cannot be first and (E) is correct.

6.   D

This question eliminates rule 6, and asks for the one answer that must be false. Even though a rule is gone, you can still use previous work to determine which choices are possible. (Just because L and V don't *have* to be separated doesn't mean they *can't* be separated.) You just saw V in the fifth position in question 5, so (A) is wrong. The answer to the acceptability question has S in second, so (B) is possible, and therefore the incorrect answer. In question 4, you tried having this:

J	M/V	V/M	L	P	S	F
1	2	3	4	5	6	7

It didn't work then because it violated rule 6, but this rule doesn't matter anymore, so you can have S F; (E) is wrong. Choice (D) cannot be true; if L is to the immediate left of V, then you have L V—making it impossible to have P V or L P, violating rule 5; (D) is the correct choice. For the record, here is a sketch that shows how (C) is possible:

J	P	V	M	L	S	F
1	2	3	4	5	6	7

This chapter has set the pattern for your work with Logic Games throughout this workbook. First, be sure you see how to approach each game type methodically, then practice the method and strategies on your own, and finally work on your pacing. Developing these skills will make you more efficient and confident on Test Day.

PRACTICE SETS

<u>Directions:</u> Each group of questions is based on a set of conditions. It may be useful to draw a rough diagram to answer some questions. Choose the response that most accurately and completely answers each question.

Game 4

Eight puppies—Grendel, Hamlet, Icarus, Jabberwocky, Kafka, Lennie, Moriarty, and Nemo—are to be adopted on a promotional "free puppy" Saturday. One puppy will be adopted at a time, and the order must be consistent with the following conditions:

Hamlet is adopted before Jabberwocky and also before Grendel.

Grendel is adopted after Icarus.

Moriarty is adopted sometime before Hamlet, but after Kafka.

Nemo is adopted sometime after Moriarty.

Lennie is adopted sometime before Moriarty.

1. Which of the following could be the order, from first to last, in which the puppies are adopted?

   (A) Lennie, Moriarty, Kafka, Nemo, Icarus, Hamlet, Jabberwocky, Grendel

   (B) Icarus, Kafka, Lennie, Moriarty, Nemo, Jabberwocky, Hamlet, Grendel

   (C) Lennie, Kafka, Moriarty, Hamlet, Jabberwocky, Nemo, Grendel, Icarus

   (D) Kafka, Lennie, Moriarty, Hamlet, Jabberwocky, Icarus, Nemo, Grendel

   (E) Kafka, Lennie, Icarus, Nemo, Moriarty, Hamlet, Jabberwocky, Grendel

2. If Lennie is adopted third, then which of the following could be true?

   (A) Grendel is adopted sixth.

   (B) Moriarty is adopted fifth.

   (C) Icarus is adopted fourth.

   (D) Nemo is adopted second.

   (E) Jabberwocky is adopted first.

3. If Icarus is adopted seventh, then which of the following must be true?

   (A) Kafka is adopted first.

   (B) Moriarty is adopted third.

   (C) Hamlet is adopted fourth.

   (D) Nemo is adopted fifth.

   (E) Jabberwocky is adopted sixth.

4. Which one of the following could be true?

   (A) Hamlet is the second puppy adopted.

   (B) Nemo is the third puppy adopted.

   (C) Icarus is the fourth puppy adopted.

   (D) Moriarty is the fifth puppy adopted.

   (E) Lennie is the sixth puppy adopted.

5. If Moriarty is adopted fourth, all of the following could be true EXCEPT

   (A) Lennie is adopted second.

   (B) Kafka is adopted third.

   (C) Nemo is adopted fifth.

   (D) Hamlet is adopted sixth.

   (E) Icarus is adopted seventh.

6. If Hamlet is adopted sometime before Icarus, then which of the following could be true?

   (A) Lennie is adopted third.

   (B) Jabberwocky is adopted eighth.

   (C) Hamlet is adopted sixth.

   (D) Nemo is adopted third.

   (E) Grendel is adopted fifth.

Game 5

Jenna will eat a dessert consisting of six pieces of fruit, an apple, a cherry, a kiwi, a mango, a plum and a tangerine. She will eat all six pieces, one at a time, and will finish each piece before starting the next piece. Jenna will eat her dessert in accordance with the following conditions:

> No matter their order relative to each other, the apple, cherry, and kiwi cannot be a series of three consecutive fruits that Jenna eats.

> No matter their order relative to each other, the mango, plum, and tangerine cannot be a series of three consecutive fruits that Jenna eats.

> She must eat the apple before she eats the plum.

> She can eat the cherry neither first nor sixth.

> She can eat the tangerine neither immediately before nor immediately after she eats the cherry.

1. Which one of the following could be the order, from first to last, in which Jenna eats the pieces of fruit?

    (A) apple, cherry, mango, plum, tangerine, kiwi
    (B) apple, mango, tangerine, kiwi, plum, cherry
    (C) kiwi, cherry, tangerine, apple, plum, mango
    (D) mango, cherry, kiwi, tangerine, apple, plum
    (E) tangerine, mango, cherry, plum, kiwi, apple

2. If Jenna eats the tangerine third, which one of the following must be true?

    (A) She eats the apple first.
    (B) She eats the cherry fifth.
    (C) She eats the kiwi fourth.
    (D) She eats the mango sixth.
    (E) She eats the plum fourth.

3. If she eats the plum third and the tangerine fourth, then which one of the following must be true?

    (A) She eats the apple second.
    (B) She eats the cherry fifth.
    (C) She eats the kiwi fifth.
    (D) She eats the kiwi first.
    (E) She eats the mango first.

4. If Jenna eats the apple fifth and the kiwi first, which one of the following must be true?

    (A) She eats the mango third.
    (B) She eats the tangerine fourth.
    (C) She eats the cherry immediately before the apple.
    (D) She eats the kiwi immediately before the tangerine.
    (E) She eats the mango immediately before the cherry.

5. If Jenna eats the mango immediately after she eats the plum and immediately before she eats the kiwi, then which one of the following could be true?

    (A) She eats the apple immediately before the plum.
    (B) She eats the apple immediately before the tangerine.
    (C) She eats the kiwi immediately before the cherry.
    (D) She eats the kiwi immediately before the tangerine.
    (E) She eats the tangerine immediately before the plum.

6. If Jenna eats the kiwi third, then any one of the following could be the fruit she eats fourth EXCEPT:

    (A) the apple
    (B) the cherry
    (C) the mango
    (D) the plum
    (E) the tangerine

Game 6

Ten Navy recruits—Harry, Inga, Jason, Kip, Larry, Mallory, Nicki, Olmos, Pam, and Quincy—will take an officer's entrance examination, each receiving a different score. Based on these results, each recruit will be assigned to one of three ranks. The top three scores will receive the rank of Admiral, the bottom three scores will receive the rank of Lieutenant, and the remaining four scores will receive the rank of Captain. The following conditions apply:

Kip scores higher than Nicki.

Nicki scores higher than Inga and Olmos.

Larry scores lower than Inga.

Quincy and Jason score lower than Larry.

Jason scores higher than Harry.

Olmos scores higher than Mallory and Pam.

1. How many different combinations of recruits could all receive the rank of Admiral?

   (A) 1
   (B) 2
   (C) 3
   (D) 4
   (E) 5

2. Which one of the following recruits could receive the rank of Captain, but not the rank of Lieutenant?

   (A) Harry
   (B) Jason
   (C) Larry
   (D) Mallory
   (E) Olmos

3. Which of the following recruits could receive any one of the three ranks?

   (A) Harry
   (B) Inga
   (C) Larry
   (D) Olmos
   (E) Pam

4. Which of the following pairs of recruits cannot both receive the same rank as Larry?

   (A) Harry and Inga
   (B) Harry and Pam
   (C) Jason and Olmos
   (D) Jason and Pam
   (E) Mallory and Quincy

5. Which one of the following must be true?

   (A) Harry receives the rank of Captain.
   (B) Jason receives the rank of Captain.
   (C) Larry receives the rank of Captain.
   (D) Mallory receives the rank of Lieutenant.
   (E) Pam receives the rank of Lieutenant.

Game 4 Answers and Explanations

Step 1: Overview

Situation: Adopting puppies

Entities: The 8 puppies—Grendel, Hamlet, Icarus, Jabberwocky, Kafka, Lennie, Moriarty, and Nemo

Action: Sequencing puppy adoptions

Limitations: 8 puppies given away one at a time

Step 2: Sketch

Your initial instinct may have been to write out eight slots, numbered 1 through 8. But glancing at the rules, you aren't given any information tying any of the puppies to specific slots. This is a classic loose sequencing game; as such, it will be best to draw your sketch as you go. You do want to list the entities, however (G, H, I, J, K, L, M, and N).

Step 3: Rules

In order to better visualize the conditions of this game, think of the order in which the puppies are given away as descending from top to bottom, rather than from left to right. When an entire game is loose sequencing, it is often easier to visualize this way. The puppies on the top of the sketch must be adopted before the ones on the bottom of the sketch.

The first condition states that Hamlet is adopted before Jabberwocky and before Grendel, which you can visualize like this:

H
/\
J   G

Rule 2 says Grendel is after Icarus, so add Icarus in before Grendel.

H   I
/\ /
J G

The next condition is that Moriarty is adopted before Hamlet but after Kafka. This rule alone gives a relative order of K…M…H, but if you add it to our sketch-in-progress, you have:

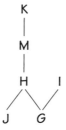

Test Prep and Admissions

Sketch out the last two conditions: Nemo is adopted after Moriarty and Moriarty is adopted after Lennie.

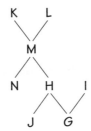

Step 4: Deductions

Since you have all of the rules in one sketch, you have been making deductions along the way. But this sketch is easily misinterpreted, so take a second to review it. First, notice that all eight puppies are in the sketch. Also, notice that K, L, *and* I can all be first, and N, J, and G can all be last. Don't think that I comes toward the end because it is drawn lower; all you know about I is that G follows it. Now look at the questions.

Step 5: Questions

1. D

This is an acceptability question. Apply each individual condition to each choice and eliminate any that violates that condition. (B) has Jabberwocky adopted before Hamlet, violating rule 1. (C) has Grendel adopted before Icarus, violating rule 2. (A) has Moriarty adopted before Kafka, violating rule 3. (E) has Nemo adopted before Moriarty, violating rule 4. (D) is the only one with an acceptable adoption order.

2. A

This "if" question stipulates that Lennie is adopted third, and requires you to find the one choice that could be true. Remember to eliminate any choice that must be false. Taking a look at the "puppy tree," note that half the puppies must be adopted after Moriarty. This means Moriarty can be adopted no later than fourth, and therefore (B) must be false. Since Moriarty and four other puppies must be adopted after Lennie, only Kafka and Icarus can be adopted first and second (though not necessarily in that order). So it follows that (C), "Icarus is adopted fourth," must also be false. (D) and (E) are also incorrect since only Kafka and Icarus can fill the first two slots. The correct answer is (A).

3. B

This "if" question stipulates that Icarus is adopted seventh. The second condition says Grendel must be adopted eighth. You are asked to find the one choice that *must* be true, so you can eliminate any that could be false. Referring to the "puppy tree," there is no conditional relation between Kafka and Lennie—either one could potentially be the first puppy adopted, so answer (A) can be eliminated. If Icarus and Grendel occupy the seventh and eighth positions, then there are three remaining puppies that must be adopted after Moriarty. These puppies must occupy the fourth, fifth, and sixth positions, and since Kafka and Lennie must be adopted before Moriarty, Moriarty must be adopted third. (B) is correct.

4.   **C**

The question asks you to find one choice that *could* be true, so eliminate answers that *must* be false. Referring to the "puppy tree," at least three puppies must be adopted before Hamlet, so Hamlet cannot be the second one adopted; eliminate (A). The same holds true for Nemo: Three puppies must be adopted before him, so Nemo can't be adopted third, eliminating (B). Remember from question 2 that Moriarty can be adopted no later than fourth; eliminate (D). Since Lennie must be adopted before Moriarty, it isn't possible for Lennie to be the sixth puppy adopted; eliminate (E). (C) is correct. Icarus's only condition is that he must be adopted before Grendel.

5.   **E**

This "if" question stipulates that Moriarty is adopted fourth and asks you to find one choice that *cannot* be true. Remember that four puppies must be adopted after Moriarty, so if Moriarty is adopted fourth, the fifth, sixth, seventh, and eighth positions, according to the "puppy tree," will be occupied by Nemo, Hamlet, Jabberwocky, and Grendel, (though not necessarily in that order). Then Kafka, Lennie, and Icarus must occupy the first three positions (though not necessarily in that order). Therefore, (E) must be false, since Icarus must be adopted in one of the first three positions.

6.   **B**

This "if" question slightly alters the form of the "puppy tree." It places Icarus's adoption sometime after Hamlet's and asks you to find the one answer that could be true. This means Icarus is no longer independent of the other puppies' conditions, and thus the "puppy tree" becomes stricter in terms of puppy arrangement.

```
    K      L
     \    /
      \  /
  N — M
       |
       H
      / \
     /   \
    J     I
          |
          G
```

This new condition now sets five puppies to be adopted after Moriarty, while still ensuring that two puppies must be adopted before Moriarty. Therefore, Moriarty must be adopted third; eliminate (A) and (D). Hamlet now precedes three puppies' adoptions, which means he cannot be adopted sixth; eliminate (C). Finally, the earliest Grendel could be adopted would be after Kafka, Lennie, Moriarty, Hamlet, and Icarus, so Grendel cannot be adopted fifth; eliminate (E), and (B) is correct; Jabberwocky precedes no other puppy, and can therefore be adopted eighth.

Game 5 Answers and Explanations

Step 1: Overview

Situation: A girl eating a fruit dessert

Entities: The pieces of fruit—A, C, K, M, P, and T

Action: Sequencing

Limitations: Six pieces, and she eats them one at a time

Step 2: Sketch

Use a standard sequencing sketch for this game, with six slots numbered 1 through 6 from left to right.

1	2	3	4	5	6

Step 3: Rules

Rule 1 states that Jenna cannot eat the apple, cherry, and kiwi as three consecutive fruits. Can she eat A and C consecutively? As long as she doesn't eat K along with them, she can. For example, A C M K would be acceptable, while A C K M would not. And order doesn't matter, so C A K does not work either. When you have a more complex rule like this one, it is important to spend the time *understanding* what the rule means, rather than just quickly figuring out how best to write it down. Once you've puzzled out this rule, "No A C K" will work.

Rule 2 is very similar to rule 1, but with the other three entities. "No M P T" will work.

Rule 3 states that Jenna must eat the apple before she eats the plum. "A … P" reflects this. Rule 4 stipulates that Jenna cannot eat the cherry first or sixth. Enter this rule directly into your sketch.

Rule 5 states that she cannot eat C and T consecutively, regardless of the order. This rule is similar to the first two rules, but with only two entities. "No T C or C T" works.

Step 4: Deductions

Most of the rules in this game specify things that can't happen, and not things that must be true. This is a good sign that there probably won't be any major deductions. And although several entities appear in more than one rule, you aren't yet able to combine them to draw concrete conclusions, so we'll head directly to the questions. But to summarize:

A, C, K, M, P, T

1	2	3	4	5	6
no C					no C

No A C K
No M P T

A … P
No T C or C T

Step 5: Questions

1. D

This acceptability question allows you to use the game's rules one at a time to eliminate answer choices. Rule 1 doesn't help you much, but rule 2 eliminates (A), since M, P, and T appear consecutively. Rule 3 eliminates (E), since P is listed before A. Rule 4 allows you to cross off (B), which lists C as being eaten sixth. Finally, rule 5 eliminates (C), in which T is eaten immediately after C. As a result, (D) is correct.

2. B

This "if" question stipulates that Jenna eats the tangerine third. What else do you know about the tangerine? She can't eat it right before or after the cherry. So you have:

		T			
1	2	3	4	5	6
no C	no C		no C		no C

As a result, she must eat C fifth; therefore, (B) is correct.

3. C

This new "if" question stipulates that Jenna eats P third and T fourth. After entering that information into a new sketch, you can check the rules for more deductions. Once again, rules 4 and 5 come into play. You know that Jenna cannot eat C first or sixth, and since T is fourth, C cannot be fifth. So C must be second. And if P is third and C is second, the only place for A that will allow it to precede P is first. So far you have:

A	C	P	T		
1	2	3	4	5	6
no C				no C	no C

You still need to place M and K. M, P, and T cannot be a series of three fruits, so since P and T are already together in slots 3 and 4, M cannot be fifth. So M must be sixth, leaving K to be fifth; (C) must be true, and (A), (B), (D), and (E) are false.

4. A

This "if" question tells you that Jenna eats A fifth and K first. Using rule 3, you can immediately deduce that Jenna eats P sixth. That leaves C, M, and T as the fruits Jenna must eat, in some order, second, third, and fourth. According to rule 5, Jenna must not eat C and T consecutively. If she eats either C or T third, there will be no way to avoid breaking rule 5. Consequently, she must eat either C or T second, and the other one fourth. She must then eat M third, and (A) is correct.

5. D

This "if" question tells you there is a P M K block, but doesn't tell you where it is. But let's work with what you do know. Because of rule 2, you know that T cannot immediately precede P. You also know that A must precede P. You have:

A	...	P	M	K
	no T			

Since A must precede this block, you're in no danger of an A C K series happening, so we've now dealt with three of the five rules.

Can you eliminate any choices? So far, only (E) can't happen. At this point, it is probably best to test each choice individually, focusing on the cherry and the tangerine (the two entities you have yet to place, and the two entities in the remaining rules).

In (A), A is immediately before P, creating an A P M K block. This leaves two entities that still must be placed: C and T. You know Jenna cannot eat them consecutively because of rule 5, so separate them on opposite sides of the A P M K block. But this forces C to be either first or sixth, which isn't allowed. So (A) can't be true.

Choice (B) creates a second block A T, which you must place ahead of the P M K block. But since you already know T can't come right before this block, you must put C in between the blocks: A T C P M K. This breaks rule 5, so (B) must be false.

Choice (C) creates a P M K C block. Jenna must eat A before this block, but there is no place where Jenna can eat T without breaking a rule. If she eats T before she eats A, C will be sixth, in violation of rule 4; rule 5 prevents her from eating T directly after C. Thus, (C) is eliminated.

Choice (D) is correct. If you've confidently eliminated four choices, don't bother taking the time to test the fifth. But to make sure you're convinced: choice (D) results in a P M K T block. So you can have:

A	C	P	M	K	T
1	2	3	4	5	6

6. A

This "if" question states that K is third. The question tells you that doing so makes it impossible for Jenna to eat one of the remaining fruits fourth. The only rule in which K appears is rule 1 "NO A C K." Because K appears in only one rule, it's almost a certainty that this rule will determine the correct answer. Therefore, start with one of the other two entities involved in rule 1. If Jenna were to eat A fourth, rule 1 would prevent her from eating C second or fifth. Since rule 4 prevents Jenna from eating C first or sixth, it would be impossible for Jenna to eat C at all. Therefore, (A) is correct.

Game 6 Answers and Explanations

Step 1: Overview

Situation: Ranking ten Navy recruits

Entities: Ten recruits H, I, J, K, L, M, N, O, P, and Q

Action: Sequencing recruits according to their test scores

Limitations: The ten recruits get 10 different scores; the top three scorers receive rank of admiral, the bottom three become lieutenants, and the remaining four scorers become captains

Step 2: Sketch

The sketch for this game will display the rankings of the recruits from top (admirals) to bottom (lieutenants) according to the rules. For a loose sequencing game like this—where it's the relationship *between* entities that's important—the sketch is created rule by rule.

Step 3: Rules

The first rule places Kip in a higher position than Nicki. This can be shown through a vertical diagram, with K in a higher position than N.

The second rule places Nicki in a higher position than both Inga and Olmos. You can add on to your sketch for rule 1, placing both I and O below N, so you have:

Continue drawing each rule by adding on to your sketch in progress. The third rule places Larry below Inga. The fourth rule places Quincy and Jason below Larry. The fifth rule places Jason higher than Harry, and the last rule places Olmos higher than both Mallory and Pam. In the end, all six rules should be sketched like this:

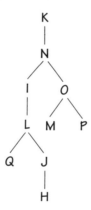

Step 4: Deduction

Technically, every time you added a new rule on to the sketch, you made a deduction. Since you've incorporated all of your rules into one sketch, there aren't any more deductions to make. Are all of the entities accounted for? Yes—so there aren't any "floaters." And remember to read the sketch carefully; H could be ranked higher than O, M, and P.

Step 5: Questions

1.   B

This question asks for the total number of *combinations* of recruits that could all receive the rank of Admiral. Take a look at your ranking tree. Since the top three test scores receive the rank of Admiral, you know from your sketch that both Kip and Nicki must receive the rank Admiral, regardless of the other recruits' scores. Also, according to your "ranking tree," you know that the third highest score must be either Inga or Olmos. Since no other recruit can score higher than Inga or Olmos, the top three scores must be one of two possibilities: Kip, Nicki, and Inga, or Kip, Nicki, and Olmos, so (B) is correct.

2.   C

This question asks you to identify a recruit that could receive the rank of Captain, but not the rank of Lieutenant. Remember that the middle four test scores receive the rank of Captain and the bottom three test scores receive the rank of Lieutenant. Since Lieutenants are the bottom three scorers, the only recruits who can receive this rank are those who have *no more than* two recruits scoring below them. Since you are interested in who *cannot* be a Lieutenant, you want those recruits who *must* score higher than at least three other recruits: Larry, Inga, Nicki, and Kip are the recruits who score higher than three or more people. In the last question you learned that Nicki and Kip must be Admirals, so Larry and Inga are the two recruits who can be Captains, but *cannot* be Lieutenants. Larry is (C), which is correct.

3.   D

From the first question, you know that Inga and Olmos are the only two recruits who could receive the rank of Admiral other than Kip and Nicki (who *must* be Admirals). Since the question asks for the one recruit who could receive all three ranks, it must be one of these two. Eliminate (A), (C), and (E). From question 2, you deduced that Inga could not receive the rank of Lieutenant, so that leaves Olmos, who can be anywhere from the third highest (if only K and N score higher) to the third lowest (if only M and P score lower). So Olmos can receive any one of the three ranks, and (D) is correct.

4.   B

Since this question asks about the recruits who can't both be the same rank as Larry, determine what rank or ranks Larry can receive. Looking at your ranking tree, you know that at least three recruits score higher than Larry, and that Larry scores higher than at least three other recruits; this means that Larry cannot be an Admiral or Lieutenant, so he is always a Captain.

Go to the choices. In (A), can H and I both be Captains? Sure—this means O is the third Admiral, and Q, M, and P are Lieutenants. Can H and P both be Captains? This would mean that the four Captains are L, J, H, and P (since J scores between L and H). But since both I and O must score higher than L and P respectively, and since our four slots for Captains are filled, I and O would both have to be Admirals. So K, N, I, and O would all be Admirals, which exceeds the limitations. Choice (B) is correct.

5.   C

You're looking for something that must be true. You just deduced that Larry must receive the rank of Captain, and sure enough, that's (C). Remember, you're done when you've reached this point. But again, to be sure you're convinced: Could (A) be true? Certainly, but it doesn't have to be. Both Harry and Jason could be Lieutenants, ruling out (A) and (B), and both Mallory and Pam could be Captains, if Q, J, and H are the Lieutenants, ruling out (D) and (E).

Chapter 5: **Strict Sequencing Games**

In the second type of sequencing game, a **strict** sequencing game, the placement of entities is very strictly defined. You may be told, for example, that "A is third," or that "X and Y are adjacent," and so on. These are definite, concrete pieces of information, and the game centers around placing as many entities into definite spots as possible. As a result, both your scratchwork and much of your reasoning will be very different from that used in relative sequencing games.

GAME 1: THE METHOD

Once again, work through the first game, focusing on applying Kaplan's 5-Step Method. If you are feeling more confident of your skills now, try to develop your own sketch based on the stimulus and rules before reading further.

Questions 1-6

Seven runners—Nat, Olga, Pam, Quon, Rita, Sue, and Tia—are to be assigned to seven starting positions arranged in a straight line and numbered consecutively 1 through 7. The runners are all assigned to the positions, one runner per position, according to the following conditions:

Olga and Pam are separated by exactly one position.

Olga and Sue cannot be assigned to positions that are immediately next to each other.

Tia is assigned to position 4.

Sue and Nat are both assigned to positions numbered lower than the position to which Quon is assigned.

Step 1: Overview

Situation: A racetrack

Entities: Seven runners (N, O, P, Q, R, S, and T)

Action: The runners must be ordered, or sequenced, into the starting positions

Limitations: There are 7 runners and 7 starting positions, all of which are used, so there is one runner per starting position

Step 2: Sketch

The sketch for this game is quite simple: seven columns, arranged horizontally. The columns should be numbered 1 through 7, from right to left. Also, list the 7 runners.

Step 3: Rules

As you saw in the previous chapter, the following are the key issues in sequencing games.

Typical Selection Game Issues

Issue	Wording of Rule
Which entities are concretely placed in the ordering?	X is third.
Which entities are forbidden from a specific position in the ordering?	Y is not fourth.
Which entities are next to, adjacent to, or immediately preceding or following one another?	X and Y are consecutive. X is next to Y. No event comes between X and Y. X and Y are consecutive in the ordering.
Which entities cannot be next to, adjacent to, or immediately preceding or following one another?	X does not immediately precede or follow Z. X is not immediately before or after Z. At least one event comes between X and Z. X and Z are not consecutive in the sequence.
How far apart in the ordering are two particular entities?	Exactly two events come between X and Q.
What is the relative position of two entities in the ordering?	Q comes before T in the sequence. T comes after Q in the sequence.

The first rule separates Olga and Pam by exactly one runner. Next to the sketch, note that O and P will make up a three position "block," with O and P on the ends and an unknown runner in the middle. Also note that you don't know who comes first, Olga or Pam. The next rule is that Olga and Sue cannot be immediately next to each other. Next to the sketch, note that the combination of O/S or S/O is not possible. The third rule places Tia in position 4; put T in the fourth column in the sketch. The last rule is that Sue and Nat must be in a lower numbered position than Quon, so S and N must be placed to the left of Q on the sketch.

Step 4: Deductions

Are there any deductions that can be made? Start with the rule with the most information—the Olga/Pam block. Because of Tina's presence in position 4, the block can only span positions 1-3, 3-5, or 5-7.

Saving Time

While it probably isn't worth the time to sketch out each of these possibilities, it is useful to spend a short amount of time thinking about where large blocks like this can go. So basically, you have:

N, O, P, Q, R, S, T

			T			
1	2	3	4	5	6	7

O/P ___ P/O (In 1-3, 3-5, or 5-7)

No O S̲ or S̲ O ___

S̲
  ⟍
    Q̲
N̲ ⟋

Step 5: Questions

1. Which of the following lists an acceptable assignment of runners to positions 1 through 7, respectively?

    (A) Nat, Quon, Pam, Tia, Olga, Rita, Sue

    (B) Pam, Sue, Olga, Tia, Rita, Nat, Quon

    (C) Nat, Rita, Sue, Tia, Pam, Quon, Olga

    (D) Rita, Sue, Tia, Olga, Nat, Pam, Quon

    (E) Rita, Pam, Olga, Tia, Sue, Nat, Quon

This is an acceptability question. Apply each rule to the choices. In (E), Pam and Olga are next to each other, violating the first rule. In (B), Sue and Olga are immediately next to each other, violating the second rule. (D) places Tia in the third position, violating the third rule. (A) places Quon in a lower numbered position than Sue, violating the fourth rule. Only (C) is an acceptable assignment of runners to positions, and is therefore correct.

2. Which of the following is a complete and accurate list of the positions to which Olga could be assigned?

    (A) 3, 5

    (B) 3, 5, 7

    (C) 3, 4, 5

    (D) 1, 3, 5, 7

    (E) 1, 2, 3, 5, 6, 7

In the deductions, you noted that the Pam/Olga block could either be in positions 1-3, 3-5, or 5-7, and that Pam and Olga do not have a fixed relation to one another: Pam could be positioned before or after Olga. Therefore, Olga could be positioned in any odd numbered position; (D) is correct.

3. If either Pam or Olga is in position 3, then which of the following must be true?

   (A) Olga is in position 5.
   (B) Rita is in a lower numbered position than Tia.
   (C) Nat is in position 2.
   (D) Quon is in a higher numbered position than Pam.
   (E) Sue is in a higher numbered position than Tia.

This "if" question places Pam or Olga in position 3; therefore, according to rule 1, the other one (Pam or Olga) must be in position 1 or 5. Choice (A) does not have to be true. Pam, Olga, and Tina are in three of the first five positions (it doesn't really matter which ones). Since Sue and Nat must be to the left of Quon, there must be at least two more "open" positions before Quon is positioned. Therefore, Quon must be in either position 6 or 7. Quon will always be in a higher numbered position than Pam; (D) is correct.

4. Which of the following CANNOT be true?

   (A) Quon is in position 3.
   (B) Quon is in position 5.
   (C) Rita is in position 3.
   (D) Sue is in position 2.
   (E) Sue is in position 5.

The best way to get through this question is to try each choice, starting with choices dealing with the most limiting entities. In this game, Quon's position determines the positions of two other entities, so start with (A) and (B). (A) is possible: if Quon is in 3, then the Olga-Pam block is in 5-7, and Nat and Sue are in positions 1 and 2. But if Quon were in position 5, the Pam-Olga block must occupy positions 1-3. This leaves position 2 open for Nat, but every position to the left of Quon is filled.

O/P	N	P/O	T	Q		
1	2	3	4	5	6	7

Since there is no room for Sue to be placed to the left of Quon, rule 4 is violated, and (B) is correct.

5. If neither Pam nor Olga is assigned to position 3, then which of the following must be false?

    (A) Sue is in position 2.
    (B) Quon is in position 3.
    (C) Olga is in position 5.
    (D) Nat is in position 6.
    (E) Pam is in position 7.

This "if" question stipulates that neither Pam nor Olga can occupy position 3. Therefore, the Pam/Olga block must occupy positions 5-7. The runner in position 6 must be either Quon or Rita, since both Nat and Sue must come to the left of Quon.

_____	_____	_____	T	P/O	Q or R	O/P
1	2	3	4	5	6	7

So (D), which places Nat in position 6, must be false.

GAME 2: PRACTICE

Now try Game 2 on the following page on your own before looking at the explanations. Once more, focus on your method and strategy in this game, not on your pacing yet.

Questions 1-6

Four students—Paolo, Raul, Sonia, and Terrence—
have been chosen to be hall monitors five days a week,
Monday through Friday. Exactly one student will be hall
monitor for each day. The schedule for appointed hall
monitors for any given week must meet the following
conditions:

Each student is a hall monitor on at least one day.

No student is a hall monitor on two consecutive
days.

Sonia is not a hall monitor on Tuesday.

Terrence is a hall monitor on either Wednesday or
Friday or both.

If Raul is a hall monitor on Tuesday, then Terrence
is not a hall monitor on Friday.

1. Which of the following could be a schedule of hall
monitors for one week, Monday through Friday,
respectively?

(A) Terrence, Raul, Sonia, Paolo, Sonia

(B) Raul, Raul, Terrence, Sonia, Paolo

(C) Paolo, Terrence, Raul, Paolo, Terrence

(D) Terrence, Paolo, Sonia, Raul, Terrence

(E) Sonia, Raul, Terrence, Raul, Sonia

2. Which of the following could be true of the
schedule of hall monitors for a given week?

(A) Sonia is hall monitor on both Wednesday
and Friday.

(B) Raul is hall monitor on both Tuesday and
Wednesday.

(C) Paolo is hall monitor on Wednesday and
Raul is hall monitor on Friday.

(D) Raul is hall monitor on Tuesday and
Terrence is hall monitor on Thursday.

(E) Sonia is hall monitor immediately after
Paolo and immediately before Terrence.

3. If, during a given week, Terrence is scheduled to be
hall monitor on Wednesday and Friday, then which
of the following must also be true of that week?

(A) Paolo is hall monitor on Tuesday.

(B) Raul is hall monitor on Monday.

(C) Sonia is hall monitor on Thursday.

(D) Paolo is hall monitor on Thursday.

(E) Raul is hall monitor on Tuesday.

4. If, during one week, Raul is hall monitor on
Tuesday and Thursday, all of the following must be
false EXCEPT:

(A) The same person is hall monitor on Monday
and Friday

(B) There are at most two different students who
could be hall monitor on Friday

(C) Terrence is not hall monitor on Wednesday

(D) There is only one person available to be hall
monitor on Monday

(E) Paolo is hall monitor on two different days

5. Which of the following CANNOT be true of the
week's schedule of hall monitors?

(A) Terrence is hall monitor on Monday and
Raul is hall monitor on Tuesday.

(B) Sonia is hall monitor immediately after Raul,
and immediately before Terrence.

(C) Sonia is hall monitor on the day between the
two days on which Terrence is hall monitor.

(D) Paolo is hall monitor on Monday and
Terrence is hall monitor on Thursday.

(E) Raul is hall monitor on Monday and
Terrence is hall monitor on Wednesday.

6. If Sonia is hall monitor twice during the week, but
not on Thursday or Friday, which of the following
must be false?

(A) Sonia is hall monitor on Monday.

(B) Paolo is hall monitor on Tuesday.

(C) Raul is hall monitor on the day between the
two days on which Sonia is hall monitor.

(D) Terrence is hall monitor on Friday.

(E) Raul is not hall monitor on Tuesday.

Use this space for scratchwork

$$\frac{S}{M} \quad \frac{\not{P}}{T} \quad \frac{T}{W} \quad \frac{R}{Th} \quad \frac{T}{F}$$

$$\frac{\cancel{S}}{R} \qquad T \qquad \cancel{T}$$

P R S T

○ 1 per da

① No consecutive

② S not Tues

③ T weds. _or_ Friday ~~of~~ weds and Friday

④ Is ~~If~~ R on Tues then T not Fri

$$\frac{}{M} \quad \frac{P}{T} \quad \frac{}{W} \quad \frac{}{Th} \quad \frac{}{Fr}$$

Turn the page when you are ready to check your answers.

Game 2 Answers and Explanations

Step 1: Overview

Situation: A school with hall monitors

Entities: Four students (P, R, S, and T)

Action: The students must be scheduled over the course of a week, Monday through Friday

Limitations: There are 4 students and 5 days, so at least one student must be scheduled for two different days

Step 2: Sketch

Before you look at the rules of the game, determine how the action of the game can best be reflected in a sketch. Since you are scheduling students to be hall monitors on a given school week, sketching out Monday through Friday, left to right, like a weekly calendar, would be best. Also, make sure to list the four students.

Step 3: Rules

The first rule is that each student is a hall monitor on at least one day. This means you must use all four students in determining the schedule of hall monitors.

The second rule says a student cannot be a hall monitor two days in a row. You might write "not consec" to remind yourself of this.

The third rule tells you that Sonia cannot be scheduled on Tuesday. Note this rule in your sketch.

The fourth rule is that Terrence must be a hall monitor on Wednesday or Friday or both. Jot this down in shorthand as in "T—Wed, Fri, or both"—note that this rule does not limit Terrence to *only* Wednesday and Friday; it just mandates that he be scheduled on at least one of these two days.

The last rule is that if Raul is a hall monitor on Tuesday, then Terrence is not a hall monitor on Friday. Write this as an *if/then* rule, and write its contrapositive as well (if Terrence is on Friday, Raul is not on Tuesday).

Step 4: Deductions

What deductions can you make? You already know that each student must be scheduled once, and since there are five days, this means *exactly* one student is scheduled twice. Note that both the fourth and fifth rules involve Terrence. In rule 5, if Raul is on Tuesday, then Terrence is not on Friday, which means Terrence *must* be on Wednesday.

Add this deduction onto the *if/then* rule. Also, if Terrence must be either on Wednesday or Friday, then he cannot possibly be on Thursday, since this would place him on two consecutive days.

Before you look at the questions, you should have a sketch of the action that looks somewhat like this:

P, R, S, T (1 twice)

M	Tu	W	Th	F
___	___	___	___	___
	no S		no T	

Nobody on two consec days

T- on Wed, Fri, or both

If R- Tues → T- not Fri (T- Wed)

If T- Fri → R- not Tues

Step 5: Questions

1.   D

This is an acceptability question. Apply each rule to the choices and eliminate any that violates a rule. (C) and (E) only schedule three students to be hall monitors, violating the first rule. (B) schedules Raul on two consecutive days, violating rule 2. (A) does not have Terrence scheduled for a Wednesday or a Friday, violating the fourth rule. Only (D) is an acceptable schedule.

2.   E

Since this question asks for the choice that *could* be true, eliminate any answer that *must* be false. (A) would not allow Terrence to be scheduled on either Wednesday or Friday, violating rule 4. (B) has Raul scheduled on consecutive days, violating the second rule. (C) does not allow Terrence to be scheduled on Wednesday or Friday. (D) is a bit more complex: Raul is scheduled for Tuesday, which means Terrence must be scheduled for Wednesday, according to the *if/then* rule.. But (D) also says that Terrence is on Thursday, meaning that Terrence is scheduled on two consecutive days, which is not allowed.

Saving Time

So (E) must be correct: You should feel comfortable choosing (E) and moving on. In (E), you are given a block of P S T, which must be on Wed-Fri. (Sonia cannot be on Tuesday, and if Sonia is on Wednesday, then Terrence would be on Thursday, which is not allowed.) If Terrence is on Friday, then Raul is not on Tuesday. Since neither Sonia (rule 3) nor Paolo (rule 2) can be on Tuesday, Terrence must be on Tuesday. This means Raul must be on Monday since he hasn't been used yet.

R	T	P	S	T
M	Tu	W	Th	F
	no S, R, P			

Since this is an acceptable arrangement of the schedule, (E) could be true and is thus correct. However, there is absolutely no reason to go through all of this work on Test Day unless you are having trouble ruling out the other four choices.

3.   A

In this "if" question, it is a good idea to put the new "if" in a sketch. (Don't draw it into your master sketch!) Terrence is on both Wednesday and Friday. Since only one student can be scheduled twice in a given week, it must be Terrence. Therefore, the remaining three students must be distributed among the remaining three days. Since Terrence is scheduled on Friday, Raul cannot be scheduled for Tuesday, and since Sonia can never be scheduled for Tuesday, this leaves only Paolo to be scheduled for Tuesday.

S/R	P	T	R/S	T
M	Tu	W	Th	F
	no S, R			

Choice (A) is correct.

4.   B

This "if" question places Raul on both Tuesday and Thursday; again it is a good idea to sketch this. Since only one student can be scheduled twice in a given week, it must be Raul here. Remember that if Raul is scheduled for Tuesday, then Terrence must be scheduled for Wednesday. This leaves Monday and Friday to be split between Paolo and Sonia. Since there are no rules governing the positions of these remaining students among the remaining days, both students could be scheduled on each remaining day.

S/P	R	T	R	P/S
M	Tu	W	Th	F
	no S, R			

However, make sure you read the question carefully. It says that all of the following must be false EXCEPT; four choices are false, and one is possible. (A) and (E) are wrong, because no one else can be scheduled on two days. You know that Terrence *is* the hall monitor on Wednesday, which rules out (C). Finally, either Paolo or Sonia could be on Monday, so (D) is false. Only (B) remains, and indeed, it must be true.

5.   D

You are looking for the one choice that cannot be true, or must be false; therefore, eliminate any choice that *could* be true.

Saving Time

If you've deduced that Terrence can never go on Thursday, you may have quickly spotted (D). Since Terrence must be scheduled for either Wednesday or Friday or both, if Terrence was ever scheduled for a Thursday, it would violate the second rule by having a student scheduled on consecutive days. (D) cannot be true, and is therefore correct.

If you had not noticed this, then you probably just went through the choices one by one. This can take some time, but is often the only way to handle a problem like this. Just remember not to take too much time trying to prove a choice false; if it looks OK, move on to the next one. A choice that violates a rule will usually jump out, and you don't want to waste too much time trying to prove a choice false when it is possible!

6.   C

This "if" question stipulates that Sonia is the student who will be scheduled twice, and that she is not on Thursday or Friday. Since Sonia cannot be scheduled on consecutive days, she must be scheduled on Monday and Wednesday. Again, sketch this new "if" out, rather than trying to keep it all in your head. Since Sonia is on Wednesday, Terrence must be scheduled on Friday (rule 4). Since Terrence is scheduled on Friday, Raul cannot be scheduled for Tuesday (rule 5); Paolo is the only remaining student who can be scheduled on Tuesday. This leaves Raul to be scheduled on Thursday.

S	P	S	R	T
M	Tu	W	Th	F
	no S, R, T			

The correct choice is the one that must be false, so eliminate any choice that can or must be true. (C) must be false, and is therefore correct.

GAME 3: PACING

Now try another test-like game on your own. Allow yourself no more than 11 minutes—less if you're up to it. Never push your pacing at the expense of learning and internalizing the methods and strategies. But developing a sense of timing and keeping up your sense of urgency about moving through each game expeditiously (rather than allowing yourself the luxury of unlimited time to solve it) is as much a part of winning Logic Games as getting the right answers.

On Test Day, you'll have to average about 8.75 minutes per game. If one game takes you 10 minutes, you'll have to do another in about 7 minutes to make up the difference. Less time than that for a Logic Game is unrealistic, so you have to get very sensitive to that 8.75 minute average, varying it only slightly for the harder games.

Five packages—T, U, W, X, and Z—are to be delivered on five consecutive days, Monday through Friday, one package per day. All of the packages must be delivered. The following restrictions governing the schedule of package deliveries must be observed:

Package X is not delivered on Monday.

If package T is delivered on Monday, then package X must be delivered on Friday.

If package X is delivered on Tuesday, package U is delivered on Monday.

Package W is delivered the day following the day of the delivery of package Z.

1. Package W could be delivered on any day except:

    (A) Monday
    (B) Tuesday
    (C) Wednesday
    (D) Thursday
    (E) Friday

2. If package U is delivered the day after package T is delivered, which of the following is a complete and accurate list of the days, any one of which is a day on which package X could be delivered?

    (A) Tuesday, Wednesday, Thursday
    (B) Wednesday, Thursday, Friday
    (C) Tuesday, Wednesday, Friday
    (D) Wednesday, Friday
    (E) Thursday, Friday

3. If package W is delivered on Wednesday, which of the following could be true?

    (A) Package U is delivered on Friday.
    (B) Package X is delivered on Tuesday.
    (C) Package X is delivered before package T.
    (D) Package X is delivered before package U.
    (E) Package X is delivered before package Z.

4. If package U is delivered on Wednesday, which of the following must be true?

    (A) Package W is delivered before package T.
    (B) Package T is delivered before package X.
    (C) Package T is delivered before package U.
    (D) Package X is delivered before package W.
    (E) Package X is delivered before package T.

5. If package W is delivered on Friday, which of the following must be false?

    (A) Package Z is delivered on Thursday.
    (B) Package X is delivered on Wednesday.
    (C) Package T is delivered on Tuesday.
    (D) Package T is delivered on Wednesday.
    (E) Package U is delivered on Tuesday.

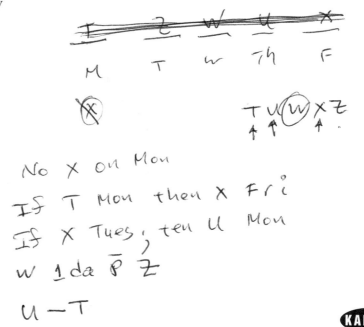

Game 3 Answers and Explanations

Were you able to finish in the time you allowed? Keep in mind that your goal is to average under 9 minutes per game on Test Day. But working methodically should come before focusing on your speed.

Step 1: Overview

Situation: Delivering packages

Entities: Five packages (T, U, W, X, and Z)

Action: The packages must be scheduled for delivery over the course of a week, Monday through Friday

Limitations: There are 5 packages and 5 days; 1 package per day

Step 2: Sketch

Since the action involves the delivery of these packages in the span of a week, you will want to sketch out a weekly calendar to denote the days of the week. You should also list the five entities.

Step 3: Rules

Now look at the restrictions. The first stipulates that package X cannot be delivered on Monday. Note this in your sketch. The second rule is a conditional: If package T is delivered on Monday, then package X is delivered on Friday. Note this next to your sketch, and write the contrapositive as well (if X is not on Friday, then T is not on Monday). The next restriction is that if package X is delivered on Tuesday, then package U is delivered on Monday. Another conditional, and of course another contrapositive: If U is not on Monday, then X is not on Tuesday. The last restriction stipulates that package W is delivered the day after package Z; this creates a two-day Z/W "block" which will appear somewhere on the delivery schedule; note this next to your sketch.

T, U, W, X, Z

____	____	____	____	____
M	Tu	W	Th	F
no X				

If T- Mon → X- Fri
If X- No Fri → T- No Mon

If X- Tues → X- Fri
If X- No Fri → U- Mon

If U- No Mon → X- No Tues

Z̲ W̲

Step 4: Deductions

There aren't really any deductions to make. Two of the four rules are conditionals (the *if/then* rules). Since they do not refer to something that *always* happens, but only to what happens in a given situation, there is nothing that *must* be true. Remember that in making deductions, you are looking for what must be true; with *if/then* rules, there are almost never any deductions to be made. The only other certainty is the "ZW" block, which can go anywhere. Now go on to the questions.

Step 5: Questions

1. A

Since package W must be delivered on the day immediately after the day on which package Z is delivered, it would not be possible for package W to be delivered on Monday; so (A) is correct.

2. D

This "if" question says that package U is delivered the day after package T. This creates another restriction similar to the fourth; you have two "blocks" that you need to fit into the weekly schedule. Since package X is the only package remaining that is not in a "block," its placement in the delivery schedule cannot impede the placement of the two "blocks." If package X were delivered on Tuesday or Thursday, one of the "blocks" would have to be split up. Therefore, package X could only be delivered on Wednesday or Friday, and (D) is correct.

3. C

This "if" question says package W is delivered on Wednesday, and it asks for the one choice that could be true. Therefore, eliminate any choice that must be false. Sketch out the new "if" next to the question. If package W is delivered on Wednesday, then package Z must be delivered on Tuesday.

	Z	W		
M	Tu	W	Th	F
no X				

Rule out (B), because Z is on Tuesday, not X. Rule out (E), because for X to be before Z, it would have to be on Monday, which is not allowed. But what about the other three choices? The *if/then* rules don't seem to trigger anything, so how can you go any further?

Limited Options

Think about the most limited entity: X (since it is in the most rules). Since X can't be on Monday, it can go either on Thursday or Friday. Sketch these two options and then use the *if/then* rules to go further. If X is on Thursday, T is *not* on Monday, which means T must be on Friday, leaving U to be on Monday. If X is on Friday, then U and T are split between Monday and Thursday. You now have:

U	Z	W	X	T
M	Tu	W	Th	F

or

T/U	Z	W	U/T	X
M	Tu	W	Th	F

Choice (A) cannot be true because according to your sketch, either X or T is delivered on Friday; (D) is incorrect for the same reason—since package X can only be delivered on Thursday or Friday, and package U cannot be delivered on Friday, package U is always delivered before package X. So (C) is the only answer that could be true, and is correct.

If you think multiple sketches will take up too much time on Test Day, consider that staring at your test takes up a lot of time as well and doesn't get you anywhere. Remember, if you find yourself stuck, start thinking about the most limited entities, and where they can go.

4. A

This "if" question places package U on Wednesday, and requires you to find the one choice that must be true. Since package U is delivered on Wednesday, according to the contrapositive of rule 4, package X cannot be delivered on Tuesday. Therefore, package X must be delivered on Thursday or Friday. This in turn forces the ZW "block" to be delivered on Monday and Tuesday respectively.

Z	W	U	X/T	T/X
M	Tu	W	Th	F
	no X			

This puts package T on either Thursday or Friday, so (A) must be true, and is the correct answer. Notice that (C) and (D) are both impossible, and (B) and (E) are both possible, but neither one *must* be true. You only know that X and T must be on Thursday and Friday; you don't know the relative order of these two packages.

5. E

In this "if" question, you are looking for the one choice that must be false, so eliminate any that could be true. Once again, unless the answer is immediately apparent, sketch out the new "if." If W is delivered on Friday, then Z must be delivered on Thursday. Since Friday's delivery is not X, Monday's delivery cannot be T. This means Monday's delivery must be U.

U	T/X	X/T	Z	W
M	Tu	W	Th	F
no T				

Choice (E), which states that package U is delivered on Tuesday, *cannot* be true and is correct.

If you've been working methodically, you should already be working through each game without forgetting any of the steps of Kaplan's Method, and two chapters of sequencing games should have built your confidence. If you're feeling strong, try doing the Practice Sets all together, averaging no more than 10 minutes for the three. But if you still feel uncertain about method or strategy, do each separately and check your results before moving on to the next, so that you improve with each.

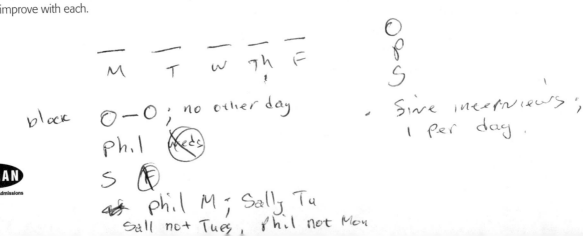

PRACTICE SETS

<u>Directions:</u> Each group of questions is based on a set of conditions. It may be useful to draw a rough diagram to answer some questions. Choose the response that most accurately and completely answers each question.

Game 4

During a single week, from Monday through Friday, Coffee Insurance will interview three applicants (Onda, Phil, and Sally). Exactly five interviews will be conducted, one interview per day. The schedule of interviews for the week must conform to the following restrictions:

Each applicant is interviewed at least once.

Onda is interviewed on two consecutive days, and on no other day.

Phil is not interviewed on Wednesday.

Sally is not interviewed on Friday.

If Phil is interviewed on Monday, then Sally is interviewed on Tuesday.

1. Which of the following could be true of the week's schedule?

   (A) The applicant who is interviewed on Tuesday is also interviewed on Thursday

   (B) The applicant who is interviewed on Wednesday is also interviewed on Friday

   (C) The applicant who is interviewed on Monday is also interviewed on Tuesday

   (D) Phil is interviewed on Monday and Thursday

   (E) Sally is interviewed on Tuesday and Thursday

2. If in addition to Onda, one other applicant is interviewed on two consecutive days, then which of the following could be true?

   (A) Phil is interviewed on Monday and Onda is interviewed on Wednesday

   (B) Phil is interviewed on Tuesday and Friday

   (C) Phil is interviewed on Tuesday and Onda is interviewed on Friday

   (D) Sally is interviewed on Tuesday and Onda is interviewed on Thursday

   (E) Sally is interviewed on Monday and Phil is interviewed on Tuesday

3. If the week's interview schedule has the same applicant scheduled for Monday and Thursday, then which is a day on which Phil must be interviewed?

   (A) Monday

   (B) Tuesday

   (C) Wednesday

   (D) Thursday

   (E) Friday

4. If the applicant who is interviewed on Thursday is different from the applicant who is interviewed on Friday, then which of the following could be true?

   (A) Phil completes his interviews earlier in the week than Sally completes her interviews

   (B) Phil completes his interviews earlier in the week than Onda completes her interviews

   (C) Onda is interviewed on Friday

   (D) Phil is interviewed on Thursday

   (E) Sally is interviewed Monday

5. If Onda is interviewed on Friday, then which of the following must be true of the week's schedule?

   (A) Phil is interviewed on Monday

   (B) Sally is interviewed on Tuesday

   (C) Sally is interviewed exactly twice

   (D) Phil is interviewed exactly twice

   (E) Phil interviews on Tuesday

Game 5

At a local newspaper, five albums—two soft jazz (F and G) and three disco (S, T, and U)—will each be reviewed by two critics, Haslem and Inge. The reviews will take place over five consecutive days. Each critic reviews exactly one album per day, and no album will be reviewed by both critics on the same day. The following rules apply:

Haslem cannot review any disco album until Inge has reviewed that album.

Inge cannot review any soft jazz album until Haslem has reviewed that album.

Inge cannot review any two soft jazz albums consecutively.

Haslem must review album T on day 4.

1. Which of the following is an acceptable review schedule, with the albums listed in order of their review for days 1 through 5?

   (A) Haslem: F, G, U, T, S
        Inge: U, F, T, S, G
   (B) Haslem: F, G, U, T, S
        Inge: T, F, S, G, U
   (C) Haslem: G, F, T, S, U
        Inge: T, S, G, U, F
   (D) Haslem: G, S, F, T, U
        Inge: S, T, U, G, F
   (E) Haslem: G, F, S, T, U
        Inge: F, S, T, U, G

2. If Haslem reviews F on day 3 and Inge reviews U on day 4, which of the following must be true?

   (A) Inge reviews G on day 2
   (B) Inge reviews S on day 1
   (C) Inge reviews T on day 3
   (D) Haslem reviews S on day 5
   (E) Haslem reviews G on day 2

3. If Haslem reviews U on day 2, then Inge must review which album on day 4?

   (A) F
   (B) G
   (C) S
   (D) T
   (E) U

4. Which of the following must be true?

   (A) Inge reviews T on day 3
   (B) Inge reviews a disco album on day 4
   (C) Haslem reviews G on day 1
   (D) Haslem reviews a soft jazz album on day 3
   (E) Haslem has at least one day between the two days on which he reviews the soft jazz albums

5. Which of the following could be true?

   (A) Haslem reviews T before G
   (B) Haslem reviews all three disco albums consecutively
   (C) Inge reviews all three disco albums consecutively
   (D) Inge reviews U on day 5
   (E) Inge reviews both soft jazz albums before she reviews S

6. Which of the following is a complete and accurate list of the days on which Haslem must review a disco album?

   (A) 2, 4
   (B) 3, 4
   (C) 4, 5
   (D) 2, 4, 5
   (E) 3, 4, 5

Game 6

Lasagna, manicotti, ravioli, spaghetti and tortellini are the signature dishes at an Italian restaurant. The Italian restaurant will make one of the dishes the special each month from January to September. Only one dish can be the special in any month, and no dish is the special for more than two months total. The restaurant's choice of specials will be consistent with the following conditions:

Manicotti is the special for exactly one month.

Tortellini is the special in February.

Lasagna is not the special in January.

Ravioli is not the special in consecutive months.

Tortellini is the special in the only month between the months in which lasagna is the special.

Spaghetti is the special in either January or September but not both.

Manicotti will be the special after both months in which tortellini is the special but before at least one month in which spaghetti is the special.

1. Which one of the following is a pair of dishes, neither of which could be the special in May?

    (A) Ravioli and lasagna
    (B) Tortellini and manicotti
    (C) Spaghetti and lasagna
    (D) Tortellini and lasagna
    (E) Spaghetti and manicotti

2. If ravioli is the special in March, then which one of the following CANNOT be true?

    (A) Ravioli is the special in September.
    (B) Tortellini is the special in June.
    (C) Spaghetti is the special in April.
    (D) Lasagna is the special in April.
    (E) Manicotti is the special in June.

3. Which one of the following dishes could be the special in two consecutive months?

    (A) Ravioli
    (B) Tortellini
    (C) Spaghetti
    (D) Lasagna
    (E) Manicotti

4. Which one of the following is a complete and accurate list of dishes, any one of which could be the special in March?

    (A) Ravioli, tortellini, spaghetti
    (B) Ravioli, spaghetti, lasagna
    (C) Ravioli, spaghetti, manicotti
    (D) Ravioli, tortellini, spaghetti, lasagna
    (E) Ravioli, tortellini, spaghetti, manicotti

5. If the months in which spaghetti is the special are separated by the maximum possible number of months, which one of the following could be true?

    (A) Ravioli is the special in June.
    (B) Lasagna is the special in July.
    (C) Both of the months in which ravioli is the special come before the month in which manicotti is the special.
    (D) Ravioli is not the special in January, March, May, July, or September.
    (E) Only one dish is a special in a month later than manicotti is the special.

6. Which one of the following is a complete and accurate list of months, any one of which could be a month in which lasagna is the special?

    (A) January, March, April, May
    (B) March, May, July, September
    (C) March, April, May, June
    (D) March, April, May, June, July
    (E) March, May, July

Game 4 Answers and Explanations

Step 1: Overview

Situation: Interviewing job applicants

Entities: Three applicants—O, P, S

Action: Sequence the three applicants for five interviews, Monday through Friday

Limitations: Exactly one interview per day, and with only three applicants for five interviews, some of the applicants must be interviewed more than once

Step 2: Sketch

The interviews are conducted one per day, Monday through Friday; therefore, you should sketch out a weekly schedule with five spaces, one for each day.

Mon	Tue	Wed	Thu	Fri	O, P, S
___	___	___	___	___	

Step 3: Rules

The first rule says each applicant will be interviewed at least once, so you know that no entity can be left out of the game. The next rule says Onda is interviewed on two consecutive days—you have an OO block. The next two rules stipulate which days Phil and Sally cannot be interviewed; mark this information directly in your sketch. The last rule says that if Phil is interviewed on Monday, Sally must be interviewed on Tuesday.

$$P_{MON} \rightarrow S_{TUE}$$

Step 4: Deductions

The most restricting facet of this game so far is the two-space "block" that Onda's interviews create. There is nothing that prevents its placement on any particular day in the schedule. But since O goes on exactly two days, and P and S are each used at least once, you have four out of the five entities. The fifth interview will go to either P or S.

And if you haven't already, now is a good time to draw out the result of the *if/then* rule. If Phil is on Monday, Sally is on Tuesday, but what else? Your OO block will be on either Wed-Thu or Thu-Fri, so you know that in this scenario, O is definitely on Thursday. And if *any of this* does not happen, the contrapositive of our rule tells you that Phil won't be on Monday.

Mon	Tue	Wed	Thu	Fri	O O	P	S	P/S
___	___	___	___	___		___	___	___
		no P		no S				

If P MON →	Mon	Tue	Wed	Thu	Fri	P	S
	O					___	___
___	___	___					

Step 5: Questions

1.   C

You are looking for the one choice that *could* be true; eliminate any answer choice that must be false. Choice (A) does not allow you to place the OO block anywhere, so it can't be true. (B) cannot be true either: since Phil is not interviewed on Wednesday and Sally is not interviewed on Friday, the only applicant who could be interviewed on both Wednesday and Friday is Onda—but her two interviews must take place on consecutive days. (D) also can't be true: If Phil is interviewed on Monday, you've already deduced that Onda will be interviewed on Thursday. Eliminate (E) for the same reason you eliminated (A): You wouldn't be able to place Onda on two consecutive days. Only (C) could be true.

2.   D

This "if" question states that another applicant besides Onda is interviewed on two consecutive days, and asks you to find the one choice that could be true. So you either have a PP block or an SS block. There are still a lot of possibilities, so start evaluating the choices.

Choice (A) triggers the *if/then* rule by putting Phil on Monday, but with S on Tuesday and O on Wednesday and Thursday, you don't have room for PP or SS, so (A) is out. Choice (B) doesn't work because Phil is interviewed on two *non*-consecutive days, which doesn't allow for someone besides Onda to go on two consecutive days.

Choice (C) is a bit trickier. O is on Friday, which means O is also on Thursday. Since both P and O can't go on Wednesday (rule 3, and O has already been used twice), S must be on Wednesday. But since Phil is on Tuesday, Phil must be the other applicant interviewed on two consecutive days—Monday and Tuesday. This seems fine, except for the fact that putting Phil on Monday requires that Sally be interviewed on Tuesday. So (C) is out.

Choice (D) is possible. If you put S on Tuesday and O on Thursday, you can also put S on Monday and O on Wednesday.

	Mon	Tue	Wed	Thu	Fri
	S	S	O	O	___

You can put Phil on Friday, and you're all set. For the record, (E) doesn't work because if S is on Monday and P is on Tuesday, P would have to be the other applicant interviewed on two consecutive days. But with Phil not allowed to go on Wednesday, and Monday already taken, this isn't possible.

3.   E

This "if" question stipulates that the same applicant is scheduled for both Monday and Thursday, and asks you to determine what day Phil must be interviewed. Who goes on Monday and Thursday? It can't be Onda, who must go on consecutive days. It can't be Phil, because the *if/then* rule deduction says when Phil is on Monday, Onda is on Thursday. So it must be Sally. And if Monday and Thursday are occupied by Sally, then Onda must be interviewed on Tuesday and Wednesday (the only two consecutive days left). You still need to put Phil somewhere, and since Friday is the only open day, Phil must be on Friday. Choice (E) is correct.

4.   E

This "if" question says that the applicant who interviews on Thursday is not the same as the applicant who interviews on Friday, and asks you to find the one choice that could be true. Since Thursday and Friday must have different applicants, it would not be possible for Onda to be interviewed on Friday due to her two-day "block." And rule 4 is that

S isn't on Friday either. So Phil must be interviewed on Friday. Thursday could go to Sally or Onda (i.e. not Phil). Eliminate (A) and (B); Phil is the last one to finish his interviews, since he goes on Friday. Also eliminate (C) and (D), since Phil is on Friday, *not* on Thursday. This leaves (E).

5.   C

This "if" question stipulates that Onda is interviewed on Friday, and asks you for the answer that *must* be true. Since Onda occupies a two-day block, Onda must also be interviewed on Thursday. Since Phil cannot be interviewed on Wednesday, Sally must be interviewed on Wednesday. Monday can either go to P or S, since we've already used O twice. If Phil is scheduled for Monday, the *if/then* rule mandates that Sally be scheduled for Tuesday. If Sally is scheduled for Monday, Phil must be scheduled for Tuesday because you have to use Phil somewhere. Either way, Sally will be scheduled exactly twice, and (C) is correct.

Mon	Tue	Wed	Thu	Fri
P	S	S	O	O

Mon	Tue	Wed	Thu	Fri
S	P	S	O	O

Game 5 Answers and Explanations

Step 1: Overview

Situation: Music reviews

Entities: 5 albums: Jazz (F, G) and Disco (s, t, u); 2 people (H and I) review the albums

Action: Double Sequencing—you need to order the 5 albums for both people

Limitations: 5 days, 5 albums, and 2 people; each album is reviewed once by each person, and an album can't be reviewed by both people on one day

Step 2: Sketch

Since you are dealing with placing albums into certain days to be reviewed, your sketch should resemble a weekly calendar with days 1 through 5 written from left to right. Because two people will be reviewing each album, you may want to place the two reviewers in two separate rows, so you can easily see the albums they are reviewing in reference to one another. Also, it is helpful to list the entities. Use lowercase letters for one kind of entity. Now go on to look at the rules.

Step 3: Rules

The first rule states that any disco album that Haslem reviews must have been reviewed by Inge first. This means that Inge must review s,t, and u before Haslem does. The second rule states that any soft jazz album Inge reviews must have been reviewed by Haslem first. This is similar to the first rule: Haslem reviews F and G before Inge does. Rules like this are easier to handle when you turn the categories (soft jazz and disco) into the specific entities (F,G, and so on). For these first two rules, you might write these restrictions next to the names you have in your sketch already.

The next rule is that Inge cannot review the two soft jazz albums consecutively. Therefore, you cannot have FG or GF; you might write this alongside your sketch. The final rule states that Haslem must review album T during day 4. Finally, a rule that can be put into the sketch! (Some people like to start with rules like this one first—they are simple, and can often inform your handling of other rules. If you take the rules out of order, just be sure you eventually deal with every rule. Overlooking a rule can ruin everything!)

Step 4: Deductions

Look at the rules to see if any deductions can be made. Haslem must review any soft jazz album before that album is reviewed by Inge, and Inge must review any disco album before that album is reviewed by Haslem. Therefore, the first album Haslem reviews must be a soft jazz album, and the first album Inge reviews must be a disco album. Likewise, the last album Haslem reviews must be a disco album (if it were a soft jazz album, when would Inge review it?), and since he reviews t on day 4, this final album must be s or u. Similarly, the last album Inge reviews must be a soft jazz album. Write this into your sketch, but use specifics (i.e., F/G instead of soft jazz). Also note that since Inge cannot review any two soft jazz albums consecutively, the album she reviews on day 4 must be a disco album. Since Haslem reviews t on day 4, this disco album must be either s or u.

Notice that you no longer need to remember that Inge cannot review F and G consecutively; by using this rule to make a deduction, and then sketching that deduction in, there is no way you can put F and G on two consecutive days for Inge. This is the power of deduction—it allows you to incorporate more rules into your sketch. Your sketch should now look something like this:

Soft Jazz: F, G
Disco: s, t, u

	1	2	3	4	5
Haslem (F & G before Inge)	F/G			t	s/u
Inge (s, t, u before Haslem)	s/t/u			s/u	F/G

Step 5: Questions

1. **A**

This is an acceptability question, so you want to apply each rule to the choices and eliminate any that contradict a rule. Often, it may be easier to start with the simpler rules; here, start with rule 4 and work your way up the list. (C) has Haslem reviewing album T on day 3, and not day 4, so eliminate (C). As for Inge not reviewing two soft jazz albums in a row (rule 3), this happens in (D). (E) has Inge reviewing album F before Haslem reviews it, violating the second rule. (B) has Haslem reviewing disco album U before Inge, violating the first rule. Only (A) is an acceptable review schedule.

2. B

This "if" question stipulates that Haslem reviews album F on day 3 and that Inge reviews album u on day 4. Resketch this information (remember that you don't need to draw *everything* from your master sketch over again, but merely a quick framework that will allow you to write down everything for this question). Since Haslem must wait to review any disco album until Inge has reviewed it, Haslem must review album u on day 5. This leaves albums G and s to be reviewed by Haslem on days 1 and 2. Since Haslem's first album must be a soft jazz album, Haslem must review album G on day 1 and album s on day 2.

	1	2	3	4	5
H:	G	s	F	t	u
I:	s			u	F

Again, Inge must review the disco albums before Haslem does; therefore, Inge must review album s on day 1. Choice (B) is correct.

3. C

This "if" question stipulates that Haslem reviews album u on day 2, and then asks which album Inge reviews on day 4. If Haslem reviews u on day 2, then the only remaining disco album for him to review on day 5 (a disco day for Haslem) is s. Since Inge must review any disco album before Haslem reviews it, Inge must review u on day 1, and t on day 2 or 3 (before Haslem reviews it on day 4). This forces Inge to review s on day 4 (since she has to review a disco album on that day), so that Haslem will be able to review it on day 5; (C) is correct.

	1	2	3	4	5
H:	F/G	u		t	s
I:	u	t or F/G	t or F/G	s	F/G

4. B

This question asks about a facet of the game that must be true at all times. This usually means the question has to do with any deductions you were able to make. (B) should look very familiar, since you made the same deduction before you began answering the questions. (B) is correct. All of the others are possible, but not mandatory.

5. B

You are looking for the one choice that could be true; therefore eliminate any that must be false. Go through the choices one by one and rule out the ones that can't happen. Haslem reviews t before only one album, and it is a disco album, so (A) cannot be true. Could Haslem review all three disco albums consecutively? Sure—on days 3, 4, and 5. Then he would have to review F and G on days 1 and 2, and Inge would be able to review two disco albums on days 1 and 2 (or 1 and 3) and still have the soft jazz albums separated. Choice (B) looks like a good bet—here's what it could look like.

	1	2	3	4	5
H:	F	G	u	t	s
I:	u	t	F	s	G

As for (C), if Inge reviewed all three disco albums consecutively, since she must begin with a disco album, this would mean she reviews the disco albums on days 1, 2, and 3. Therefore, the two soft jazz albums would have to be reviewed consecutively as well (on days 4 and 5), violating the third rule. Choice (C) cannot be true. Since Inge must review a soft jazz album on day 5, (D) and (E) cannot be true either; (B) is correct.

6. C

The question asks for the days on which Haslem *must* review a disco album. Reviewing the initial set-up, you know that he must review one on day 5, and since t is fixed on day 4, Haslem must also review a disco album on that day as well. Day 1 is reserved for a soft jazz album. This leaves days 2 and 3 left over for reviewing both one soft jazz album and one disco album. However, the two albums can be switched around between the two days, so Haslem is only guaranteed to review disco albums on days 4 and 5. Choice (C) is correct.

Game 6 Answers and Explanations

Step 1: Overview

Situation: A restaurant with a "special dish of the month"

Entities: The dishes: L, M, R, S, T

Action: Sequencing—the months are consecutive. The rules also use words like "consecutive," "before," and "after"— signs that order is important.

Limitations: Only one dish is the special each month; and no dish is the special in more than two months. Since you only have 5 dishes to choose from, each dish must be the special twice, except for one dish, which is only the special during one month. Taking these limitations to this conclusion is crucial, and should leave you wondering "which dish is only used once?" But before you get to that...

Step 2: Sketch

We can use nine blanks for the month. In the sketch, you labeled the months with the first few letters, since many of the months start with the same letter. However, calendar months are fairly familiar, so you may find it sufficient to just use the first letter (as long as you don't mix up June and July).

You can also write out the entities, keeping in mind that you will have to use most of them twice.

L, M, R, S, T

| ___ | ___ | ___ | ___ | ___ | ___ | ___ | ___ | ___ |
| Jan | Feb | Mar | Apr | May | Jun | Jul | Aug | Sep |

Step 3: Rules

There are many rules for this game, and they contain a great deal of useful information. Rule 1 states that manicotti is the special for exactly one month. That's what you were looking for! Rather than simply writing down "M = 1," add to your entity roster. You now have "L, L, M, R, R, S, S, T, T."

Thinking through the limitations in step 1 allowed you to make this deduction immediately; if something like this occurs to you (as, with practice, it will) you should factor it in.

Now you have nine dishes and nine months. Already, the game is a little less complicated. Rule 2 tells you that tortellini is the special in February. Put this into your sketch. According to rule 3, lasagna is not the special in January. This can also be indicated in your sketch. Rule 4 states that ravioli is not the special in consecutive months. You can write this as a restricted block separate from our sketch: "No R R." Rule 5 tells you that tortellini is the special in the only month between the months in which lasagna is the special. This gives you another block, though you don't yet know where it goes: "L T L." According to rule 6, spaghetti is the special in either January or September, but not both. You can make a note: "S = Jan or Sep, not both." Rule 7 tells you that manicotti will be the special after both months in which tortellini is the special, but before at least one month in which spaghetti is the special. This gives you a relative order of "T…T…M…S." you now have:

L, L, M, R, R, S, S, T, T

	T							
Jan	Feb	Mar	Apr	May	Jun	Jul	Aug	Sep
no L								

No R R
L T L
S = Jan or Sep, not both
T … T … M … S

Step 4: Deductions

Most of the entities in this game show up in multiple rules, and you have several blocks of data to work with. As a result, this game is rich in deductions. But where to start?

Let's look at the common entities. Tortellini is, by far, the most common, and therefore most limited, entity. Rule 5 establishes a block of "L T L," and rule 7 gives you "T…T…M…S." The T in rule 5 must be one of the Ts in rule 7 (since there are only two total), but which one? Rule 2 tells you that T is the special in February—this must be the first T in the "T…T…M…S" block. Otherwise, you couldn't surround either of the tortellini with lasagna. Therefore, it must be the second "T" in "T…T…M…S" that is the one surrounded by the Ls. you now have: "T…L T L…M…S."

This is a huge block—six dishes out of nine! And you know that the first T is in February, so in effect, you have seven dishes accounted for. How can you incorporate this big block of data into a sketch, rather than just leaving it off to the side?

Let's keep looking—we know that spaghetti is either the special in January or September, but not both. This calls for using limited options. Remember, if you see a potential limited option, think about what else you have available. Here, you have a huge block of data just begging to be placed, and there is a much better chance of doing this if you use limited options. If spaghetti is the special in January, then something else must be in September. The only thing left is ravioli. And since you can't have two consecutive months of ravioli (rule 4), spaghetti must be the special in August. Likewise, if spaghetti is the special in September, ravioli must be the special in January.

You now have:

Option 1:
One R left

S	T	...L T L...M...	S	R
Jan	Feb		Aug	Sep

Option 2:
One R, one S left

R	T	...L T L...M...	S
Jan	Feb		Sep

Notice that you did a few things. One, you didn't worry about the specific month assignments during the middle of the sequence—those are more flexible. But the limited options allowed you to incorporate EVERY SINGLE RULE into the sketch. That's powerful sketching!

Step 5: Questions

1. E

You know from your deductions that manicotti cannot be the special in May, so it makes sense to look at the choices that include manicotti. Start with (B). Can tortellini be the special in May? Sure—put one of your "leftover" dishes into March, and tortellini will be bumped to May. So turn to (E); sure enough, spaghetti can never be the special in May. In option 1 spaghetti is already placed, and in option 2, while you have a spaghetti left to place, the "L T L" block will prevent you from putting spaghetti in May.

2. E

Enter this new "if" into option 1 first, since you will then have a complete scenario. You now have:

S	T	R	L	T	L	M	S	R
Jan	Feb	Mar	Apr	May	Jun	Jul	Aug	Sep

If you put your remaining spaghetti into April, you rule out (C). You also rule out (B); when spaghetti is in April here, tortellini is in June. Therefore, since (E) is the last choice remaining, it must be correct. Indeed, unless you place all of our "leftovers" *after* the manicotti (i.e., in July and August), it is impossible to place manicotti in June.

3. C

Wow—your options are really helpful here. So far, you don't have any consecutive dishes; the only way this can happen is to place option 2's "leftover" spaghetti in August. Choice (C) is correct. Without the options, you can still reason it out. You know from rule 4 that ravioli cannot be the special for two consecutive months, so (A) is incorrect. Rule 5 establishes the "L T L" block, which means that neither lasagna nor tortellini can be the special in consecutive months, eliminating (B) and (D). Choice (E) is incorrect because rule 1 says that manicotti is the special in only one month; there's no way it can be the special in two consecutive months. Choice (C) is the only one remaining.

4. B

This "complete and accurate list" question rewards you for taking the time to make your original deductions. From your two options, you know that lasagna, ravioli, and spaghetti can all be the special in March. This is (B).

5. A

This new "if" question tells you that the months in which spaghetti is the special must be as far apart from each other as possible. Looking at your options, you know this question refers to option 1, in which spaghetti is the special in January and August. Based on this information, you can eliminate (C), since one of the ravioli months is September, after everything else. (D) is gone for the same reason. You can also eliminate (E) because you know that at least two dishes are the specials after manicotti. (A) and (B) require you to look a little bit closer. In (A), ravioli can be the special after the "L T L" block, putting it in June. (B) can't happen because the latest you can put the lasagna is June, but putting the remaining ravioli in March.

6. D

This "complete and accurate list" question asks you to identify all the months in which lasagna could be the special. That means you can eliminate any choice that lists an inaccurate month or that does not list an accurate month. Once again, this question pays dividends on the time you spent making deductions.

Rule 3 says lasagna cannot be the special in January, so (A) is incorrect. Your deductions told you that lasagna could not be the special in August or September, so (E) is incorrect. February is occupied by tortellini, which leaves March, April, May, June, and July as months where lasagna can possibly be scheduled. Hence, (D) is correct.

You can also use work you have done on previous questions to help you answer "complete and accurate list" questions that, like this one, ask you for what *could* be true, instead of what *must* be true. For example, on question 2, the work you did showed that lasagna *could* be the special in April, May, June, and July. You can use that work to eliminate (C) and (E).

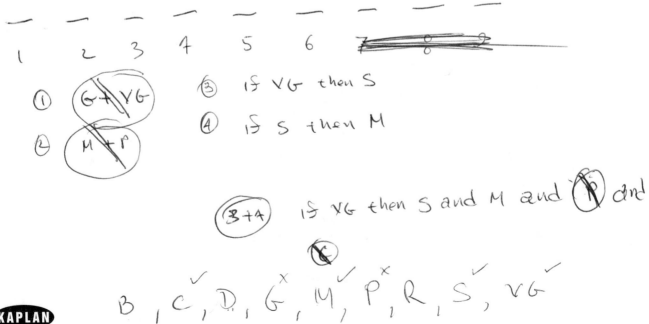

Chapter 6: **Selection Games**

In grouping games of **selection**, you are given the cast of characters and told to select a smaller group based on the rules. For example, a game may include eight DVDs from which you must choose four.

Sometimes the test makers specify an exact number for the smaller group, sometimes they don't. In an occasional variation, the initial group of entities is itself broken into subgroups at the start of the game: an example would be a zookeeper choosing three animals from a group of three apes and five lizards.

GAME 1: THE METHOD

Start, as usual, with a game setup, and work your way through applying Kaplan's 5 Step Method. As your confidence improves, be sure to stop and work on your own sketch based on the stimulus and rules before reading further, and work out the answer to each question before reading its explanation.

Questions 1-6

From a group of nine paintings, a curator will select exactly six paintings to display in a gallery. Of the nine paintings, exactly one was created by each of the following artists: Bazille, Cezanne, Degas, Guillaumin, Monet, Pissarro, Renoir, Seurat, and Van Gogh. The curator's selection of paintings for the gallery must conform to the following guidelines:

The Guillaumin and the Van Gogh are not both selected.

The Monet and the Pissarro are not both selected.

If the Van Gogh is selected, the Seurat is also selected.

If the Seurat is selected, the Monet is also selected.

Step 1: Overview

Situation: Paintings being displayed in a gallery

Entities: Nine paintings: B, C, D, G, M, P, R, S, V

Action: To select a group of paintings for display

Limitations: Exactly six of the nine paintings must be displayed, and three are NOT displayed

Step 2: Sketch

The master sketch for selection games is a roster of all the entities. If there are no specific numbers, circle the entities when they are selected and cross them out when they're rejected. But sometimes you have specific number limitations. Blanks can often be a helpful way of making these number limitations explicit:

B C D G M P R S V

YES   NO

_____   _____   _____   _____   _____   _____

_____   _____   _____

Step 3: Rules

The following is a list of the key issues in grouping games of selection, each followed by a corresponding rule—in some cases, with several alternative ways of expressing the same rule. These rules all refer to a scenario in which you are to select a subgroup of four from a group of eight entities—Q, R, S, T, W, X, Y, and Z:

Typical Selection Game Issues

Issue	Wording of Rule
Which entities are definitely chosen?	Q is selected.
Which entities rely on a different entity's selection in order to be chosen?	If X is selected, then Y is selected. X will be selected only if Y is selected. X will not be selected unless Y is selected.

Which entities must be chosen together, or not at all?	If Y is selected, then Z is selected,
	   and if Z is selected, then Y is selected.
	Y will not be selected unless Z is selected,
	   and vice versa.

Which entities cannot both be chosen?	If R is selected, then Z is not selected. If Z is selected, then R is not selected. R and Z won't both be selected.

Note that a rule like "If X is selected, then Y is selected" works only in one direction. If X is chosen, Y must be, but if Y is chosen, X may or may not be.

Rule 1: G and V are not both selected: No G V.

Rule 2: M and P are not both selected: No M P.

Rule 3 is a standard *if/then* rule: If V is selected, S is also selected (and the contrapositive).

$$V \rightarrow S \quad No\ S \rightarrow No\ V$$

Rule 4 is another conditional statement: If S is selected, M is also selected.

$$S \rightarrow M \quad No\ M \rightarrow No\ S$$

Step 4: Deduction

There are some common entities here: combining rules 2 and 4, for instance, will give you:

$$S \rightarrow M\ and\ no\ P$$

But this is still a conditional, and in deductions, you need to focus on what *must* be true.

Rules 1 and 2 here are the definites, so focus attention there. You can't have both G and V, so at least one of the blanks in the "No" column will be filled by either G or V. Similarly, one of the blanks will be filled by either M or P.

Yes				No		
____	____	____		G/V	M/P	____
____	____	____				

This does not mean you can't reject *both* M and P, but you must leave room to reject at least one of them.

Lastly note that this game has an unusually high number of identical, unrestricted elements: B, C, D, and R.

Step 5: Questions

1. Which one of the following is an acceptable selection of paintings for the gallery?

    (A) The Bazille, the Degas, the Guillaumin, the Monet, the Pissarro, the Seurat
    (B) The Bazille, the Guillaumin, the Monet, the Renoir, the Seurat, the Van Gogh
    (C) The Bazille, the Cezanne, the Degas, the Renoir, the Seurat, the Van Gogh
    (D) The Bazille, the Degas, the Monet, the Renoir, the Seurat, the Van Gogh
    (E) The Bazille, the Cezanne, the Degas, the Monet, the Renoir, the Van Gogh

You can use the rules one at a time to eliminate choices in this acceptability question. Rule 1 eliminates (B) because both V and G are selected. Rule 2 eliminates (A) because both M and P are selected. Rule 3 allows you to cross off (E) because V is selected but S is not. Rule 4 eliminates (C) because S is selected but M is not. So (D) is correct.

2. If the Van Gogh and the Cezanne are among the paintings selected, which one of the following could be true?

    (A) The Guillaumin is selected.
    (B) The Pissarro is selected.
    (C) The Renoir is selected.
    (D) Neither the Bazille nor the Monet is selected.
    (E) Neither the Degas nor the Seurat is selected.

This new "if" question tells you that both V and C are selected. Rule 1 tells you that V and G cannot both be selected, so you must reject G. By selecting V, rules 3 and 4 tell you you must also select S and M. Rule 2 then tells you that in selecting M, you must reject P.

Yes			No		
V	C	S	G	P	___
M	___	___			

Four of the choices will be false, and the correct one will be possible. The diagram shows that (A), (B), (D), and (E) are all false. (C) is correct.

In a "could be true" question, focus on the answers that use the unrestricted entities. Since B, D, and R are identical elements, any two of them could be selected.

3. Each of the following is a pair of paintings that could be selected together EXCEPT:

    (A) The Guillaumin and the Degas
    (B) The Van Gogh and the Seurat
    (C) The Seurat and the Pissarro
    (D) The Cezanne and the Monet
    (E) The Pissarro and the Bazille

Attack this question by focusing on the most limited entities: B, C, D, and R are all unlimited; any one could be selected with any other entity. Choices (A), (D), and (E) are all possible, and therefore wrong. Looking at both (B) and (C), they both include the Seurat. If you select the Seurat, you must also select the Monet (rule 4), and then reject the Pissarro (rule 2). So you can't select both S and P, and (C) is correct.

4. If the curator does not select the Bazille, which one of the following must be true?

    (A) The Seurat is not selected.
    (B) The Monet is selected.
    (C) The Pissarro is selected.
    (D) The Van Gogh is selected.
    (E) The Guillaumin is not selected.

This new "if" question specifies that B is not selected. But if B is a "floater," how can you deduce anything? This is where the earlier deduction will come in handy. If you reject B, you effectively fill up the "No" column; all of the other entities must be selected.

Yes				No		
G/V	M/P	C		G/V	M/P	B
D	R	S				

But wait—you aren't done! Since you must select the Seurat, you must also select the Monet, so you must then reject the Pissarro. So you actually have:

Yes				No		
G/V	M	C		G/V	P	B
D	R	S				

So (B) must be true, (A) and (C) must be false, and (D) and (E), which deal with G and V, are both possible.

5. If the Pissaro is selected, which one of the following is a pair of paintings that must also be selected?

    (A)   The Guillaumin and the Degas

    (B)   The Degas and the Van Gogh

    (C)   The Seurat and the Cezanne

    (D)   The Seurat and the Renoir

    (E)   The Cezanne and the Monet

This new "if" question uses the same kind of deduction as the previous question. Because P is selected, rule 2 prohibits M from being selected. With M out, the contrapositive of rule 4 states that S is also out, and the contrapositive of rule 3 forces V out. Once again, M, S, and V are not selected, so everything else *must* be selected.

Yes				No		
P	B	C		M	S	V
D	G	R				

The sketch shows that (A) is the correct response because both G and D are selected. (B) is wrong because V cannot be selected. (C) and (D) are wrong because S cannot be selected. (E) is wrong because M cannot be selected.

6. Which one of the following cannot be true?

    (A)   Neither the Seurat nor the Pissarro is selected.

    (B)   Neither the Pissarro nor the Guillaumin is selected.

    (C)   Neither the Renoir nor the Van Gogh is selected.

    (D)   Neither the Van Gogh nor the Seurat is selected.

    (E)   Neither the Seurat nor the Bazille is selected.

This question asks you to find two paintings that cannot both be excluded from the curator's selections. Start out using your previous work. The sketch that you generated for question 2 or 4 allows you to cross off (B). The sketch from question 5 eliminates (D). You'll have to test the remaining choices individually. If neither S nor P were selected, the contrapositive of rule 3 tells you that V also could not be selected. This is a total of three "rejects," and since you have a G/V and an M/P in the reject list, we've satisfied all of the rules and (A) is possible.

For (C), failing to select either R nor V does not trigger any of the four rules, so you can't possibly break any rules by doing so. But (E) is tricky. It looks like it should be possible to reject both S and B. After all, B is one of the unlimited entities, right? Remember the master sketch: After rejecting G/V and M/P, you only have room to reject one more. You can't say no to both S and B, so (E) must be false, and is correct.

GAME 2: PRACTICE

Now that you have a good sense of the issues you can face in a game of selection, try working methodically through the next game on your own. By this time, you should be picking up some speed—allow yourself no more than 11 minutes, always keeping in mind that your goal is an average of less than 9 minutes per game.

However, don't focus on timing at the expense of your primary goal—in this game be sure you use the right strategies. Use the extra space provided to keep your scratchwork clear, and check all aspects of your own work against the explanations provided to see where you went wrong or could have worked more efficiently.

Questions 1-5

From a group of nine employees, a newspaper will assign six people to cover a story. Of the nine employees, three are reporters (Janice, Karina, and Laylan), three are editors (Omar, Rindy, and Siobhan), and three are photographers (Vasin, Wanda, and Zach). The employees are assigned in a manner consistent with the following:

There are more reporters covering the story than there are editors.

Either Omar or Siobhan, but not both, must cover the story.

If Karina covers the story, then Omar does not.

1. Which of the following is an acceptable assignment of newspaper employees to the story?

   (A) Karina, Laylan, Omar, Vasin, Wanda, Zach

   (B) Janice, Laylan, Omar, Siobhan, Vasin, Wanda

   (C) Janice, Karina, Laylan, Vasin, Wanda, Zach

   (D) Janice, Karina, Laylan, Rindy, Siobhan, Vasin

   (E) Karina, Laylan, Rindy, Siobhan, Vasin, Wanda

2. If Rindy covers the story, then which one of the following must be true?

   (A) Omar and Vasin are not assigned to the story.

   (B) Janice and Omar are assigned to the story.

   (C) Laylan and Siobhan are assigned to the story.

   (D) Karina and Wanda are assigned to the story.

   (E) Zach and Janice are not assigned to the story.

3. If all three photographers cover the story, then which one of the following must be true?

   (A) Omar is assigned to the story.

   (B) Janice is not assigned to the story.

   (C) Karina is assigned to the story.

   (D) Rindy is not assigned to the story.

   (E) Laylan is assigned to the story.

4. If Karina is not assigned to the story, then who else must also not be assigned to the story?

   (A) Omar

   (B) Rindy

   (C) Siobhan

   (D) Vasin

   (E) Wanda

5. Which one of the following must be false?

   (A) Neither Siobhan nor Karina covers the story

   (B) Rindy covers the story and Laylan does not.

   (C) Exactly two photographers cover the story.

   (D) Neither Wanda nor Vasin covers the story

   (E) Omar covers the story and Rindy does not.

Use this space for scratchwork

Emp   J$_r$, K$_r$, L$_r$ O$_e$, R$_e$, S$_e$ Y$_p$, W$_p$, Z$_p$

① r → e

② O$_e$ or S$_e$ must cover (not both)

③ If k then O$_e$

___ ___ ___ ___ ___ ___
 1   2   3   4   5   6

When you're ready to check your answers, turn the page.

Game 2 Answers and Explanations

Step 1: Overview

Situation: A newspaper handing out assignments

Entities: Three reporters J,K,L, three editors O,R,S, and three photographers V,W, Z

Action: Selection—to select a group of people to cover a story

Limitations: Exactly six of the nine people must cover the story

Step 2: Sketch

Create a roster of entities for this game, which is a standard selection game sketch. Keep track of the three different types of entities—reporters, photographers and editors—separately.

Rep	Ed	Pho
J K L	O R S	V W Z

Step 3: Rules

Rule 1 specifies that more reporters than editors cover the story. Make a note next to the sketch to the effect of "Rep > Ed" and come back to this rule later for deductions.

Rule 2 states that either O or S, but not both, is selected. "O or S, No OS" works well.

Rule 3 is a straightforward conditional rule: $K \rightarrow \textbf{\textit{no}}\ O$

$O \rightarrow \textbf{\textit{no}}\ K$

Step 4: Deduction

Even though you only have three rules, they are powerful. The first rule covers the numbers of the different types of entities, which can often lead to deductions. Think about this rule in terms of precise numbers. There are more reporters than editors, so if there were one reporter, there would be no editors, and with a max of three photographers, you'd only have four employees. There must therefore be at least two reporters, with one editor and three photographers. There could also be three reporters, with editors and photographers filling in the rest. In effect:

Rep		Ed		Pho
J K L		O R S		V W Z
2	:	1	:	3
3	:	2	:	1
3	:	1	:	2

Why can't there be three reporters and three photographers? Nothing says you need at least one from each group, but rule 2 says you need either O or S, so this eliminates the 3:0:3 possibility.

Limited Options

One strategy is to draw out two limited options: when there are two and alternately three reporters:

Rep	Ed	Pho
J K L	O R S	V W Z

Opt I: ___ ___   ___   ___   ___ ___

OR

Opt II: ___ ___ ___   ___   ___

This might not seem like a lot, but in both options, one category is completely picked. In option I, all three photographers are selected, and then either O or S is in the editor column. In option II, all three reporters are selected. Using rule 3, this means O is not picked, so S must be. You therefore have:

Rep	Ed	Pho
J K L	O R S	V W Z

Opt I: ___ ___   O/S   V   W Z   K → no O

OR   O → no K

Opt II: J K L   S   ___

                        not O

There is another, more noticeable limited option: rule 2 is an "either/or" rule. Either O or S is picked, but not both. You could also set up the game based on what happens when each one is picked.

Step 5: Questions

1.   D

Eliminate choices one rule at a time in this acceptability question. Rule 1 eliminates choice (E), which includes equal numbers of reporters and editors. Rule 2 eliminates choices (B) and (C); in (B), both O and S are selected, and in (C), neither one is selected. Finally, rule 3 eliminates (A): K has been selected, and so has O. Therefore, (D) is correct.

2.   C

This new "if" question tells you that R is selected. Using the two limited options, R can only be selected in option II. The only choice that *must* be true in this option is (C); L and S are both selected. Selecting R means selecting only one photographer, but it could be any one of the three, with the other two not being picked. This rules out (A), (D), and (E). And of course, O is *not* selected, ruling out (B).

3. **D**

This new "if" question tells you that all three photographers cover the story. You're dealing with option I: Exactly two reporters and exactly one editor also cover the story. Since the one editor is either O or S, R must not be selected, and (D) is correct.

4. **B**

This new "if" question tells you that K is not selected. This can only happen in option I, because option II requires selecting all three reporters. Therefore, all three photographers are definitely selected, but only one editor is selected. This could be either O or S (since K isn't picked), but there is no room for R, so (B) is correct.

5. **B**

This question asks you to find the choice that *cannot* be true. Once again, use the options to help find the answer. Choice (A) is possible in option I; (B), however, cannot happen in either option. R can only be selected in option II, but in option II you must select all three reporters. Therefore, (B) is correct. Choices (C) and (D) are possible in option II, and choice (E) is possible in option I.

GAME 3: PACING

Finally, try a selection game on your own under test-like conditions.

Work on all aspects of your timing. For example, allowing an average of only 1 minute per question for 6 questions, in order to finish the game in 8.75 minutes you must do your overview, sketch, and deductions in under 3 minutes. Notice where you're losing time, and focus on improving there.

Allow yourself no more than 10 minutes for this game. If you're still having trouble finishing in time, try to identify patterns in your work that are holding you back: Are you missing key deductions or an opportunity to use a contrapositive to your advantage? If you can recognize what's slowing you down, you can make sure you focus on that in future practice.

Questions 1-5

An all-star basketball team will be made up of five basketball players. The players will be selected from a pool of three guards—Ardebelli, Breshears, and Creek, three centers—Haratani, Keller, and Luskey, and three forwards—Paul, Russell, and Stevens. Players are selected in accordance with the following guidelines:

If more than one forward is selected, then at most one center is selected.

Russell and Breshears cannot both be selected.

Breshears and Ardebelli cannot both be selected.

If Ardebelli is selected, both Luskey and Keller must be selected.

1. Which one of the following is an acceptable selection of players for the basketball team?

(A) Ardebelli, Luskey, Keller, Paul, Stevens
(B) Breshears, Creek, Keller, Paul, Stevens
(C) Ardebelli, Breshears, Luskey, Keller, Stevens
(D) Breshears, Haratani, Paul, Russell, Stevens
(E) Ardebelli, Creek, Haratani, Luskey, Stevens

2. If Luskey is the only center selected, which one of the following must be true?

(A) If Breshears is selected, Paul cannot be selected.
(B) If Creek is selected, Russell cannot be selected.
(C) If exactly one guard is selected, it must be Breshears.
(D) If exactly two guards are selected, Russell cannot be selected.
(E) If exactly two guards are selected, Paul cannot be selected.

3. If both Paul and Stevens are among the players selected, then the basketball team must include either:

(A) Russell or else Breshears
(B) Russell or else Ardebelli
(C) Breshears or else Ardebelli
(D) Ardebelli or else Haratani
(E) Luskey or else Haratani

4. If Ardebelli is the only guard selected for the team, which one of the following must be true?

(A) Russell and Paul are both selected.
(B) Paul and Stevens are both selected.
(C) Stevens and Luskey are both selected.
(D) Russell, Paul, and Stevens are all selected.
(E) Luskey, Haratani, and Keller are all selected.

5. If four of the players selected are Russell, Creek, Haratani, and Keller, which one of the following must be the fifth player selected?

(A) Ardebelli
(B) Breshears
(C) Luskey
(D) Paul
(E) Stevens

Game 3 Answers and Explanations

Step 1: Overview

Situation: Picking players for a basketball team

Entities: Nine total players, three different types of players

Action: To select players for the team

Limitations: Exactly five of the nine players must be selected

Step 2: Sketch

This game allows you to use the master sketch for selection games: a roster of entities, either circled or crossed off, based on whether they are selected or not. Now look at the rules.

Step 3: Rules

Guard	Cen	Forw
A B C	L H K	P R S

Rule 1 can't be entered directly into the sketch, but make the appropriate notations of this *if/then* statement and its contrapositive:

$$2+ \text{Forw} \rightarrow \text{exactly 1 Cen}$$
$$\text{Not exactly 1 Cen} \rightarrow 1 \text{ or } 0 \text{ Forw}$$

Rule 2 can be noted with a restricted block: No B R.

Rule 3 is also noted with a restricted block: No A B.

Rule 4 is another *if/then* rule:

$$A \rightarrow L \text{ and } K$$
$$\text{No K or No L} \rightarrow \text{No A}$$

Step 4: Deduction

Make note of the fact that P and S are identical, unrestricted elements. But as is the case in any selection or distribution game with unspecified number requirements, you want to look at the numbers in more detail.

Saving time

Rule 1 is the only piece of information you have here. Since the trigger deals with the forwards, start there.

You could pick zero forwards (nothing says you can't!). In that case you would need to have all 5 from the guards and centers; since you can't pick both A and B, you would have two guards (one of which is C) and then all three centers. Picking one forward is less specific: You would have four players total from the guards and centers. But since you couldn't have all three guards, you'd have to select at least two centers.

Picking two forwards triggers the *if/then* rule; you can only pick one center, and you then must have two guards (you can't pick three guards and no centers because of rule 3). And by picking three forwards, you only have room for two more. Since R is picked, B can't be (rule 2), and since selecting A would mandate two more entities, A can't be picked either. Since selecting three forwards also triggers rule 1, you can't pick more than one center, so if you pick three forwards, you must also pick one guard (C) and one center.

Guard	Cen	Forw
A B C	H K L	P R S
2 :	3 :	0
1/2 :	2/3 :	1
2 :	1 :	2
1 :	1 :	3

This seems like a lot of work, and with this many numerical possibilities, it probably isn't worth it to draw them all out. But you should practice thinking along the lines of "number deductions"—the LSAT loves to test it. You also may have noticed that the vagueness of rule 1 is now a lot easier to deal with.

Step 5: Questions

1. B

As always with acceptability questions, use the rules one at a time to eliminate choices. Rule 1 eliminates (A), which includes two forwards and two centers. (D) breaks rule 2 because it has both R and B. Rule 3 allows you to cross off (C). Rule 4 does away with (E), which includes A and L but not K. Thus, (B) is correct.

2. D

Working through this new "if" question turns out to be fairly time-consuming. However, all of that work you did with the numbers will be extraordinarily helpful. If L is the only center, you must pick at least 2 forwards. And the contrapositive of rule 4 tells you that since K is not selected, A is not selected either.

So you have:

Guard	Cen	Forw
A B C	H̶ K̶ Ⓛ	P R S

However, you're not able to determine who else is or is not selected, so you'll have to address the choices individually. If B is picked, you can't pick R, but that isn't what (A) says, so (A) is wrong. Picking C doesn't mandate anything, so (B) is wrong. (C) also is not necessarily true; either B or C or both can be selected. But if you pick both, as you must do in (D), then R cannot be selected (rule 2). So (D) is correct.

3.   A

This new "if" question presents an opportunity to capitalize on previous work. Question 3 stipulates that both P and S are selected; using the number deductions, exactly one center is selected, along with one or two guards. Look at both. As we've already discussed, selecting one guard means that C must be selected. Selecting two guards means that both B and C must be selected (again, selecting A mandates selecting both K and L, and you only have one center):

Guard	Cen	Forw
A B̶ Ⓒ	H K L	Ⓟ Ⓡ Ⓢ
A Ⓑ Ⓒ	H K L	Ⓟ R Ⓢ

Since you can never select Ardebelli, eliminate (B), (C), and (D). And since nothing tells you which center to select, (E) is out, and (A) is correct: either B or R is selected.

4.   E

This new "if" question stipulates that A is the only guard selected. Rule 5 tells you that when A is selected, L and K must also be selected. From the number deductions, you know that one forward is selected. Because exactly one forward and exactly one guard are selected, all three centers—H, K, and L—must join A on the team, so (E) is correct. Choices (A), (B), and (D) are not possible, since only one forward is selected. The final spot must be filled by a forward. Any of P, R, or S can fill that final spot, so (C) could be true but does not have to be.

5.   C

This new "if" question gives you a lot of information to work with, placing R, C, H, and K on the team. Because R is on the team, rule 3 prohibits B from being on the team. Because both H and K are on the team, the number deductions tell you that there can be a max of one forward on the team. Since R is already on the team, neither P nor S can be selected. Finally, whenever A is selected, rule 5 mandates that L and K must both be selected as well. Only one spot remains on the team, so it is not possible to select both A and L. Therefore, you can't pick A and the only remaining entity is Luskey, so (C) is correct.

Unless selection games are a special problem for you, you should be able to do all three practice sets in 20 minutes.

PRACTICE SETS

Directions: Each group of questions is based on a set of conditions. It may be useful to draw a rough diagram to answer some questions. Choose the response that most accurately and completely answers each question.

Game 4

Ron is packing for his upcoming vacation, trying to decide among the following types of clothing: belts, hats, jackets, neckties, T-shirts, vests, and caps. Ron has several of each of the seven types of clothing, and makes choices consistent with following guidelines:

If he packs neckties, he does not pack caps.

If he packs belts, he does not pack jackets.

If he packs belts, he packs at least one cap.

If he packs jackets, he packs at least one cap.

If he packs caps, he packs at least one vest.

If he packs vests, he packs at least one cap.

If he packs caps, he packs at least two.

1. Which one of the following could be a complete and accurate list of the items Ron packs for his vacation?

   (A) one belt, one T-shirt, one vest, two caps

   (B) one belt, one necktie, one T-shirt, three caps

   (C) two belts, one necktie, three T-shirts

   (D) one jacket, one T-shirt, two vests, one cap

   (E) one belt, one jacket, one vest, two caps

2. If Ron does not pack any caps, what is the maximum number of different types of clothing that he could pack?

   A) two

   B) three

   C) four

   D) five

   E) six

3. Which one of the following statements must be false?

   (A) Ron packs exactly three items of clothing, one of which is a vest.

   (B) Ron packs exactly four items of clothing, one of which is a hat.

   (C) Ron packs exactly three items of clothing, one of which is a cap.

   (D) Ron packs exactly four items of clothing, one of which is a T-shirt.

   (E) Ron packs exactly three items of clothing, one of which is a belt.

4. If Ron packs as many different types of clothing as possible, then it must be true that he does not pack any of which one of the following types of clothing?

   (A) belts

   (B) hats

   (C) neckties

   (D) jackets

   (E) vests

5. If Ron packs at least one item, which one of the following are the minimum and maximum numbers, respectively, of types of clothing that he could pack?

   (A) 1, 4

   (B) 1, 5

   (C) 1, 6

   (D) 2, 5

   (E) 2, 6

6. If Ron does not pack any vests, then it could be true that he packs one or more

   (A) neckties and jackets

   (B) T-shirts and belts

   (C) neckties and belts

   (D) T-shirts and neckties

   (E) hats and caps

Game 5

Each of a group of seven business executives—Bateer, Garrity, Korver, Ming, Odom, Ramos, and Walker—are serving on panels at a trade conference. The business executives serve on the panels either alone or in groups together, consistent with these conditions:

Bateer serves on every panel that Korver serves on.

Korver serves on every panel that Walker serves on.

Ming serves on every panel that Ramos does not serve on.

If Bateer serves on a panel, then neither Garrity nor Ming serves on that panel.

1. Which one of the following could be a complete and accurate list of the business executives who serve together on one panel?

   (A) Garrity, Korver, Ramos, Walker
   (B) Garrity, Ming, Odom, Ramos
   (C) Bateer, Korver, Ming, Odom
   (D) Bateer, Odom, Ramos, Walker
   (E) Garrity, Korver, Odom, Walker

2. What is the maximum number of business executives who could serve on a panel that Ramos does not serve on?

   (A) two
   (B) three
   (C) four
   (D) five
   (E) six

3. If exactly three business executives serve together on a panel, then each of the following could be true EXCEPT:

   (A) Bateer and Korver both serve on the panel.
   (B) Ramos and Odom both serve on the panel.
   (C) Odom and Ming both serve on the panel.
   (D) Korver and Odom both serve on the panel.
   (E) Garrity and Ramos both serve on the panel.

4. If Walker and Odom serve together on a panel, then exactly how many of the other business executives must also serve on that panel?

   (A) one
   (B) two
   (C) three
   (D) four
   (E) five

5. If Garrity and Odom serve on a panel together, then which one of the following must be true?

   (A) Walker does not serve on the panel.
   (B) Bateer also serves on the panel.
   (C) Ramos also serves on the panel.
   (D) Korver also serves on the panel.
   (E) Ming does not serve on the panel.

Game 6

A group of ten friends—Adriel, Chamique, Darius, Guillermo, Hillary, Joaquin, Lisa, Promod, Quentin, and Soon—is at a nightclub. Some of the friends are dancing, and the other friends are not dancing. The following restrictions are in place:

> If both Soon and Adriel are dancing, then both Promod and Quentin are dancing.
>
> If both Chamique and Guillermo are dancing, then neither Hillary nor Joaquin is dancing.
>
> If neither Chamique nor Guillermo is dancing, then Soon is dancing.
>
> If either Hillary or Joaquin is dancing, then neither Promod nor Quentin is dancing.
>
> Adriel is dancing.
>
> Darius is not dancing.

1. Which one of the following could be a complete and accurate list of the friends who are dancing?

    (A) Adriel, Chamique, Guillermo, Hillary, Lisa
    (B) Adriel, Chamique, Joaquin, Promod
    (C) Adriel, Hillary, Joaquin, Lisa
    (D) Adriel, Lisa, Promod, Soon
    (E) Adriel, Guillermo, Promod, Quentin

2. If Promod is not dancing, then which one of the following must be true?

    (A) Hillary is not dancing.
    (B) Hillary is dancing.
    (C) Lisa is not dancing.
    (D) Either Guillermo or Chamique is not dancing.
    (E) Either Soon or Adriel is not dancing.

3. If Chamique and Guillermo are dancing, which one of the following is the minimum number of people that also could be dancing?

    (A) one
    (B) two
    (C) three
    (D) four
    (E) five

4. If Guillermo and Chamique are not dancing, then each of the following must be true EXCEPT:

    (A) Lisa is dancing.
    (B) Hillary is not dancing.
    (C) Joaquin is not dancing.
    (D) Promod is dancing.
    (E) Quentin is dancing.

5. If Promod is dancing but neither Soon nor Chamique is dancing, then which one of the following CANNOT be true?

    (A) Guillermo is not dancing.
    (B) Lisa is not dancing.
    (C) Joaquin is not dancing.
    (D) Quentin is dancing.
    (E) Quentin is not dancing.

6. Which one of the following CANNOT be a partial list of friends, none of whom is dancing?

    (A) Darius, Hillary, Joaquin, Lisa
    (B) Chamique, Darius, Guillermo, Lisa
    (C) Darius, Lisa, Promod, Quentin
    (D) Chamique, Darius, Guillermo, Soon
    (E) Chamique, Guillermo, Hillary, Joaquin

Game 4 Answers and Explanations

Step 1: Overview

Situation: Packing for a vacation

Entities: Different types of clothing—B, H, J, N, T, V, C

Action: Selection—to select different types of clothing

Limitations: There are seven different types of clothing but no restrictions on how many must be selected. There's also the twist that you can select more than one of each type of clothing.

Step 2: Sketch

Use a roster of the entities to keep track of which ones are selected and which ones are excluded. Simply list the seven entities.

Step 3: Rules

This game has an unusually large number of rules, and they're all *if/then* statements:

Rule 1:
$$N \rightarrow no\ C \qquad C \rightarrow no\ N$$

Rule 2:
$$B \rightarrow no\ J \qquad J \rightarrow no\ B$$

Rule 3:
$$B \rightarrow C \qquad No\ C \rightarrow no\ B$$

Rule 4:
$$J \rightarrow C \qquad no\ C \rightarrow no\ J$$

Rule 5:
$$C \rightarrow V \qquad no\ V \rightarrow no\ C$$

Rule 6:
$$V \rightarrow C \qquad no\ C \rightarrow no\ V$$

Rule 7:
$$C \rightarrow 2+\ Cs \qquad not\ 2+\ Cs \rightarrow no\ C$$

Step 4: Deduction

One entity, C, appears in six of the seven rules. That is a dead giveaway that it will be the most important entity in this game. Rules 5 and 6 are kind of a pair; combine them to learn that whenever C or V is selected, the other one is selected as well. In other words, you either select C V, or reject C V. Before you move to the questions, you should also note that H and T are identical, unrestricted elements.

Step 5: Questions

1. A

Using the rules individually allows you to eliminate choices one at a time on acceptability questions. Rule 1 eliminates (B) because it includes both N and C. (E) contains both J and B, which breaks rule 2. Choice (C) includes B but no C, so it is eliminated by virtue of rule 3. Lastly, rule 7 allows you to eliminate (D) because it contains only one C, which leaves (A) as correct.

2. B

This new "if" question tells you that C is not selected and asks for the maximum types of clothing. If C is not selected, B, J, and V must also not be selected. That creates the following roster:

$$\text{B̶ H J̶ N T V̶ C̶}$$

H and T are unrestricted, and the only restriction on N is that it cannot be selected alongside C. Therefore, all three of them can be selected, and (B) is correct.

3. E

This question differs from the others in this game because it deals with the number of individual items of clothing, not just the different types of clothing. The only rule that deals with the number of items is rule 7: Ron must pack at least two Cs if he packs any, so you'll pay close attention to C as you work through this question.

In (A), if Ron packs one V, rule 6 says that he also packs two Cs. However, he's not compelled to pack any other items, so (A) could be true. H and T are both unrestricted elements, so Ron can simply pack four Hs or four Ts, and (B) and (D) could be true. Choice (C) could be true for the same reason that (A) could be true. If Ron packs one C, rule 7 says he must pack at least two. Rule 6 says he also must pack one V, but the rules do not require him to pack anything else. This leaves (E). If Ron packs a B, rule 3 and rule 7 combine to say he must also pack at least two Cs. Rule 5 requires him to also pack at least one V, mandating at least four articles of clothing, so (E) must be false.

4. C

This new "if" question requires that you maximize the number of types selected. Since C is such a major player, what happens if you reject C? You also reject J, V, and B. This leaves a maximum of three types (H, T, and N). But selecting C (if you don't reject C, you must select it) allows you to select V, as well as H and T. You have at least four types, so you will want to select C. According to rule 1, Ron therefore can't pack N, which is (C).

5. B

You might have already figured out the maximum number of types of clothing for the previous question, but even if you didn't, the work you did there is relevant. To maximize the types, you need to pick C, which brings along V. H and T are unrestricted, so they can be selected without incident. B and J are all that is remaining; rule 2 tells you that if Ron includes one, he must reject the other. So the maximum is five; eliminate (A), (C), and (E) immediately. Now you have to determine the minimum number of clothing types he can pack. Technically, the minimum is zero, but you're told in the question that Ron must pack at least one type of clothing. Since H and T are identical, unrestricted elements, Ron could pack either one by itself. None of the rules force Ron to pack one type of clothing if he excludes another, so the minimum number is one, which allows you to eliminate (D); (B) is correct.

6. D

This new "if" question specifies that Ron does not pack any V. As a result, the contrapositive of rule 5 requires that he not pack any C; as we've already seen, he must then also reject B and J. Eliminate (A), (B), (C), and (E), leaving (D) as correct.

Game 5 Answers and Explanations

Step 1: Overview

Situation: Panels at a conference

Entities: Seven business executives: B, G, K, M, O, R, and W

Action: Selection—to select executives to serve on panels

Limitations: Panelists serve either alone or together in groups

Step 2: Sketch

Neither the number of executives who serve nor the number of panels formed is specified. Nonetheless, you can sketch this game using a simple roster of entities:

B G K M O R W

Step 3: Rules

Though the wording is not standard, each of the four rules is an *if/then* statement. Double-check to make sure that you have each entity placed on the correct side of each conditional.

Rule 1:

$K \rightarrow B$ No B $\rightarrow$ No K

Rule 2:

$W \rightarrow K$ No K $\rightarrow$ No W

Rule 3:

No R $\rightarrow$ M No M $\rightarrow$ R

Rule 4:

$B \rightarrow$ No M and no G M or G $\rightarrow$ No B

Step 4: Deduction

You could combine these conditionals into longer chains, but since you won't learn anything new, it is best to go on to the questions.

Step 5: Questions

1. B

Rule 1 allows you to eliminate (A), in which K appears but B does not. Rule 2 eliminates (D), since there is W but no K. Rule 3 eliminates (E). R is not selected, but neither is M. Rule 4 eliminates (C); both B and M are selected. Thus, (B) is correct.

2. B

This question works just like a new "if" question. If R is not on a panel, you know from rule 3 that M must be on the panel. The contrapositive of Rule 4 tells you that because M is selected, B cannot be. Because B is not selected, the contrapositive of rule 1 requires that K not be selected, which triggers the contrapositive of rule 2 and prevents W from being selected. As a result, the roster of entities now looks like this:

$$\cancel{B}\ G\ \cancel{K}\ \boxed{M}\ O\ \cancel{R}\ \cancel{W}$$

Four elements have been excluded, and none of the rules prevent G or O from serving on a panel with M, so (B) is the correct response.

3. D

This new "if" question stipulates that exactly three of the executives make up one panel, and asks you to find the two executives who cannot serve together on that panel. Previous work can get you started. In question 2, you saw that G, M, and O can serve together on a three-person panel, so eliminate (C). You need to test the remaining choices. If B and K both serve on a panel, M and G cannot serve, so R must be selected. Only O and W remain unaccounted for, and none of the rules compel either of them to serve on the panel, so the sketch produces this roster:

$$\boxed{B}\ G\ \boxed{K}\ M\ O\ \boxed{R}\ W$$

That allows you to cross off (A). R and O serving together on a panel does not trigger any of the four rules, so you have flexibility in filling in the third member of the panel. None of the rules prevent G from serving on a panel with R and O, which leaves you with:

$$\cancel{B}\ \boxed{G}\ \cancel{K}\ M\ \boxed{O}\ \boxed{R}\ W$$

That enables you to eliminate both (B) and (E). If K and O both serve on a panel, then rule 1 requires that B also serve on the panel. Rule 4 then mandates that neither G nor M serve on the panel. According to the contrapositive of rule 3, if M is not on the panel, R must be, and R represents the panel's fourth member. It is thus impossible for K and O to serve together on a three-person panel, and (D) is the correct response.

4. C

This new "if" question tells you that W and O serve together on a panel. Based on rule 2, you know that if W serves on the panel, K must also serve on the panel. That means that, based on rule 1, B must also serve on the panel. As a result, neither G nor M can serve on the panel, as stipulated in rule 4. Because M is not on the panel, the contrapositive of rule 3 requires that R serve on the panel, and the final roster looks like this:

$$\boxed{B}\cancel{G}\boxed{K}\cancel{M}\boxed{O}\boxed{R}\boxed{W}$$

There is a total of five executives on the panel, which means that three others besides W and O must serve on the panel; (C) is correct. Watch out for (E); five people total are chosen, but the question does not ask for the total number of people.

5. A

In this new "if" question, G and O must serve on a panel together. The contrapositive of rule 4 thus requires that B does not serve on the panel. Because B is not on the panel, rule 1's contrapositive states that K cannot be on the panel either. The contrapositive of rule 2 states that W cannot be on the panel when K is not on the panel, so (A) is correct. Both (C) and (E) could be true, but they do not have to be.

Game 6 Answers and Explanations

Step 1: Overview

Situation: Dancing at a nightclub
Entities: Ten friends: A, C, D, G, H, J, L, P, Q, S
Action: Selection—to select which of the friends are dancing
Limitations: None—there is no set number of friends who must or must not be dancing

Step 2: Sketch

This game has a large number of entities, so it will be important to make good use of a roster-type sketch to keep track of them all.

Step 3: Rules

The first four rules are all conditional statements. Just be careful that you don't read 'neither…nor' and think 'or':

Rule 1:

S and A → P and Q   No P or No Q → No A or No S

Rule 2:

C and G → No H and No J   H or J → No C or No G

Rule 3:

No C and No G → S   No S → C or G

Rule 4:

H or J → No P and No Q   P or Q → No H and No J

The last two rules can be entered directly into the roster, which now looks like this:

$$\boxed{A}\,C\,\cancel{D}\,G\,H\,J\,L\,P\,Q\,S$$

Step 4: Deduction

Rule 6 tells you that A is always dancing, so simply amend rule 1 as follows:

$$S → P \text{ and } Q \qquad No P \text{ or } No Q → No S$$

Otherwise, it's not efficient to explore the myriad ways that these rules can be combined. You'll combine them as needed as you work through the questions.

Step 5: Questions

1.   E

On this acceptability question, rule 1 eliminates (D), as both S and A are dancing, but Q is not. Rule 2 eliminates (A), as C and G are both dancing, and so is H. Rule 3 lets you eliminate (C), because while neither G nor C is dancing, S is also not dancing. Rule 4 allows you to eliminate (B) because J is dancing and so is P. Therefore, (E) is correct.

2.   E

This new "if" question specifies that P is not dancing. As a result, by the contrapositive of rule 1, you know that either S or A must also not be dancing, so (E) is correct. Note that since Adriel must be dancing (rule 5), you know that it is actually Soon who must not be dancing. However, do not let the phrasing of the answer cause you to dismiss it as the correct choice; it is true that either S or A is not dancing. The LSAT loves to give answers like this. Based on the fact that P is not dancing, the rules tell you nothing about the other four choices.

3.   A

In this new "if" question, G and C are dancing, and you're asked to find the smallest number of people who could be dancing with them. Rule 5 requires that A be dancing, so at least one other person has to dance alongside G and C.

You know that D never dances. According to rule 2, if G and C both dance, then neither H nor J can dance. The game places no restrictions on L, so there's no reason she has to dance. The only remaining entities are P, Q, and S, and none of the rules force you to select any of those three elements. the roster, with the minimum number of dancers, looks like this:

$$\boxed{A}\boxed{C}\cancel{D}\boxed{G}\cancel{H}\cancel{J}\cancel{L}\cancel{P}\cancel{Q}\cancel{S}$$

It's possible that A could be the only person dancing with G and C, so (A) is correct—there is *one other* person dancing.

4. A

This new "if" question stipulates that G and C are not dancing. As a result, rule 3 tells you that S must be dancing. Rule 1 states that if S is dancing, P and Q must also be dancing. Because P and Q are dancing, the contrapositive of rule 4 requires that neither H nor J dance.

$$\boxed{A}\cancel{C}\cancel{D}\cancel{G}\cancel{H}\cancel{J}L\boxed{P}\boxed{Q}\boxed{S}$$

There are no limitations on L, so L either can be dancing or not dancing, and (A) is correct. Lisa could be dancing, but it isn't necessary. All of the other choices must be true, as the above sketch shows.

5. A

This new "if" question provides a lot of information, settling the status of three of the 10 entities. Because P is dancing, the contrapositive of rule 4 requires that neither H nor J be dancing. The contrapositive of rule 3 states that if S is not dancing, either G or C must be dancing. Since the question tells you C does not dance, G must be dancing. You have:

$$\boxed{A}\cancel{C}\cancel{D}\boxed{G}\cancel{H}\cancel{J}L\boxed{P}Q\cancel{S}$$

The question provides you with no information about either L or Q, so (B), (D), and (E) all could be true, but do not have to be; (C) must be true, and (A) cannot be true. Since you're looking for the answer that cannot be true, (A) is correct.

6. D

This is a tricky partial acceptability question: not only are you *not* given the list of people who dance, you aren't even given a *complete* list of the non-dancers. Be careful here—read this question too quickly and you may be fooled into selecting (E), which is the only choice without Darius. But since this is only a partial list, Darius doesn't have to be on it. The answer lies in rule 3—it is the only rule that mandates that when you reject some people, you select others. If both C and G do not dance, S must dance. In (D), C, G, and S are all listed as not dancing, so (D) cannot be a partial list.

Chapter 7: **Distribution Games**

In grouping games of **distribution**, you're concerned with who goes where, rather than who's chosen and who isn't. Sometimes, every entity will end up in a group—like placing eight marbles into two jars, four to a jar. Or a game might mandate the placement of three marbles in each jar, leaving two marbles out in the cold.

It's important to be aware of the numbers that govern each particular game, because although all grouping games rely on the same general skills, you have to adapt these skills to the specific situation. Like sequencing games, grouping games have a language all their own, and it's up to you to speak that language fluently.

Note, too, that in grouping games, knowing an entity is rejected is as helpful as knowing one is selected.

To get started, work through Game 1.

GAME 1: THE METHOD

By this time, you should always make your own sketch and draw your own inferences based on the stimulus and rules before reading further. Respond to each question on your own, following Kaplan's Method, before continuing through the explanations below them. However, since the work done on one question may help on another, it's still useful in this first distribution game to make sure you understand each question and its explanation before moving on to the next.

Questions 1–6

Exactly eight sprinters—Aisha, Drew, Emily, Jeanne, Kedrick, Nick, Rianna, and Sammy—will participate in a relay race. The eight sprinters will be divided into two teams of exactly four sprinters each. One team will be called the Gold Team. The other will be called the Blue Team. Each sprinter is assigned to exactly one of the two teams according to the following conditions:

Aisha must be on the same team as Kedrick.

Drew must be on a different team from Rianna.

If Emily is on the Gold Team, then Nick must also be on the Gold Team.

If Sammy is on the Blue Team, then Drew must be on the Gold Team.

Step 1: Overview

Situation: Sprinters being assigned to relay teams

Entities: Two teams—gold and blue—and eight runners: A, D, E, J, K, N, R, and S

Action: Distribution—the eight runners must be distributed between the two teams

Limitations: Exactly four runners per team

Step 2: Sketch

For this game, you need a sketch with spots for both teams and all eight runners. You should also list the sprinters:

Blue   Gold

_____ _____ _____ _____   _____ _____ _____ _____

A, D, E, J, K, N, R, S

Step 3: Rules

Here are the issues involved in grouping games of distribution—along with the rules that govern them. These rules refer to a scenario in which the members of another group of eight entities—Q, R, S, T, W, X, Y, Z—have to be distributed into three different classes:

Typical Issues—Grouping Games of Distribution

Issue	Wording of Rule
Which entities are concretely placed in a particular subgroup?	X is placed in Class 3.
Which entities are barred from a particular subgroup?	Y is not placed in Class 2.
Which entities must be placed in the same subgroup?	X is placed in the same class as Z.
Which entities cannot both be chosen?	If R is selected, then Z is not selected. If Z is selected, then R is not selected. R and Z won't both be selected. Z is placed in the same class as X. X and Z are placed in the same class.
Which entities cannot be placed in the same subgroup?	X is not placed in the same class as Y. Y is not placed in the same class as X. X and Y are not placed in the same class.
Which entity's placement depends on the placement of another entity?	If Y is placed in Class 1, then Q is placed in Class 2.

Rule 1: Aisha and Kedrick must be assigned to a team together. You can use a block to note this rule:

$$\boxed{A\ K}$$

Rule 2: Drew must be on a different team from Rianna. Use a big NO to make sure you remember this rule: NO DR

Rule 3: If Emily is on the Gold Team, then Nick must also be on the Gold Team. This is a straightforward conditional clue:

$$E_G \rightarrow N_G$$

$$\text{Not } N_G \rightarrow \text{not } E_G$$

Since there are only two teams, you can also write the contrapositive as

$$N_B \rightarrow E_B$$

Get used to noticing this kind of thing *as* you write your contrapositives—it can save a lot of writing space (not to mention time).

Rule 4: If Sammy is on the Blue Team, then Drew must be on the Gold Team.

$$S_B \rightarrow D_G$$

$$D_B \rightarrow S_G$$

Step 4: Deduction

Because D and R can never be on the same team, you know that one spot on each team is always already spoken for by either D or R, even if you don't know which one:

	Blue					Gold			
D/R	___	___	___		D/R	___	___	___

This is a powerful deduction because you are **taking up space**. This is a big issue in grouping games, and you should try to do it whenever you can.

D is common to two rules, so you can also work rule 2 into rule 4:

$$S_B \rightarrow D_G \text{ and } R_B$$

$$D_B \text{ or } R_G \rightarrow S_G$$

Since there are no other common elements, those are the only deductions you can make.

Step 5: Questions

1. The Gold Team could consist of:

   (A) Aisha, Drew, Emily, Kedrick
   (B) Aisha, Emily, Nick, Rianna
   (C) Aisha, Kedrick, Jeanne, Nick
   (D) Drew, Emily, Nick, Sammy
   (E) Drew, Jeanne, Rianna, Sammy

Think of this as a "partial acceptability" question, which allows you to use the rules to eliminate answer choices. Start with the easier, non-conditional rules. With rule 1, you need to see A and K, or else *neither* A *nor* K. Anything else violates a rule. Choice (B) includes A but not K, which violates rule 1. Choice (E) breaks rule 2 by including both D and R. Though it's more difficult to identify, (C) also breaks rule 2. Neither D nor R is among the four runners listed in (C), which would force them to be together on the Blue Team. Rule 3 eliminates (A): E is on the Gold Team, but N is not. Choice (D) is correct.

On "partial acceptability" questions like this one, it's common for one or more answers to be incorrect because of what *isn't* shown, like (C). A good strategy is to think about what you should see to satisfy/violate a particular rule. For example, a choice will violate rule 2 if it has either *both* Drew or Rianna, or else *neither one*.

2. If Jeanne is on the same team as Sammy, which one of the following must be true?

   (A) Drew is on the Gold Team.
   (B) Emily is on the Blue Team.
   (C) Kedrick is on the Gold Team.
   (D) Jeanne is on the Blue Team.
   (E) Rianna is on the Gold Team.

This new "if" question tells you that J and S must be on the same team. However, it doesn't tell you which team they must be on. Since the question asks you to find what must be true, try both possibilities. If J and S are on the Blue Team, rule 2 (and your deduction) tells you that D is on the Gold Team and R is on the Blue Team. Because J, S, and D take up three spots on the Blue Team, A and K must be on the Gold Team because of rule 1. With only one spot left on each team, you can use rule 3 to determine that E must be on the Blue Team. As a result, your diagram looks like this:

Blue				Gold			
J	S	R	E	D	A	K	N

That eliminates only one choice, (E). Now start by putting J and S on the Gold Team. With J, S, and *either* D or R occupying three slots on the Gold Team, A and K are again forced onto the Blue Team. That leaves only one slot remaining on the Gold Team, so you know by rule 3 that E cannot be on the Gold Team (there isn't enough room for N to be there as well).

Blue					Gold			
A	K	D/R	E		J	S	R/D	N
___	___	___	___		___	___	___	___

Your second sketch eliminates choices (A), (C), and (D), which means that (B) is correct.

Saving Time

Is there a quicker way to do this, short of trying both scenarios? Keep in mind the *kind* of information you are given. Since you aren't told which team J and S are on, maybe it doesn't matter! J and S are together, with either D or R, and A and K are together (on the other team) with either D or R:

Blue				Gold			
A	K	D/R		J	S	R/D	
___	___	___	___	___	___	___	___

You don't know which team is which, but who cares? You still need to place E and N. But if E is on the Gold Team, then N is as well, and neither of your "anonymous" teams have room for two sprinters. Therefore, E must be on the Blue Team.

3. If Aisha is on the same team as Emily, which one of the following must be true?

   (A) Drew is on the Blue Team
   (B) Kedrick is on the Gold Team
   (C) Jeanne is on the Gold Team
   (D) Nick is on the Blue Team
   (E) Rianna is on the Blue Team

Saving Time

This is a great example of how you can use previous work to your benefit. The question asks what must be true if A and E are on the same team. If E is with A, you must include K, and then either D or R, so you are back to a scenario from question 2! A, E, and K must be on the Blue Team. This eliminates (B) and (D). Choices (A) and (E) deal with D and R; nothing must be true about them in this question. This leaves (C) as the correct answer.

4. If Nick and Rianna are on the Blue Team, then a sprinter who could be assigned to the Gold Team, or alternatively to the Blue Team, is:

   (A) Aisha
   (B) Drew
   (C) Emily
   (D) Kedrick
   (E) Sammy

This is another new "if" question, and it gives you very specific information to work with: N and R are on the Blue Team. So you know that D is on the Gold Team (rule 2), which eliminates (B). You also know that E must be on the Blue Team (rule 3), which eliminates (C). With N, R, and E occupying three spots on the Blue Team, A and K must be on the Gold Team, which eliminates (A) and (D). That leaves only J and S unassigned, and none of the rules compel you to place either of those entities on either team:

Blue					Gold			
N	R	E	J/S		D	A	K	S/J

So (E) is correct.

5. Each of the following is a pair of sprinters who could be on the Gold Team together EXCEPT:

    (A) Aisha and Drew

    (B) Aisha and Emily

    (C) Aisha and Nick

    (D) Emily and Drew

    (E) Emily and Sammy

One way to do this new "if" question is to look at the choices and place an entity common to many choices on the Gold Team; E is a common entity, so place E on the Gold Team. Rule 3 then forces you to place N on the Gold Team as well. E, N, and either R or D now occupy three of the Gold Team's slots, which forces A and K onto the Blue Team. Thus, (B) is correct; whenever E is on the Gold Team, there is not enough room for both A and K.

Saving Time

This question presents another opportunity to use previous work to your advantage. The question asks for a pair of sprinters who cannot be on the Gold Team together. That means you can cross off any two sprinters who have already appeared together on the Gold Team in a previous sketch. The sketch you just created for question 4 eliminates (A), the answer to question 1 eliminates (D) and (E), and question 2 eliminates (C), leaving (B) as the only pair that *cannot* be together on the Gold Team.

6. If Nick is on the Blue Team, then each of the following is a pair of people who could be on the Gold Team together EXCEPT:

    (A) Aisha and Rianna

    (B) Drew and Sammy

    (C) Kedrick and Sammy

    (D) Jeanne and Rianna

    (E) Rianna and Sammy

This new "if" question specifies that N is on the Blue Team. Rule 3 tells you that E must also be on the Blue Team. Either D or R fills in the Blue Team's third slot, so A and K must be on the Gold Team.

At this point, four entities—N, E, A, and K—are assigned, and the other four are still up in the air. Rule 4 tells you that if S is on the Blue Team, D must be on the Gold Team, so sketch out that possibility first. Because of rule 2, R must occupy the fourth slot on the Blue Team, which forces J onto the Gold Team:

Blue					Gold			
N	E	S	R		A	K	D	J

Unfortunately, this doesn't allow you to eliminate any answer choices, so try the other possibility: S is on the Gold Team. Under this scenario, either D or R is the Gold Team's fourth member:

Blue					Gold			
N	E	D/R	J		A	K	S	D/R

You can now eliminate (A), (B), (C), and (E), so (D) is correct.

GAME 2: PRACTICE

Now that you're familiar with the issues you'll face in distribution games, try the following one on your own, using the extra space we've provided for your sketches and notes. By this time, you should be doing all practice games under timed conditions, so allow youself no more than 10 minutes.

<u>Questions 1-6</u>

Five police officers (Allen, Belinda, Clint, Danielle, and Erwin) and four firefighters (Ramona, Samuel, Teresa and Vince) will conduct four public safety workshops and one home safety lecture. The workshops will be composed of exactly two persons each, and exactly one person will conduct the lecture. Each person will conduct either one of the workshops or the lecture in accordance with the following guidelines:

> At least one person in each workshop must be a police officer.
>
> Neither Erwin nor Ramona nor Vince can conduct a workshop with Allen.
>
> If Teresa conducts a workshop, either Belinda or Danielle must also conduct that workshop.
>
> Clint cannot conduct a workshop with Ramona.

1. Which one of the following is a firefighter who can conduct a workshop with Allen?

    (A) Danielle
    (B) Ramona
    (C) Samuel
    (D) Teresa
    (E) Vince

2. Which one of the following is a pair of people who can conduct a workshop together?

    (A) Allen and Vince
    (B) Clint and Erwin
    (C) Clint and Ramona
    (D) Clint and Teresa
    (E) Samuel and Vince

3. If Teresa conducts a workshop, and if Samuel conducts another workshop with a police officer who could also have conducted a workshop with Teresa, then the only person with whom Allen could conduct a workshop is

    (A) Belinda
    (B) Clint
    (C) Erwin
    (D) Ramona
    (E) Vince

4. If Belinda does not conduct a workshop, then Clint must conduct a workshop with

    (A) Allen
    (B) Danielle
    (C) Erwin
    (D) Teresa
    (E) Vince

5. If all of the firefighters conduct workshops, and neither Ramona nor Teresa nor Vince conducts a workshop with Belinda, then Samuel must conduct a workshop with either:

    (A) Allen or else Belinda
    (B   Allen or else Erwin
    (C) Belinda or else Erwin
    (D) Clint or else Danielle
    (E) Clint or else Erwin

6. Suppose the condition that Allen and Erwin not conduct a workshop together is lifted. If the two of them conduct a workshop together, which one of the following must be false?

    (A) Ramona conducts a workshop with Belinda or else Danielle.
    (B) Clint conducts a workshop with Vince, and Danielle conducts a workshop with Teresa.
    (C) Samuel conducts the lecture.
    (D) Clint conducts a workshop with Samuel, and Belinda conducts a workshop with Teresa.
    (E) Samuel conducts a workshop with Belinda, and Vince conducts a workshop with Danielle.

Use this space for scratchwork

Turn the page when you are ready to check your answers.

Game 2 Answers and Explanations

Step 1: Overview

Situation: Conducting workshops and lectures

Entities: 5 Police officers and 4 firefighters

Action: To distribute all nine entities among four workshops and one lecture

Limitations: Exactly two people per workshop, and one person for the lecture

Step 2: Sketch

Use your standard sketch for a distribution game and create lists to keep track of the two people conducting each workshop and the one person who is conducting the lecture. You have exact numbers, so you can use blanks to incorporate this information.

Workshops: ___ ___ | ___ ___ | ___ ___ | ___ ___

Lecture: ___

Police: A, B, C, D, E   Fire: r, s, t, v

Step 3: Rules

For rule 1, you can make a note next to the sketch: "At least one pol in each Work." Think about what this means: There are five police, and four are accounted for in the four workshops. The fifth can be in either a workshop or the lecture. Another strategy is to write a small "p" below the first blank in each of the four workshop groups.

Rule 2 gives you three pieces of information, each of which can be reflected with a big "NO":

No AE

No Ar

No Av

Rule 3 is a classic *if/then* statement:

$T_W \rightarrow t\ B$ or $t\ D$
No $t\ B$ and No $t\ D \rightarrow$ not T_W, which is equivalent to:
No $t\ B$ and No $t\ D \rightarrow T_L$

Rule 4 is just like rule 2, and can be represented the same way:

NO C r

Step 4: Deduction

There are some common elements among these clues: r shows up twice. By combining rules 2 and 4, you know that if r conducts a workshop, then she conducts it with B, D, or E. The only other point to note before moving to the questions is that B and D are identical, unrestricted elements. And among the nine people, the rules place no restrictions on s—a "floater."

Step 5: Questions

1. C

This "partial acceptability" question deals with A, an element about which you received a lot of information in the rules. Eliminate (A) immediately because D is a police officer, not a firefighter. Rule 2 disqualifies (B) and (E). Eliminate (D) because of rule 3.

2. B

This is another "partial acceptability" question. Eliminate (E) because it contains two firefighters, and thus breaks rule 1. Rule 2 is violated in (A), (D) breaks rule 3, and (C) breaks rule 4.

3. B

This new "if" question is wordy and sounds complicated, but it actually deals with the entities that you know the most about. According to rule 3, the only two police officers with whom t can conduct workshops are B and D. Thus, the question tells you t and s both conduct workshops, one with B and the other with D.

$$\text{Workshops:} \quad \underline{\text{B/D}} \ \underline{t} \ \bigg| \ \underline{\text{B/D}} \ \underline{s} \ \bigg| \ \underline{A} \ \underline{\quad} \ \bigg| \ \underline{\quad} \ \underline{\quad}$$

$$\text{Lecture:} \quad \underline{\quad}$$

That eliminates (A). Rule 2 tells you that Allen can never conduct workshops with E, r, or v, which eliminates (C), (D), and (E). The only remaining entity is Clint, so (B) is correct.

4. E

If B does not conduct a workshop, that means she must conduct the lecture, and one of the four remaining police officers must be in each of the workshops to avoid breaking rule 1. Consequently, each workshop will have one police officer and one firefighter. That eliminates (A), (B), and (C), all of which pair Clint with other police officers. Because of Rule 3, since t must conduct a workshop, she must do it with D, which eliminates (D). Having already eliminated four choices, (E) must be correct, but to prove it, you can go on. Rule 2 means s must conduct the workshop with A. Rule 4 prohibits r from conducting a workshop with C, so your final sketch looks like this:

$$\text{Workshops:} \quad \underline{D} \ \underline{t} \ \bigg| \ \underline{A} \ \underline{s} \ \bigg| \ \underline{C} \ \underline{v} \ \bigg| \ \underline{E} \ \underline{r}$$

$$\text{Lecture:} \quad \underline{B}$$

Saving Time

You would not need to take it this far on Test Day; if four choices are eliminated, the one that remains must be correct.

5. A

This new "if" question gives you a lot of information to work with. All four of the firefighters are assigned to workshops, and three of the firefighters—r, t, and v—cannot conduct a workshop with B. That means that either B conducts a workshop with s, or B conducts the lecture.

Limited Options

Knowing that B can conduct a workshop with s eliminates (B), (D), and (E). Because of rule 3, you also know that D must conduct the workshop with t. Rule 2 tells you that A cannot conduct a workshop with either r or v, which means that A, like B, has only two options: conducting the lecture or conducting the workshop with s. Hence, (A) is the right answer. If you used your sketch to work through this question, it should look something like this:

Workshops: ___ r | A/B s | ___ t | ___ v
            No A   D   No A

Lecture: A/B

6. E

In addition to providing more information, this new "if" question changes the rules of the game. It pairs A and E together in a workshop, and asks you to find the answer that must be *false*.

Because of rule 1, you know that each of the remaining three firefighters conducts a workshop. However, you can't determine anything else, so you'll have to check each choice with a sketch: (A), (B), and (C) all can be eliminated with one sketch:

Workshops: A E | B r | C v | D t
Lecture: s

Similarly, you can see that (D) could be true—and thus is incorrect:

Workshops: A E | B t | C s | D r/v
Lecture: r/v

If s and v conduct workshops with B and D respectively, then either r or t would be forced to conduct the workshop with C, breaking either rule 3 or rule 4. Choice (E) is correct.

Saving Time

As an alternative to working out numerous sketches, look for entities common to the answer choices. Either Belinda or Danielle is in almost every choice, and you know it is likely that one of them will be paired with Teresa; (B) and (D) both do this, but (E) does not. This alone doesn't mean (E) must be false, but catching this might help you zero in on (E) and test it first.

GAME 3: PACING

Now do another, in test-like conditions. You should be pushing yourself to spend no more than an *average* of 9 minutes on each game.

Questions 1-6

During a certain week, a temping agency places six temporary employees—Brett, Charles, Kiana, Rob, Shauna and Tomas—with three employers: a law firm, an insurance company, and a hospital. Each employee is placed with exactly one employer. Each employer will receive two employees. The employees are placed in accordance with the following constraints:

If Tomas is placed with the hospital, Brett is placed with the insurance company.

If Kiana is placed with the law firm, Rob is placed with the insurance company.

Shauna is placed with the same employer as Charles.

Rob is not placed with the same employer as Brett.

1. Which of the following could be a complete and accurate placing of employees with employers?

   (A) Law firm: Shauna, Charles
       Insurance company: Rob, Kiana
       Hospital: Brett, Tomas

   (B) Law firm: Shauna, Charles
       Insurance company: Brett, Kiana
       Hospital: Rob, Tomas

   (C) Law firm: Kiana, Tomas
       Insurance company: Rob, Brett
       Hospital: Shauna, Charles

   (D) Law firm: Rob, Shauna
       Insurance company: Brett, Charles
       Hospital: Kiana, Tomas

   (E) Law firm: Rob, Kiana
       Insurance company: Shauna, Charles
       Hospital: Brett, Tomas

2. Which one of the following must be true?

   (A) Rob is with the same employer as Tomas.

   (B) Brett is with the same employer as Kiana.

   (C) Tomas is not with the same employer as Brett.

   (D) Kiana is not with the same employer as Rob.

   (E) Kiana is not with the same employer as Tomas.

3. If Charles is placed with the insurance company, then which one of the following could be true?

   (A) Shauna is with the law firm.

   (B) Kiana is with the law firm.

   (C) Rob is with the law firm.

   (D) Tomas is with the hospital.

   (E) Brett is with the insurance company.

4. If Rob is with the same employer as Kiana, which one of the following must be true?

   (A) Brett is with the law firm.

   (B) Tomas is not with the hospital.

   (C) Shauna is with the law firm.

   (D) Charles is not with the hospital.

   (E) Kiana is with the insurance company.

5. If Tomas is placed with the insurance company, then which one of the following CANNOT be true?

   (A) Brett and Tomas are with the insurance company.

   (B) Kiana is with the hospital and Rob is with the insurance company.

   (C) Shauna and Charles are with the law firm.

   (D) Kiana is with the law firm and Brett is with the insurance company.

   (E) Tomas and Rob are with the insurance company.

6. Suppose that the rule mandating that Shauna and Charles are placed with the same employer is changed to state that they CANNOT be placed together. If all other rules remain in place and Kiana is placed with the law firm, which of the following CANNOT be true?

   (A) Shauna is with the hospital.

   (B) Brett is with the hospital.

   (C) Tomas is with the hospital.

   (D) Tomas is with the law firm

   (E) Charles is with the insurance company.

KAPLAN
Test Prep and Admissions

Game 3 Answers and Explanations

Step 1: Overview

Situation: A temp agency

Entities: The six employees (B, C, K, R, S, and T), and three employers (a law firm, an insurance company and a hospital)

Action: Placing employees to employers. Because the entities are used exactly once, and the rules talk about who can and can't be placed together, this is really more of a distribution game. However, if you see it as matching, you should be fine; the distinction in this case is less important than on some other games.

Limitations: Each employee is placed with exactly one company, and each company gets exactly two employees

Step 2: Sketch

The game asks you to place employees with employers, so organize your sketch with the three employers in three separate columns, and create two spots for employees with each employer. It may be helpful to write out the first few letters of the companies. You should also list the 6 employees.

B, C, K, R, S, T

Law	Ins	Hos

Step 3: Rules

Rule 1 states that if Tomas is placed with the hospital, Brett is placed with the insurance company. This gives us:
T - hos → B - ins / If B not ins → T not hos

Rule 2 states that if Kiana is placed with the law firm, Rob is placed with the insurance company. This can be written as:
K - law → R - ins / R not ins → K not law

Rule 3: Shauna is placed with the same employer as Charles. We can use a block to sketch this clue:

S
C

According to rule 4, Rob is not placed with the same employer as Brett. We can use a restrictive block to sketch this clue:

not R
B

Step 4: Deductions

Both Rob and Brett are mentioned in more than one rule, so look for deductions using either of them. Rule 4 states that Brett and Rob are not placed with the same employer. Based on a combination of that rule and rules 1 and 2, you can conclude that Tomas and Kiana are not both placed to the law firm. If they were, rule 1 and 2 would force both Brett and Rob, respectively, to be placed with the insurance company.

Saving Time

That's the only concrete deduction you can make before moving to the questions. However, the blocks of data in rule 3 and 4 allow you to have a pretty good idea of how the employees will be placed together, even though you don't yet know which employers they'll be placed with. There are only three employers, and Shauna and Charles are always placed with one. Between the remaining two employers, you know that Brett and Rob must not be placed together. As a result, you know that the employees must be distributed among the employers like this:

$$S \quad R \quad B$$
$$C \quad T/K \quad K/T$$

Step 5: Questions

1. **B**

This is an "acceptability" question, so use the rules one at a time to eliminate choices. Rule 1 eliminates (A) because Tomas is at the hospital but Brett is not at the insurance company. Rule 2 eliminates (E) because Kiana is at the law firm but Rob is not at the insurance company. Rule 3 eliminates (D) because Shauna is at the law firm but Charles is at the insurance company. Rule 4 eliminates (C) because Rob and Brett are placed with the same employer.

2. **E**

Often, with "not-if" questions like this one, it can be helpful to look at the answer choices to figure out what aspect of the game the question is testing. Here, all of the choices deal with who can or can't be placed together; the specific companies don't matter as such. This question allows you to make use of the sketch you drew after making your deductions.

Choice (E) is correct because placing Kiana to the same employer as Tomas would force Rob and Brett to be placed together, in violation of rule 4. Tomas and Kiana can never be placed together. (A) is wrong because Rob could be placed with Tomas but does not have to be. (B) is wrong because Kiana and Brett could be placed together, but they do not have to be. (C) is wrong because Tomas could be placed with Brett with either the insurance company or the law firm. (D) is wrong because Kiana could be placed with Rob at the insurance company or at the hospital.

3. **C**

This is a new "if" question, so you'll deduce whatever you can from what the question tells you. It may be helpful to draw this new information into a new sketch. If Charles is placed with the insurance company, Shauna must also be placed with the insurance company. Since both of the spots at the insurance company are taken, Tomas must not be placed with the hospital (contrapositive of rule 1) and Kiana must not be placed with the law firm (contrapositive of rule 2).

Law	Ins	Hos
T	C	K
	S	

There are no other restrictions on Brett and Rob's placement—they just can't be placed together (and they can't be now!). (C) is correct because either of them could be placed with either remaining employer. (A) is wrong because Shauna must be placed with the insurance company alongside Charles. (B) is wrong because if Kiana is placed with the law firm, rule 2 states that Rob must be placed with the insurance company, but Shauna and Charles have both spots at the insurance company. (D) is wrong because placing Tomas with the hospital requires that Brett be placed with the insurance company. (E) is incorrect because Shauna and Charles must be the two employees placed with the insurance company.

4.   **B**

This new "if" question tells you that Rob and Kiana are placed together, but it doesn't tell you the employer to which they are placed. Because of rule 2, you know that they cannot be placed at the law firm, so you'll look at what happens when they're placed with each of the other two employers. If you place Rob and Kiana together at the insurance company, you know that Tomas must not be at the hospital because of the contrapositive of rule 1.

Law	Ins	Hos
T	R	S
B	K	C

Eliminate (E) immediately because you know that Kiana does not have to be placed with the insurance company. (D) is also wrong since your sketch has placed Charles with the hospital. (C) is wrong because you are not forced to place Shauna with the law firm. However, you can't choose between (A) and (B) without looking at the possibility of Rob and Kiana being placed at the hospital.

Law	Ins	Hos
		K
		R

There's nothing in the rules forcing you to place Shauna and Charles or Brett and Tomas to either employer. (A) is incorrect because Brett and Tomas could be placed to the insurance company, placing Shauna and Charles with the law firm. Choice (B) is correct.

Saving Time

Is there a faster way to do this question, short of drawing out these two scenarios? If you were stuck here, the quickest way is actually to start drawing out some possibilities, and use them to rule out answer choices, as you did above. But you can answer this question without drawing out the scenarios: the question stipulates that Rob and Kiana be placed together, and Shauna and Charles are always placed together, so Tomas and Brett must be placed with the same employer. Using rule 1, if Tomas is placed to the hospital, Brett is placed with the insurance company. Since Tomas and Brett must be together in this question, Tomas cannot be placed with the hospital, which is what (B) says.

5. D

This new "if" question gives you new information to work with—namely, that Tomas is placed with the insurance company—but that information doesn't get you very far. Try looking at the answer choices to see if anything pops out.

In (A), Tomas is already at the insurance agency, and placing Brett there doesn't trigger any of the conditional rules, so (A) seems to be fine. In (B), placing Kiana with the hospital means that Shauna and Charles are at the law firm (it's the only company left with two spaces). Rob and Brett are now split between the insurance company and the hospital. Again, you haven't broken any rules. You can also eliminate (C), because you just saw this when you evaluated (B). In (D), however, if you place Kiana with the law firm, rule 2 states that Rob goes to the insurance agency. If Rob is there (along with Tomas), there is no room for Brett (who, in any case, can't be with Rob). Therefore, (D) can't be true and is the answer.

Alternatively, you might try sketching out the different possibilities right from the start: Shauna and Charles can either be placed at the hospital or the law firm. Start by placing Shauna and Charles together at the hospital. Rule 4 mandates that Rob and Brett must not be placed together, so you can fill in our diagram as follows:

Law	Ins	Hos
K	T	S
B	R	C

Now try placing Shauna and Charles at the law firm. Again, you know that Rob and Brett must be placed with different employers, so you can fill in our diagram as follows:

Law	Ins	Hos
S	T	K
C	R/B	B/R

With these two diagrams, you can eliminate (A), (B), (C), and (E); they all occur in one of your two sketches. (D) must be correct; when you placed Kiana at the law firm, Brett was there as well.

6. C

This question changes rule 3: Instead of Shauna and Charles being placed together, they must now be placed with different employers. The question also tells you that Kiana is placed with the law firm, placing Rob at the insurance company (rule 2). You know that, because of rule 4, Brett cannot be at the insurance company with Rob. The contrapositive of rule 1 tells you that, as a result, Tomas cannot be at the hospital. Therefore, (C) is correct.

Law	Ins	Hos
K	R	No T

PRACTICE SETS

<u>Directions:</u> Each group of questions is based on a set of conditions. It may be useful to draw a rough diagram to answer some questions. Choose the response that most accurately and completely answers each question.

Game 4

A chef is adding the final ingredients to three dishes. She will add one ingredient to an appetizer, two to a bisque, and three to a casserole. Two of the ingredients are herbs: rosemary and thyme; two are vegetables: jalapenos and leeks; two are meats: duck and elk. The ingredients are added in accordance with the following:

The chef adds at least one vegetable to the dish to which she adds duck.

The chef does not add the two herbs to the same dish.

Jalapenos are not added to the same dish as either herb.

1. Which of the following could be an accurate matching of dishes to added ingredients?

   (A) appetizer: elk; bisque: thyme, jalapenos; casserole: duck, rosemary, leeks

   (B) appetizer: thyme; bisque: duck, jalapenos; casserole: leeks, rosemary, elk

   (C) appetizer: jalapenos; bisque: rosemary, duck; casserole: elk, thyme, leeks

   (D) appetizer: leeks; bisque: rosemary, thyme; casserole: duck, elk, jalapenos

   (E) appetizer: leeks; bisque: duck, jalapenos; casserole: elk, rosemary, thyme

2. If the chef adds elk and rosemary to the same dish, which one of the following must be true?

   (A) The rosemary is in the casserole.

   (B) The jalapenos are in the bisque.

   (C) The thyme is in the bisque.

   (D) The thyme is in the appetizer.

   (E) The leeks are in the casserole.

3. Which one of the following must be true?

   (A) An herb and a meat are added to the bisque.

   (B) A vegetable and a meat are added to the bisque.

   (C) At least one herb and at least one meat are added to the casserole.

   (D) At least one vegetable and at least one meat are added to the casserole.

   (E) At least one vegetable and at least one herb are added to the casserole.

4. If the chef does not add the duck to the casserole, which of the following could be true?

   (A) She adds the rosemary to the bisque.

   (B) She adds the elk to the bisque.

   (C) She adds the thyme to the casserole.

   (D) She adds the jalapenos to the casserole.

   (E) She adds the leeks to the bisque.

5. If the chef adds both meats to the same dish, which one of the following could be true?

   (A) She adds the rosemary to the casserole.

   (B) She adds a vegetable to the appetizer.

   (C) She adds both vegetables to the bisque.

   (D) She adds the duck to the bisque.

   (E) She adds the rosemary to the appetizer.

6. Each of the following could be true EXCEPT:

   (A) A meat is added to the appetizer.

   (B) An herb is added to the same dish as the elk.

   (C) A vegetable is added to the appetizer.

   (D) The two vegetables are added to the same dish.

   (E) Neither herb is added to the appetizer.

Game 5

Each of a group of seven students—Alvarez, Burton, Cooke, Driskill, Ernest, Gray, and Higgins—majors in exactly one of two disciplines: philosophy or sociology. The students choose their majors in accordance with the following:

If Driskill majors in sociology, then Burton majors in philosophy.

If Ernest majors in sociology, then Higgins and Alvarez both major in philosophy.

Gray does not choose the same major as Cooke.

Alvarez does not choose the same major as Driskill.

If Cooke majors in sociology, then Burton also majors in sociology.

1. Which one of the following could be a complete and accurate list of students who major in sociology?

    (A) Driskill, Ernest, Cooke

    (B) Higgins, Alvarez, Gray

    (C) Burton, Higgins, Cooke

    (D) Burton, Alvarez, Gray, Cooke

    (E) Driskill, Burton, Higgins, Gray

2. If Driskill majors in philosophy, then which one of the following must be true?

    (A) Ernest majors in philosophy.

    (B) Gray majors in philosophy.

    (C) Burton majors in sociology.

    (D) Cooke majors in sociology.

    (E) Higgins majors in sociology.

3. If Higgins and Gray both major in sociology, then which one of the following could be true?

    (A) Ernest and Alvarez both major in philosophy.

    (B) Cooke and Alvarez both major in sociology.

    (C) Driskill and Alvarez both major in philosophy.

    (D) Burton and Cooke both major in sociology.

    (E) Driskill and Ernest both major in sociology.

4. What is the maximum number of students who could major in sociology?

    (A) two

    (B) three

    (C) four

    (D) five

    (E) six

5. Which one of the following is a pair of students who CANNOT major in philosophy together?

    (A) Higgins and Gray

    (B) Driskill and Burton

    (C) Driskill and Gray

    (D) Higgins and Alvarez

    (E) Burton and Gray

Game 6

Each of exactly six radio stations—Hip-hop, Jazz, News, Rock, Sports, and Talk—is broadcast on exactly one of two frequencies: AM or FM. The following conditions apply:

If Hip-hop is broadcast on AM, then both Rock and Sports are broadcast on FM.

Sports is broadcast on FM if News is broadcast on AM.

If Talk is broadcast on FM, then both Jazz and Hip-hop are broadcast on AM.

Rock is broadcast on AM if News is broadcast on FM.

If Jazz is broadcast on AM, then so is Sports.

1. Which one of the following could be a complete and accurate list of the stations that are broadcast on FM?

   (A) Jazz, News, Rock, Sports
   (B) Hip-hop, Jazz, News, Sports
   (C Rock, Sports, Talk
   (D) Jazz, Sports
   (E) Hip-hop, Jazz

2. If Jazz and Sports are broadcast on different frequencies, then which one of the following must be true?

   (A) News is broadcast on FM.
   (B) Rock is broadcast on FM.
   (C) Hip-hop is broadcast on AM.
   (D) Four stations are broadcast on FM.
   (E) Four stations are broadcast on AM.

3. Each of the following could be a pair of stations broadcast on AM EXCEPT:

   (A) News and Rock
   (B) News and Hip-hop
   (C) Rock and Sports
   (D) Jazz and Sports
   (E) Jazz and Hip-hop

4. If Rock is broadcast on FM, then which one of the following must be true?

   (A) News is broadcast on FM.
   (B) Jazz is broadcast on FM.
   (C) Sports is broadcast on AM.
   (D) Hip-hop is broadcast on FM.
   (E) Hip-hop is broadcast on AM.

5. What is the minimum number of stations that could be broadcast on FM?

   (A) zero
   (B) one
   (C) two
   (D) three
   (E) four

6. If Hip-hop is broadcast on AM, then which one of the following must be true?

   (A) News is broadcast on AM.
   (B) Rock is broadcast on AM.
   (C) Talk is broadcast on FM.
   (D) Jazz is broadcast on AM.
   (E) Sports is broadcast on AM.

Game 4 Answers and Explanations

Step 1: Overview

Situation: Adding ingredients to dishes

Entities: Seven ingredients: Herbs R and T, Vegetables J and L, Meats D and E, and three dishes: App, Bis, Cas

Action: To distribute the ingredients among the dishes

Limitations: Each dish must have a specific number of ingredients

Step 2: Sketch

Create three lists to organize the ingredients according to the dish they go in, with one available slot under "Appetizer," two available slots under "Bisque," and three available slots under "Casserole."

You also need to figure out how best to represent the different kinds of entities. One strategy is to use uppercase and lowercase, but what about the third kind of ingredient? You can have a list (herbs: R, T), or you can use subscript: R_H, T_H, etc. Most of the questions here refer to the different entities by name, so it is probably easiest to primarily use the letters in the sketch, and just refer to the categories when necessary:

App	Bis	Cas		Herbs R, T
				Veg J, L
___	___ ___	___ ___ ___		Meat D, E

Step 3: Rules

There's no easy way to incorporate rule 1 into your sketch, so make a shorthand note of it: "D J or D L." Notice how the vague "vegetable" turned into two specific letters, J and L.

You can represent rule 2 as a restricted block:

No R T

Use two restricted blocks for rule 3:

No J R
No J T

Step 4: Deduction

Because the game specifies that the chef adds only one ingredient to the appetizer, you know based on rule 1 that the chef does not add the duck to the appetizer. Beyond that, it may seem like this game is lacking for deductions.

But wait—there are a bunch of "No" rules, and they have entities in common. Is there anything you can do here? R and T cannot go together, and neither can go with J. Three entities all must be separated from each other, and only three different groups—this means that one of each of these three *must* go in each group. It doesn't matter which one—you can still take up space.

App	Bis	Cas	Herbs R̶,̶ T̶
R/T/J	R/T/J ___	R/T/J ___ ___	Veg J̶, L
			Meat D, E

Now you only have three entities left, and only one rule to keep track of: D J or D L.

This may not seem like a powerful deduction, but it will prove its worth many times in the questions.

Step 5: Questions

1. B

With your deduction, you can eliminate (A), (D), and (E). Rule 1 eliminates (C), leaving (B) as the answer.

If you didn't make this big deduction, you can still eliminate answer choices one at a time to answer this "acceptability" question. Rule 1 eliminates (C) because neither J nor L is in the same dish as D. Rule 2 eliminates (D) and (E), as R and T are in the same dish. Rule 3 eliminates (A), as J and T are both in the bisque.

2. E

This new "if" question tells you that the chef adds both R and E to the same dish, but it does not specify which dish. Therefore, try both possibilities. If the chef adds both R and E to the casserole, the third slot in the casserole must be filled by L: D requires a "partner" and there is only one open slot in the casserole. So D and J are in the bisque, and T is in the appetizer:

App	Bis	Cas
T	J D	R E L

If R and E are in the bisque, D must be in the casserole with L. Normally, L doesn't have to be with D, but in this case, since L can never be in the appetizer (this is from the big deduction) and the bisque is now full as well, you have:

App	Bis	Cas
J/T	R E	T/J D L

What must be true? Only (E); the leeks are always in the casserole.

3. D

Here's your first opportunity to take advantage of the work you did on question 2. You can eliminate any choice that doesn't have to be true, so the first sketch you drew for question 2 eliminates (A), the second sketch eliminates (B), (C), and (E), and (D) is correct. Of the three remaining entities D, E (both meats), and L (vegetable), two must go in the casserole. If you add L and either D or E, you'll have a meat and vegetable. If you add both D and E, you'll then have to add J (rule 1), so again, there will be a meat and a vegetable.

4.   C

This new "if" question specifies that D is not added to the casserole. D also can't be in the appetizer, so it is in the bisque. There is one remaining spot in the bisque. Rule 1 mandates that it is J or L, and rules 2 and 3 require that it is J or R or T. So J must be the other ingredient in the bisque. Your deduction tells you that R and T are now split between the appetizer and the casserole, and the only space left for E and L is in the casserole:

App	Bis		Cas		
R/T	J	D	T/R	E	L

Therefore, (C) is correct; the other choices are not possible.

5.   E

This new "if" question tells you that both meats are added to the same dish. The meats are D and E, and your deduction tells you that the only space for both D and E is in the casserole. D also requires J or L, but since one of the casserole slots is for R/T/J, the third spot in the casserole belongs to J. L is now in the bisque, with R and T split between the appetizer and bisque:

App	Bis		Cas		
R/T	T/R	L	J	D	E

Once again, you're looking for the one answer that could be true, so there will be four choices that are false. Choices (A), (B), (C), and (D) are all false, leaving (E) as the correct answer.

6.   A

Again, you are looking for the answer that must be false. If you had made the deduction about the appetizer being R or T or J, (A) may have jumped right out at you. A meat can never be in the appetizer.

But failing this, you can draw on previous work to answer this question. The second sketch you drew for question 2 eliminates (B), (C), and (E) by putting J in the appetizer, and (D) by putting J in the casserole.

Game 5 Answers and Explanations

Step 1: Overview

Situation: Students choosing majors

Entities: Two majors and seven students: A, B, C, D, E, G, H

Action: Distribution—to distribute the students between the two majors

Limitations: Each student picks exactly one major; there is no specified number of students per major

Step 2: Sketch

Use the two majors to organize the lists you create in your sketch. Remember that there is not a specified number of slots for each major. Your basic framework:

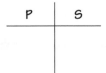

Step 3 Rules:

The first two rules are *if/then* rules that you can note, along with their contrapositives, like this:

Rule 1:

$D_S \rightarrow B_P$

Not $B_P \rightarrow$ not D_S, which is equivalent to $B_S \rightarrow D_P$

Rule 2:

$E_S \rightarrow H_P$ and A_P

H_S or $A_S \rightarrow E_P$

For rules 3 and 4, you can use "No" or ≠.

No G C (or G ≠ C)

No A D (or A ≠ D)

You can also use placeholders to note that these entities appear in different parts of your sketch, as follows:

P	S
A/D	D/A
G/C	C/G

This is especially helpful for questions that ask about maximum and minimum numbers.

The last rule is another *if/then* that can be written as follows:

$C_S \rightarrow B_S$

$B_P \rightarrow C_P$

Step 4: Deduction

There are a number of common entities in these rules; A, B, C, and D all appear in more than one rule. But don't take the time to write down all of the "chains" that exist within the *if/then* rules. You won't be learning anything *new*. When making deductions, focus on that which *must* be true. Remember, *if/then* rules are not always triggered—they don't always come into play. If you keep your *if/then* rules neat (lining up the arrows is a good organizational tactic), you will be able to scan the triggers of the *if/then* rules for anything that occurs in a particular question.

Step 5: Questions

1. B

You can answer this "partial acceptability" question by using the rules. Since the answer choices are potential lists of sociology majors, remember that if an entity is *not* on the list, it must be in the philosophy column.

Rule 1 eliminates (E): D majors in sociology, so B must major in philosophy. Rule 2 doesn't eliminate anything, but rule 3 eliminates (D): G and C have chosen the same major. Rule 4 requires that A and D be separated. While they are not together in any of the remaining answer choices, they are both missing from (C), meaning both would major in philosophy, breaking rule 4. Going on to rule 5, Cooke majors in sociology in (A). Since Burton is not there as well, (A) violates rule 5. Thus, (B) is correct.

2. A

This is a new "if" question. On games with a lot of *if/then* rules (like this one), it is *always* helpful to draw out the new ifs. Even though it may sometimes not seem necessary, you never know when a sketch for one question will be useful "previous work" later on. Since D majors in philosophy, rule 4 tells you A must major in sociology. Hence, the contrapositive of rule 2 allows you to determine that E must major in philosophy, which leads you to choice (A).

P	S
D	A
E	G/C
C/G	

3. A

This new "if" question specifies that H and G both major in sociology. Because of rule 3, you know that C must major in philosophy, and because of rule 2, E must major in philosophy. A and D, as always, are split between the two, and that is all you can do.

P	S
C	H
E	G
A/D	D/A

Choice (A) is definitely possible. If you are short on time, or confident in your work, you can feel free to pick (A) and move on. But with your work, you can quickly eliminate the others. C does not major in sociology, eliminating (B) and (D). Likewise, E doesn't major in sociology, eliminating (E). Rule 4 states A and D never choose the same major, so (C) is eliminated and (A) is correct.

4.   C

This is a great question to answer at the end of the game, or to guess on strategically if you are short on time. Because rules 3 and 4 give you two pairs that must be separated, you know right away that at least two students always choose each major, so you can eliminate (E). And question 1 showed you that three students could major in sociology, eliminating (A). Keeping in mind that maximizing the sociology majors also means minimizing the philosophy majors, you can go on to the rules.

Rule 5 is a great place to start in this kind of situation. You can start by placing C, and therefore B, in sociology. D is therefore in philosophy (contrapositive of rule 1), placing A in sociology (rule 4). The contrapositive of rule 3 then tells you that E is in philosophy. Because C is in sociology, G must be in philosophy (rule 3). H is the only one left, so you can put it in sociology to maximize your sociology majors.

P	S
D	C
E	B
G	A
	H

So far your max is four—can you get five in sociology? Start with the same rule. You can use the contrapositive and put both B and C in philosophy, but since either A or D will be there as well, you're already at three in philosophy; sociology couldn't have more than four majors here. The only other possibility (using rule 5) is to split up B and C: B goes in sociology and C goes in philosophy. You end up with this:

P	S
C	B
D	G
E	A

H is a "floater" again, but even by putting H in sociology, you will still only get a max of four. Choice (C) is correct.

5.   E

A question that asks for something that *cannot* be true: use previous work and then test the remaining choices. In the sketch for question 4, you saw that (C) was possible. And question 1, with B, C, D, and E all in philosophy, proves that (B) is also possible. Choices (A) and (D) both have H. But putting H in philosophy doesn't tell you anything else. This means that H can go in philosophy with any other entity, so (A) and (D) are both possible as well. Choice (E) is all that remains, and is correct. If B majors in philosophy, then C must as well. But if C majors in philosophy, G cannot.

Game 6 Answers and Explanations

Step 1: Overview

Situation: Finding frequencies for radio stations

Entities: Six radio stations (H, J, N, R, S, T) and two frequencies

Action: Distribution—to distribute the stations between the two frequencies

Limitations: Six total stations; each station appears on exactly one frequency; no set number of stations per frequency

Step 2: Sketch

A simple two-column list is the easiest way to sketch this game, with one column for each radio frequency. Remember that there is no set number of slots for each frequency.

Step 3: Rules

Every rule in this game is an *if/then* rule that, along with its contrapositive, can be diagrammed in a standard way alongside your sketch.

Rule 1:

$$H_{AM} \rightarrow R_{FM} \text{ and } S_{FM}$$
$$R_{AM} \text{ or } S_{AM} \rightarrow H_{FM}$$

Rule 2:

$$N_{AM} \rightarrow S_{FM}$$
$$S_{AM} \rightarrow N_{FM}$$

Rule 3:

$$T_{FM} \rightarrow J_{AM} \text{ and } H_{AM}$$
$$J_{FM} \text{ or } H_{FM} \rightarrow T_{AM}$$

Rule 4:

$$N_{FM} \rightarrow R_{AM}$$
$$R_{FM} \rightarrow N_{AM}$$

Rule 5:

$$J_{AM} \rightarrow S_{AM}$$
$$S_{FM} \rightarrow J_{FM}$$

Step 4: Deduction

There are numerous common elements in these conditional clues. They could be combined in dozens of ways, but doing so before attacking the questions would consume too much time to be productive. Instead, move directly to the questions and combine these conditional statements as needed.

Step 5: Questions

1.   B

You can use the rules to eliminate choices on this "partial acceptability" question, and also consider how each choice would impact the lineup of stations broadcast on AM. Rule 1 eliminates (D); if Hip-hop is not on your FM list (meaning it is on the AM list), then both Rock and Sports must be. Rule 2 eliminates (E): Both News and Sports are on AM, which is not allowed. Rule 3 doesn't help us, but rule 4 eliminates (A); when N is on FM, R must be on AM. You can use rule 5 to eliminate (C); since Jazz is not on the list, it is broadcast on AM, so Sports should be broadcast on AM, too. Hence, (B) is correct.

2.   A

This new "if" question specifies that J and S are broadcast on different frequencies. Rule 5 tells you that they must be broadcast on the same frequency when J is broadcast on AM, so distribute J to FM and S to AM. By the contrapositive of rule 3, you know that T must be broadcast on AM. The contrapositive of rule 1 tells you that H is on FM. By the contrapositive of rule 2, you know that N must be broadcast on FM, and then to finish it off, rule 4 requires that R is on AM.

AM	FM
S	J
T	H
R	N

So (A) is correct.

3.   E

You're looking for an answer that is NOT possible. The sketch shows you that both stations in (C) can be on AM, so (C) is out. You can test (A) and (B) at once by putting N on AM. In doing so, you end up with:

AM	FM
N	J
T	S

But since either R or H could be on AM, both (A) and (B) are possible. You're left with (D) and (E); once again, test both at once by putting Jazz on AM. Jazz on AM means that Sports is on AM (already implying that (D) is possible, and therefore the wrong answer). Because of the contrapositive of rule 1, this means that H must be broadcast on FM. When Jazz is on AM, Hip-hop cannot be, making (E) correct.

4.   B

This new "if" question tells you that R is broadcast on FM. Because of the contrapositive of rule 4, N must be broadcast on AM. In turn, by rule 2, S must be broadcast on FM. The contrapositive of rule 5 then requires that J be broadcast on FM, triggering the contrapositive of rule 3, resulting in T being broadcast on AM. H can be broadcast on either AM or FM.

AM	FM
N	R
T	S
	J

Choice (B) is correct.

5.   C

A minimum question; using previous work, you've seen that it is possible to have three stations on FM, so you can quickly eliminate (E). In order to minimize the number of FM stations, you want to maximize the number of AM stations. Rule 5 tells you that if you put J on AM, then S goes there as well. The contrapositive of rule 2 means that N is on FM. Rule 4 is triggered, so R is on AM. The contrapositives of rules 1 and 3 then tell you that H is on FM and T is on AM.

AM	FM
J	N
S	H
R	
T	

So you can get the number of FM stations down to two; can you get the number even lower? Going back to rule 5, if both S and J are on FM, you're already at two stations. If J and S are split, you can refer to the sketch from question 2, showing you that you'll have three stations on each. Two is the minimum, and (C) is correct.

6.   A

This new "if" question tells you that Hip-hop is broadcast on AM. Rule 1 stipulates that R and S must be broadcast on FM. The contrapositive of rule 5 states that broadcasting S on FM means J must also be broadcast on FM. The contrapositive of rule 3 states that broadcasting R on FM means T must be broadcast on AM. According to the contrapositive of rule 4, N must be broadcast on AM whenever R is broadcast on FM.

AM	FM
H	R
N	S
T	J

So (A) must be true.

Chapter 8: **Matching Games**

Matching games ask you to match up various characteristics—frequently more than a single type of characteristic—about a group of entities: perhaps three animals, each assigned a name, color, and size (the example used in chapter 1). The sheer numbers are often difficult to handle, unless you develop a methodical, organized approach, like a table or grid.

You already know you should help keep the entities and characteristics distinguished by using variations in your notations, such as lowercase and uppercase letters, subscripts—whatever works for you. To get the data under control, center your sketch around the most important characteristic—that is, the one with the most information attached to it. Going back to the animals example, don't assume that you should organize your sketch around the animals—there may be a better attribute, one that you know more about, that should take center stage. Visualize the action and create a mental picture or a sketch that puts the elements into a logical order. If you think through the scenarios and don't get scared off by their seeming complexity, you can find matching games accessible and even fun.

Most matching games require scratchwork in the form of a list: grids work only when there is a low number of entities to match up—3 × 3 or 4 × 2, say—and all entities are used.

GAME 1: THE METHOD

Don't forget to pause and work through the setup and each question on your own, as much as possible, before reading on.

> Questions 1-6
> Over a period of one week, Monday through Friday, M. Gorbachev Community
> College will host a Russian literature conference. The conference consists of six
> seminars: Bulgakov, Dostoyevsky, Gogol, Lermontov, Pushkin, and Turgenev.
> Jackson and Kingman are students at the college and will attend one seminar per
> day, but will not both attend the same seminar on any given day, nor will either one
> attend any seminar more than once. The seminars they choose to attend must meet
> the following conditions:
>
> > Bulgakov, Dostoyevsky, Gogol, and Pushkin are offered on Monday.
> >
> > Gogol, Lermontov, and Pushkin are offered on Tuesday.
> >
> > Dostoyevsky, Lermontov, Pushkin, and Turgenev are offered on Wednesday.
> >
> > Lermontov, Pushkin, and Turgenev are offered on Thursday.
> >
> > Gogol and Lermontov are offered on Friday.

On Tuesday, Jackson attends the Lermontov seminar.

On Thursday, Kingman attends the Pushkin seminar.

Step 1: Overview

Situation: Attending seminars on Russian literature

Entities: Two students (J and K) and six seminars (B, D, G, L, P, T)

Action: To match students with seminars

Limitations: Each student attends a *different* seminar each day. Students don't attend same seminar on the same day.

Step 2: Sketch

Sketch out a weekly calendar, Monday through Friday, and leave room to note which seminars will be presented on each day (notice rules 1-5). Since you also know that both Jackson and Kingman will be attending separate seminars each day, you will want to have a row for each.

	M	T	W	Th	F
J					
K					

Step 3: Rules

The following is a list of the key issues in matching games, each followed by a corresponding rule or set of rules. All of these rules refer to a situation in which you have three animals—a dog, a cat, and a goat. Each animal has a name (Bimpy, Hank, and Sujin), a color (brown, black, or white), and a size (large or small).

Typical Matching Game Issues

Issue	Wording of Rule
Which entities are matched up?	The dog is brown. The black animal is small.
Which entities are not matched up?	Blimpy is not white. The goat is not large.
Which entities' matchups depend on the matchups of other entities?	If the cat is large, then Hank is brown. If the white animal is small, then Sujin is not the dog.

Notice that these last rules take the form of *if/then* statements, which means, as you know, that the contrapositive can be employed.

The first five rules in Game 1 tell you the days on which certain seminars are presented. These can be written directly into your sketch. The last two rules state that Jackson must attend the Lermontov seminar on Tuesday, and Kingman must attend the Pushkin seminar on Thursday. Write in these seminars in the room provided. Your sketch should look something like this:

	M B D G P	T G L P	W D L T P	Th L P T	F G L
J		L			
K				P	

Step 4: Deduction

This is a game where the rules are fairly straightforward, but the deductions all stem from the limitations in the opening paragraph. Remember these limitations: Jackson and Kingman cannot take the same seminar more than once, and they cannot attend the same seminar as each other on any given day. Therefore, if Jackson attends the Lermontov seminar on Tuesday, he cannot attend the Lermontov seminar on Friday. Since only two seminars are presented on Friday, Jackson must attend the Gogol seminar. Since the two students cannot attend the same seminar on any given day, Kingman must attend the Lermontov seminar on Friday.

Also note that since Jackson attends the Lermontov seminar on Tuesday, and since Kingman attends the Pushkin seminar on Thursday, this leaves only the Turgenev seminar for Jackson to attend on Thursday.

Finally, review Kingman's schedule for the week. Notice that Kingman is scheduled to attend the Pushkin and Lermontov seminars. From all these deductions, your new sketch should look something like this:

	M B D G P	T G L̶ P̶	W D L̶ T P	Th L̶ P̶ T̶	F G̶ L̶
J		L		T	G
K		G		P	L

Notice that with these deductions, you are only dealing with four empty spaces and six seminars to position into those spaces. Now the game is not so daunting.

Step 5: Questions

1. Which of the following statements must be true?

    (A) Jackson attends the Dostoyevsky seminar on Monday
    (B) Jackson attends the Pushkin seminar on Wednesday
    (C) Kingman attends the Gogol seminar on Tuesday
    (D) Kingman attends the Pushkin seminar on Wednesday
    (E) Kingman attends the Turgenev seminar on Wednesday

This question asks about one of the deductions you already made. Since Kingman must attend the Gogol seminar on Tuesday, you know that (C) must be true.

2. It CANNOT be true that both Jackson and Kingman attend which seminar during the week?

    (A) Bulgakov
    (B) Dostoyevsky
    (C) Gogol
    (D) Lermontov
    (E) Turgenev

This question asks for the one seminar that Jackson and Kingman could not both attend during the given week. Since you already deduced that they both must attend the Gogol and Lermontov seminars, you can eliminate (C) and (D). Now take a closer look at the remaining choices. Notice that the Bulgakov seminar is only offered on Monday. Since Jackson and Kingman cannot attend the same seminar on a given day, only one of the two would be able to attend the Bulgakov seminar on Monday. Therefore, they both cannot attend the Bulgakov seminar during the week; (A) is the correct response.

3. If Jackson attends the Dostoyevsky seminar on Monday, then which one of the following statements must be true about Wednesday?

    (A) Jackson attends the Pushkin seminar
    (B) Jackson attends the Turgenev seminar
    (C) Kingman attends the Dostoyevsky seminar
    (D) Kingman attends the Pushkin seminar
    (E) Kingman attends the Turgenev seminar

With new "if" questions, you should always redraw your master sketch. Don't think you will be saving time by skipping this redrawing. If you don't redraw, you will waste time trying to figure out what is "master sketch" info and what is only good for the question you just finished.

Saving Time

But don't feel like you need to redraw the entire sketch. Here, you can easily get away with redrawing just the rows for J and K. We redrew everything in this explanation just for ease of reference.

The question stipulates that Jackson attends the D on Monday, and asks you to find the one choice that must be true based on this additional rule. Since Jackson already attends T on Thursday, and now must attend D on Monday, this leaves only the Pushkin seminar for him to attend on Wednesday. This leaves Kingman to choose either Dostoyevsky or Turgenev for Wednesday.

	M B D G̶ P	T G̶ L̶ P	W D L̶ P̶ T	Th L̶ P̶ T̶	F G̶ L̶
J	D	L	P	T	G
K		G	D/T	P	L

Since the question asks for the one answer that must be true, (A) is correct.

4. Which one of the following statements must be false?

   (A) Jackson attends the Pushkin seminar on Monday

   (B) Jackson attends the Gogol seminar on Friday

   (C) Kingman attends the Dostoyevsky seminar on Wednesday

   (D) Kingman does not attend the Turgenev seminar on Wednesday

   (E) Kingman does not attend the Gogol seminar on Tuesday

The question asks for the one answer choice that must be false. Looking at your master sketch, Kingman must attend G on Tuesday. Therefore, (E) must be false, since it says Kingman does not attend the Gogol seminar on Tuesday.

5. Which of the following statements must be false?

   (A) Jackson does not attend the Dostoyevsky seminar

   (B) Kingman does not attend the Bulgakov seminar

   (C) Neither Jackson nor Kingman attends the Bulgakov seminar

   (D) Neither Jackson nor Kingman attends the Dostoyevsky seminar

   (E) Both Jackson and Kingman attend the Turgenev seminar

This question asks for another choice that cannot be true. Choice (A) could be true, and can be eliminated; (B) and (C) are also possibilities and can also be eliminated; (D) might first appear to be possible, but in fact is not. If neither Jackson nor Kingman attends the Dostoyevsky seminar, then on Wednesday, Jackson must attend the Pushkin seminar, and Kingman must attend the Turgenev seminar. This leaves Jackson able to attend the Bulgakov seminar only on Monday, and Kingman can only attend the Bulgakov seminar on Monday as well. Since both Jackson and Kingman cannot attend the same seminar on the same day, it is not possible for *both* Jackson and Kingman *not* to attend a Dostoyevsky seminar.

	M B D G P	T G L P	W D L P T	T L P T	F G L
J	~~DGP~~ B	L	P	T	G
K	~~DGP~~ B	G	T	P	L

6. If the rule stating that Kingman attends the Pushkin seminar on Thursday were changed to state that Kingman attends the Pushkin seminar on Wednesday, and all other conditions remain the same, which of the following could be true?

    (A) Jackson attends the Pushkin seminar on Monday

    (B) Jackson attends the Turgenev seminar on Wednesday

    (C) Jackson attends the Turgenev seminar on Thursday

    (D) Kingman attends the Gogol seminar on Monday

    (E) Kingman attends the Lermontov seminar on Thursday

This new "if" question changes the rule of Kingman attending P on Thursday with a new rule: Kingman attends P on Wednesday. You are asked to find the one answer choice that could be true. The best thing to do here is to start with two empty rows for Jackson and Kingman.

Kingman attends P on Wednesday, and Jackson still attends L on Tuesday. If Jackson attends L on Tuesday, he must attend G on Friday, so Kingman attends L on Friday. If Kingman attends P on Wednesday, then, since he must attend L on Friday, Kingman is forced to attend T on Thursday. This forces Jackson to attend the Pushkin seminar on Thursday. This leaves Jackson and Kingman to split the Monday seminars between Bulgakov and Dostoyevsky, and Jackson to choose between Dostoyevsky and Turgenev for Wednesday. Therefore, only (B) could be true.

	M B D G P	T G L P	W D L P T	Th L P T	F G L
J	B/D	L	D/T	P	G
K	B/D	G	P	T	L

GAME 2: PRACTICE

As you can see, the work done up front organizing the data is especially important—and especially effective—in matching games. Now try a game on your own, focusing on applying Kaplan's Method and strategies, before reviewing the explanations.

Remember that all practice should include some emphasis on timing now: allow yourself 10 minutes for the following game. We're still allowing a lot of space for your scratchwork, because we want you to be able to easily compare your scratchwork with ours, but remember that you won't have that luxury on Test Day. Look for ways to make it smaller, quicker, and clearer as you perfect your approach to the games. It only has to be clear and legible while you work on that game.

Questions 1-6

Seven cities—Burton, Delareaux, Enbury, Fesburg, Giddings, Hathaway, and Jovenship—are each hosting a visiting foreign dignitary. Three cities will host ambassadors, three will host consuls, and one will host a premier. The choice of which cities will host which dignitaries must adhere to the following:

> Fesburg hosts the same type of dignitary as Enbury.
>
> Delareaux hosts a different type of dignitary from Hathaway.
>
> If Jovenship hosts a consul, then Giddings hosts an ambassador.
>
> Delareaux hosts an ambassador.

1. Which one of the following could be a complete and accurate matching of the dignitaries to the cities that host them?

    (A) Premier: Giddings
       Ambassador: Delareaux, Fesburg, Enbury
       Consul: Hathaway, Burton, Jovenship

    (B) Premier: Giddings
       Ambassador: Hathaway, Burton, Jovenship
       Consul: Delareaux, Fesburg, Enbury

    (C) Premier: Jovenship
       Ambassador: Delareaux, Hathaway, Giddings
       Consul: Burton, Enbury, Fesburg

    (D) Premier: Jovenship
       Ambassador: Delareaux, Fesburg, Burton
       Consul: Hathaway, Giddings, Enbury

    (E) Premier: Jovenship
       Ambassador: Delareaux, Burton, Giddings
       Consul: Hathaway, Fesburg, Enbury

2. If Jovenship does not host an ambassador, then which of the following could be true?

    (A) Delareaux and Fesburg both host consuls.

    (B) Fesburg and Giddings both host consuls.

    (C) Delareaux and Enbury both host ambassadors.

    (D) Hathaway and Giddings both host ambassadors.

    (E) Fesburg and Giddings both host ambassadors.

3. Each of the following could be an accurate partial list of the cities that host consuls EXCEPT:

    (A) Hathaway, Burton

    (B) Hathaway, Jovenship

    (C) Hathaway, Enbury

    (D) Fesburg, Giddings

    (E) Fesburg, Jovenship

4. Which one of the following is a complete and accurate list of cities, each of which CANNOT host an ambassador?

    (A) Hathaway

    (B) Burton, Hathaway

    (C) Enbury, Fesburg

    (D) Enbury, Fesburg, Hathaway, Jovenship

    (E) Burton, Delareaux, Hathaway, Jovenship

5. If Delareaux hosts the same type of dignitary as Jovenship, then each of the following could be true EXCEPT:

    (A) Hathaway hosts a consul.

    (B) Fesburg hosts an ambassador.

    (C) Burton hosts a consul.

    (D) Giddings hosts a premier.

    (E) Giddings hosts an ambassador.

6. Which of the following statements, if true, allows a complete determination of which type of dignitary is hosted by each city?

    (A) Delareaux and Giddings both host ambassadors.

    (B) Hathaway and Enbury both host consuls.

    (C) Burton and Giddings both host consuls.

    (D) Burton and Giddings both host ambassadors.

    (E) Burton and Jovenship both host ambassadors.

Use this space for scratchwork

Turn the page when you are ready to check your answers.

Game 2 Answers and Explanations

Step 1: Overview

Situation: Cities hosting dignitaries

Entities: Cities B, D, E, F, G, H, J and types of dignitaries a, c, and p

Action: To match the dignitaries to the cities, one per city. But some matching games may lend themselves to being set up using distribution techniques. Signs are specific numbers of each entity (you know exactly how many of each type of dignitary you have to use) and a 1:1 matchup between the two kinds of entities. Here, you can also think of this as distributing the cities to each of the three types of dignitaries. The "premier group'" will have three cities, and so on. When in doubt, sometimes the answer choices can be a clue. The choices to question 1 are set up in groups.

Limitations: One dignitary per city; three ambassadors, three consuls, and one premier

Step 2: Sketch

Create lists distributing the cities according to the type of dignitary they host:

Amb	Con	Pre
___ ___ ___	___ ___ ___	___

Step 3: Rules

Rule 1 can be rendered with a block: $\boxed{\text{E F}}$

We can note rule 2 as a restricted block: **No D H**

Rule 3 is an *if/then* statement, which can be noted along with its contrapositive:

$$J_c \;\rightarrow\; G_A$$
$$\text{Not } G_A \;\rightarrow\; \text{Not } J_c$$

Rule 4 should be entered directly into the sketch.

Step 4: Deduction

Combine rule 2 with rule 4 to deduce that H does not host an ambassador, which should be noted either inside or directly above our diagram. Can you do anything else?

Often, with *if/then* rules that seem to have involved consequences, it can be helpful to draw out the result; do that here. If J is in the consul group, then G is in group Amb. You have two cities hosting ambassadors, so since E and F must host the same type of dignitary, they must host consuls. This leaves H—which can't be the same as D—with the premier, and B with the final ambassador.

$$Jc \quad \rightarrow$$

	Amb			Con			Pre
D	G	B	J	E	F	H

This pre-thinking of the *if/then* rule will be quite helpful later on. Keep in mind the contrapositive here as well; since the trigger led you to this one specific result, if *anything* in this result sketch does not happen, you can conclude that J does not host a consul.

Step 5: Questions

1. E

Answer this acceptability question by using the rules one at a time. Rule 1 eliminates (D), since F hosts an ambassador while E hosts a consul. Rule 2 eliminates (C), since D and H are both hosting an ambassador. Rule 3 allows you to rule out (A), because J hosts a consul but G hosts a premier. Finally, Rule 4 eliminates (B) because D hosts a consul.

2. C

This *new "if"* question tells you that J does not host an ambassador, so it must host either a consul or a premier. We already have the result for J hosting a consul (rule 3), but none of the answer choices occur in this result.

Limited Options

So what happens when J hosts a premier? The combination of rule 4 and rule 2 determines that D must host an ambassador and H must host a consul. F and E must always host the same kind of dignitary, leaving G and B to host the other kind of dignitary:

	Amb			Con		Pre
D	G	B	H	E	F	J

or

	Amb			Con		Pre
D	E	F	H	G	B	J

The second sketch reveals that (C) is correct. (A) is wrong because D always hosts an ambassador. (D) is wrong because the combination of rule 4 and rule 2 prohibits H from hosting an ambassador. Both (B) and (E) are wrong because F and E always host the same type of dignitary. Pairing them with G would force either H or J to host an ambassador.

3. B

There are several ways to approach this question; it is probably easiest to start by using previous work to eliminate choices. Choice (C) is in the answer to question 1, and you see (E) in the result of the *if/then* rule you drew out earlier. A savvy test-taker will notice the *if/then* and use it to advantage. If J hosts a consul, the *if/then* rule requires that E and F also host consuls. Since this question asks for a partial list that *cannot* host consuls together, if you see J and something *other* than E or F you have found our answer, and you see that in (B). If H and J both host consuls, rule 3 requires that G host an ambassador. That creates a diagram that looks like this:

Amb	Con	Pre
D G ___	H J ___	___

Under this scenario, it's not possible for F and E to host the same type of dignitary.

Short of noticing this, you can try each remaining answer in turn. It may seem like this will take a long time, but it is better than doing nothing. You can also see what happens when H hosts a consul. Hathaway is in two answer choices (three, counting (C)), and by assigning H to the consul group you can test both (A) and (B) at the same time.

4.   A

Because this is a "complete and accurate list" question, you can eliminate any choice that includes an incorrect item (here, one that *can* host an ambassador) and any answer choice that does not include a correct item. Rule 4 says D must host an ambassador, so you can eliminate (E). The combination of rule 4 and rule 2 means H cannot host an ambassador, so Hathaway must be in the list; eliminate (C). Once again, you can use previous work. The result of our *if/then* (or the answer to question 1), shows that Burton can host an ambassador, so (B) is gone. For (D), look to question 2. The second diagram you generated there, in which E and F both host an ambassador, eliminates (D). Choice (A) is correct; Hathaway is the *only* city that cannot host an ambassador.

5.   B

This new "if" question tells you that D and J host the same type of dignitary, which means that they both host ambassadors. Because E and F must host the same type of dignitary, and only three cities can host ambassadors, E and F both have to host consuls. (B) is therefore correct.

6.   C

There are lots of ways to attack this question, but you will probably have to test at least some of the choices. You can focus on your limited entities: D always hosts an ambassador, so half of (A) is old news. (A) is most likely not enough information. Choice (D) occurs in the result of the *if/then* rule, but be careful; this does not mandate that J hosts a consul in (D). More subtle is the fact that in (B), (C), and (E), the information does *not* match with the result of the *if/then*. The contrapositive tells you that J does *not* host a consul in these choices.

Choice (C) is the correct response because if B and G both host consuls, F and E must join D in hosting ambassadors. By the contrapositive of rule 3, J cannot host a consul, so J hosts a premier and H hosts a consul. All other choices result in at least one entity that could be distributed to more than one category.

GAME 3: PACING

By this time, you should be pushing yourself to complete every game in under 10 minutes. Keep your scratchwork to the space available on the test page, as you'll have to do on Test Day.

<u>Questions 1-6</u>

On seven consecutive days (Sunday through Saturday), a travel agency discounts vacations to exactly one of three countries—Togo, France, and Gabon—and exactly one of three cities—Atlanta, Boston, and Chicago. Discounts are made in accordance with the following constraints:

No vacation is discounted on any two consecutive days.

Any vacation discounted Sunday is not discounted Saturday.

Vacations to Boston are discounted on exactly three days, but not Sunday.

Vacations to Togo are not discounted Saturday, nor on any day when those to Boston are discounted.

Vacations to Gabon are discounted Sunday.

1. Which one of the following could be the listing of discounted city vacations, from Sunday to Saturday?

   (A) Chicago, Boston, Chicago, Boston, Atlanta, Chicago, Atlanta

   (B) Chicago, Boston, Atlanta, Boston, Chicago, Boston, Chicago

   (C) Atlanta, Boston, Atlanta, Boston, Chicago, Atlanta, Boston

   (D) Boston, Chicago, Atlanta, Boston, Chicago, Boston, Atlanta

   (E) Atlanta, Boston, Chicago, Boston, Atlanta, Atlanta, Boston

2. Which of the following could be true if vacations to Boston are not discounted Saturday?

   (A) Those to Togo are discounted only Tuesday.

   (B) Those to France are discounted Tuesday.

   (C) Those to Gabon are discounted Thursday.

   (D) Those to Togo are discounted exactly three days.

   (E) Those to Togo are discounted Friday.

3. Which one of the following could be true?

   (A) Vacations to Gabon are discounted each day that vacations to Boston are.

   (B) Vacations to Togo are discounted each day that vacations to Boston are not.

   (C) Vacations to Boston are discounted each day that vacations to Togo are not.

   (D) Vacations to exactly four locations are each discounted on three different days.

   (E) Vacations to Boston are discounted each day that vacations to Gabon are.

4. If vacations to Boston are not discounted on Saturday, then the agency CANNOT discount vacations to both the same city and country on which of the following?

   (A) Sunday and Tuesday

   (B) Monday and Friday

   (C) Tuesday and Thursday

   (D) Wednesday and Friday

   (E) Thursday and Saturday

5. Which one of the following could be true?

   (A) Vacations to Togo and Boston are both discounted Wednesday.

   (B) Vacations to Gabon and Boston are both discounted Saturday.

   (C) Vacations to Gabon and Atlanta are both discounted Monday.

   (D) Vacations to France and Chicago are both discounted Friday.

   (E) Vacations to Togo and Chicago are both discounted Thursday.

6. Which of the following could be true if vacations to Boston are not discounted Monday?

   (A) Those to Gabon are discounted Saturday.

   (B) Those to Boston are discounted Friday.

   (C) Those to Togo are discounted Thursday.

   (D) Those to Chicago are discounted Tuesday.

   (E) Those to Atlanta are discounted Wednesday.

Game 3 Answers and Explanations

Step 1: Overview

Situation: A travel agency discounting trips to cities and countries

Entities: Three countries (T, F, and G) and the three cities (a, b, and c)

Action: Matching the cities and countries to the day(s) on which they are discounted. Don't be misled by the days of the week; sequencing is not an issue here.

Limitations: Exactly one city and one country are discounted each day. Note that nothing states you need to use all of the entities at least once. In fact, before you look at the rules, it is conceivable that the same city or country is discounted every day! Don't make assumptions that aren't supported by the game.

Step 2: Sketch

The days of the week provide a natural order to this matching game. You'll need to keep track of both the countries and the cities, so two rows, each with seven boxes for the days of the week, will fill the need.

	Su	M	Tu	W	Th	F	Sa
T/F/G							
a/b/c							

Step 3: Rules

Let's look at the rules. Rule 1 says no vacation is discounted on any two consecutive days. You can draw this into the sketch by using "does not equal" signs in between each day of the week, both for countries and for cities. According to rule 2, any vacation discounted on Sunday is not discounted on Saturday. This should be noted next to your sketch as Su≠Sa. Rule 3 says Boston is discounted on exactly three days, but not on Sunday. The first part of the rule should be noted next to your sketch (something like "b.../...b.../...b," since you know there must be days in between the discounts), but the second part can be included in the sketch in the Sunday column. Rule 4 tells you that Togo is not discounted on Saturday, nor on any day when Boston is discounted. The first part of this clue can be entered directly into the sketch (Sa≠T), while the second should be written separately as a restricted block (e.g., not T/b). Rule 5 tells you that Gabon is discounted on Sunday. Be sure to note this on your sketch.

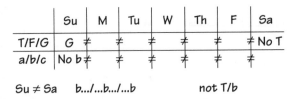

Step 4: Deductions

There are numerous common elements between these clues, which means that you should be able to make some deductions. But where to start? You have a large piece in the 'b.../...b.../...b' rule; this takes *at least* 5 spaces (the b's can't be consecutive), and since you know b can't go on Sunday, this means this piece can either start on Monday or Tuesday.

Given that Boston appears in some other rules, it may be helpful to draw out these two scenarios. Now if Boston is discounted on Monday, it could also be discounted on Wednesday and Friday, Wednesday and Saturday, or Thursday and Saturday; in option 1, you should just put b in Monday for now. But in the second scenario, b can *only* be discounted on Tuesday, Thursday, and Saturday. This is a lot of information, and now you have incorporated rule 3 into the sketch, for the most part. What else can you do? Combining rule 5 with rule 2, you know Gabon is not discounted on Saturday. Since you already know from rule 4 that Togo is not discounted Saturday, France must be the country that is discounted on Saturday. And in option 1, since Boston is discounted on Monday, you know from rule 4 that Togo cannot be. Gabon also cannot be discounted on Monday (since it is discounted on Sunday), so France must be discounted then as well.

Limited Options

Rule 1 also allows you to generally limit many of the discounted cities down to Atlanta and Chicago, since Boston can't be discounted on consecutive days. (In general, if there are only two remaining choices for any given slot, it is often helpful to write those two in, rather than writing what CAN'T go in the slot.) So now you have:

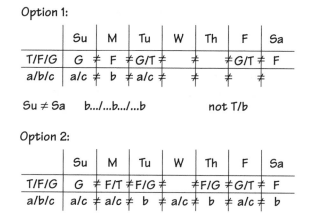

Option 1:

	Su	M	Tu	W	Th	F	Sa
T/F/G	G ≠	F	≠ G/T ≠	≠		≠ G/T ≠	F
a/b/c	a/c ≠	b	≠ a/c ≠	≠		≠	≠

Su ≠ Sa   b.../...b.../...b   not T/b

Option 2:

	Su	M	Tu	W	Th	F	Sa
T/F/G	G ≠	F/T	≠ F/G ≠		≠ F/G	≠ G/T ≠	F
a/b/c	a/c ≠	a/c	≠ b	≠	a/c ≠	b ≠ a/c ≠	b

Before you move on to the questions, note that Atlanta and Chicago are identical, unrestricted elements.

Saving Time

Drawing out these two options is not necessary, and it may even seem laborious. But with a complex game like this one, drawing out two options can often help incorporate more rules into the sketch. It can also help you get a sense for how the entities "behave," so when you move on to the questions, you can place the entities that much more quickly.

Step 5: Questions

1. **C**

This is an "acceptability" question, so use the rules one-by-one to eliminate wrong answer choices. It is often best to start with the easiest rule, but here, rule 5 is no help. However, rule 1 eliminates choice (E), since Atlanta is discounted back-to-back. Rule 2 eliminates choice (B), since Chicago is discounted on Sunday and Saturday. Rule 3 eliminates choice (D) because Boston is discounted on Sunday. It also eliminates choice (A), since Boston is discounted only twice.

2. A

This "if" question introduces the key idea in this game. Having drawn the two options, you have already explored this issue. If Boston is not discounted on Saturday, you must be in option 1, and Boston is discounted on Monday, Wednesday, and Friday. And if Boston is discounted on Friday, then Togo cannot be discounted on Friday (rule 4) which means Gabon is the only country that is left. You now have:

Option 1:

	Su	M	Tu	W	Th	F	Sa
T/F/G	G ≠	F	≠ G/T	≠ F/G≠		≠ G	≠ F
a/b/c	a/c ≠	b	≠ a/c	≠ b ≠		≠ b	≠

Choice (A) is possible, as you can see from the sketch. If you're unsure, look at the other choices. For (B), France is not on Tuesday, because it is on Monday. (C) can't be true, since Gabon cannot be on Thursday, because it is on Friday. In (D), Togo can't be discounted on three days, because those days would have to be Tuesday, Wednesday, and Thursday, which is not allowed. And for choice (E), Togo can't be discounted on Friday because Gabon already is discounted then. All this from one option; you just filled it in a bit more (in a new sketch, of course!).

You could have done this question without having the two options, of course; it just would have taken longer. You would need to take the hint from the question and focus on the days that Boston could be discounted. Because Boston must be discounted exactly three times but never on consecutive days, if Boston isn't discounted Saturday, it can only go on Monday, Wednesday, and Friday. Then we'd fill in the countries based on this, like you did above. Remember—if you don't make a deduction, it won't mean you CAN'T do the game; it may just take you longer.

3. D

Questions like this one, with no new "if" information given, are exactly what the limited options technique is made for. Can (A) be true? No, because in each option, France is discounted on a day that Boston is discounted. What about (B)? No—just look at Sunday. Boston is NOT discounted then, but neither is Togo. Sunday also helps eliminate choice (C), as well as (E). We're only left with (D); if it seems complicated, don't worry about it! After confidently eliminating four choices, you should pick the remaining one and move on. For the record, here's a sketch showing how choice (D) is possible (and you may notice it is a continuation of the sketch you drew for question 2). In the sketch, F, G, a, and b are each discounted for three days:

Option 1:

	Su	M	Tu	W	Th	F	Sa
T/F/G	G ≠	F	≠ G	≠ F	≠ T	≠ G	≠ F
a/b/c	c ≠	b	≠ a	≠ b	≠ a	≠ b	≠ a

4. B

The action of this new "if" question is identical to the action of question 2. If Boston is not discounted on Saturday, it must be discounted on Monday, Wednesday, and Friday. Because Boston and Togo never appear together on the same day, you know by default that France is discounted on Monday and Gabon on Friday. Therefore, (B) is correct: Trips to different nations are discounted on Monday and Friday.

5. E

Again, the options can really help you out here. In option 1 (and in the sketches you drew for questions 2 and 4), Togo and Chicago both could have been discounted on Thursday, which is what you see in choice (E). Rule 4 says Togo and Boston are never discounted on the same day, so (A) is wrong. Both of the options show that France is discounted on Saturday, so (B) is wrong. Gabon is discounted Sunday, and therefore cannot be discounted on Monday, so (C) is wrong. Similarly, France is discounted Saturday and thus cannot be discounted on Friday, so (D) is wrong.

6. E

This question refers you to option 2: If Boston is not discounted on Monday, then it must be discounted on Tuesday, Thursday, and Saturday. Looking at this option, you know right away that (E) is the only choice that is possible; all of the others must be false. In any case, Boston being discounted on these three days rules out choices (B), (C), and (D), since Boston can't be discounted on two consecutive days (B), Togo can't be discounted when Boston is discounted (C) and nor can Chicago (D). As for (A), since you know Gabon is discounted on Sunday, it can't be on Saturday.

Unless matching games are a special problem for you, try the three practice sets together in about 30 minutes. If you are having trouble with this game type, though, do each game separately in 10 minutes or less and check your results to learn where you can improve before moving on to the next practice game.

PRACTICE SETS

<u>Directions:</u> Each group of questions is based on a set of conditions. It may be useful to draw a rough diagram to answer some questions. Choose the response that most accurately and completely answers each question.

Game 4

A car dealership sells four types of vehicles—mopeds, roadsters, sedans, and trucks—in both new and used condition, for a total of eight different categories. The vehicles are displayed in eight different lots, numbered 1 through 8; each lot contains only one of the eight categories. The following conditions apply:

Lot 3 contains the same type of vehicle lot 4 does.

Lot 5 contains a different vehicle type than lot 6 does.

The used roadsters are located in lot 3 or else in lot 6.

The new sedans are located in lot 3 or else in lot 6.

The used trucks are not in lot 1.

Lot 2 contains the same type of vehicle that lot 8 does.

1. Which of the following would be an appropriate display of vehicles in order from lot 1 to lot 8, respectively?

   (A) new moped, used roadster, new sedan, used sedan, used moped, used truck, new truck, new roadster

   (B) new truck, new moped, used roadster, new roadster, used sedan, new sedan, used truck, used moped

   (C) new truck, used moped, used roadster, new roadster, used truck, new sedan, new moped, used sedan

   (D) new roadster, new truck, new sedan, used sedan, new moped, used roadster, used moped, used truck

   (E) used truck, new moped, new sedan, used sedan, new truck, used roadster, new roadster, used moped

2. Which one of the following statements could be true?

   (A) Used sedans are in lot 2.

   (B) New sedans are in lot 6 and new roadsters are in lot 4.

   (C) New trucks are in lot 6 and used mopeds are in lot 8.

   (D) New roadsters are in lot 3.

   (E) Used roadsters are in lot 3 and neither mopeds nor trucks are in lot 5.

3. If the used sedans are in lot 4 and new mopeds are in lot 8, then which of the following statements could be true?

   (A) New sedans are in lot 5.

   (B) New roadsters are in lot 2.

   (C) New roadsters are in lot 7.

   (D) Used trucks are in neither lot 5 nor lot 7.

   (E) Neither truck type is in lot 5.

4. Which of the following statements must be false?

   (A) New trucks are in lot 5.

   (B) New roadsters are in lot 5.

   (C) New sedans are in lot 3.

   (D) Used trucks are in lot 2.

   (E) Used mopeds are in lot 1.

5. Which of the following lists two lots that must contain two different vehicle types?

   (A) 1 and 5

   (B) 1 and 6

   (C) 1 and 7

   (D) 5 and 7

   (E) 6 and 7

Test Prep and Admissions

Game 5

A cruise ship offers exactly six activities—dancing, games, karaoke, swimming, tennis, and volleyball—to its passengers. The activities take place in three different areas on the ship. Area 1 is closest to the bow, or front of the ship, area 3 is closest to the stern, or rear of the ship, and area 2 is in between areas 1 and 3. Two of the activities take place in each of the three areas. The activities are offered to two different groups of people: Three of the activities are offered to adults, and the other three are offered to children. Adults and children are each offered one activity in each of the three different areas, consistent with the following restrictions:

Volleyball, which is offered to adults, is offered in a part of the ship that is closer to the bow than karaoke, which is offered to children.

Games are not offered closer to the bow than tennis.

Swimming is offered in area 2.

1. Which one of the following could be an accurate list of the activities offered by the cruise ship, in order of location (from bow to stern)?

   (A) children: games, swimming, karaoke
        adults: dancing, volleyball, tennis

   (B) children: volleyball, karaoke, games
        adults: tennis, swimming, dancing

   (C) children: dancing, karaoke, games
        adults: volleyball, swimming, tennis

   (D) children: tennis, games, karaoke
        adults: volleyball, dancing, swimming

   (E) children: karaoke, tennis, dancing
        adults: volleyball, swimming, games

2. If volleyball is offered in area 2, which of the following could be two of the three activities offered to adults?

   (A) games and karaoke

   (B) dancing and tennis

   (C) dancing and swimming

   (D) dancing and karaoke

   (E) tennis and karaoke

3. Which one of the following is a complete and accurate list of activities, any one of which could be the activity offered to adults in area 1?

   (A) dancing, games

   (B) dancing, volleyball

   (C) dancing, tennis, volleyball

   (D) dancing, games, tennis, volleyball

   (E) dancing, karaoke, tennis, volleyball

4. If volleyball is offered in area 2, then which one of the following activities could be offered to the same group of people as games and be offered in an area that is one area closer to the bow than the area in which games is offered?

   (A) dancing

   (B) volleyball

   (C) tennis

   (D) swimming

   (E) karaoke

5. If karaoke is offered to the same group of people as tennis and is offered in an area that is one area closer to the bow than the area in which tennis is offered, then which one of the following must be true?

   (A) Games are offered in area 3.

   (B) Games are offered to children.

   (C) Dancing is offered to adults.

   (D) Dancing is offered in area 3.

   (E) Dancing is offered to the same group of people as swimming.

Game 6

In the town of Westburg, exactly four families—the Arnolds, the Bakers, the Coopers, and the Dwights—each have exactly three children. Of the three children, exactly one is the oldest, exactly one is the youngest, and exactly one is the middle child. There are both boys and girls. The following is known about the families:

Each family has at least one girl.

Exactly two families have a boy as their oldest child.

There is at least one boy and at least one girl who are the youngest children of their respective families.

The Dwights' oldest child and the Coopers' middle child are both boys.

The Arnolds' middle child and the Dwights' middle child are the same gender.

If the Arnolds' oldest child is a girl, then each family's oldest and youngest children are the same gender.

1. If the Dwights' youngest child is a girl, then which one of the following must be true?

    (A)   The Arnolds' youngest child is a girl.

    (B)   The Dwights' middle child is a boy.

    (C)   The Bakers' oldest child is a girl.

    (D)   The Arnolds' youngest child is a boy.

    (E)   The Coopers' youngest child is a girl.

2. If the middle children in all four families are boys, then which one of the following must be false?

    (A)   Both the Arnolds' oldest child and the Bakers' youngest child are boys.

    (B)   Both the Bakers' youngest child and the Coopers' youngest child are girls.

    (C)   Both the Arnolds' youngest child and the Dwights' youngest child are girls.

    (D)   Both the Coopers' youngest child and the Bakers' youngest child are boys.

    (E)   Both the Dwights' youngest child and Coopers' youngest child are girls.

3. If the Dwights are the only one of the four families whose youngest child is a girl, then which one of the following could be true?

    (A)   The Coopers' oldest child is a boy.

    (B)   The Bakers' middle child is a girl.

    (C)   The Arnolds' middle child is a boy.

    (D)   The Bakers' oldest child is a boy.

    (E)   The Arnolds' oldest child is a girl.

4. If the oldest child and the youngest child in each family are the same gender, then each of the following could be true EXCEPT:

    (A)   The Browns' oldest child is a girl.

    (B)   The Coopers' middle child is a boy.

    (C)   The Browns' middle child is a girl.

    (D)   The Coopers' youngest child is a boy.

    (E)   The Arnolds' oldest child is a boy.

5. Which of one the following, if true, makes it impossible to assign gender to all twelve children without breaking the game's rules?

    (A)   The Arnolds' oldest child is a girl, and the Coopers' oldest child is a boy.

    (B)   The Arnolds' oldest child is a boy, and the Coopers' youngest child is a girl.

    (C)   The Arnolds' oldest child is a girl, and the Bakers' middle child is a girl.

    (D)   The Arnolds' oldest child is a boy, and the Dwights' youngest child is a boy.

    (E)   The Arnolds' oldest child is a girl, and the Dwights' middle child is a girl.

Game 4 Answers and Explanations

Step 1: Overview

Situation: A car dealership

Entities: Eight categories—four types of vehicles M, R, S, T; each type is both new and used

Action: Match the categories to the eight lots

Limitations: Eight lots and eight categories; one category per lot

Step 2: Sketch

There are a couple of ways to sketch out the action of this game. The most direct way is to number the lots in order from left to right, leaving room above or below each column to designate the vehicle category that is to be placed in it. You should also list the entities. Here, you have new and used mopeds, new and used roadsters, etc. One strategy is to use subscripts: M_N and M_U. You can also just use capital and lower case letters: M for new mopeds, m for used mopeds.

<table>
<tr><td>___</td><td>___</td><td>___</td><td>___</td><td>___</td><td>___</td><td>___</td><td>___</td></tr>
<tr><td>1</td><td>2</td><td>3</td><td>4</td><td>5</td><td>6</td><td>7</td><td>8</td></tr>
</table>

Step 3: Rules

Rule 1 says lots 3 and 4 contain the same type of vehicle. Note this in your sketch, perhaps with a simple equal sign (=) between the two adjacent numbers. The next rule states that column 5 does not contain the same vehicle type as column 6. Note this with a "does not equal" sign (≠) between the two adjacent numbers. Rule 3 puts the used roadsters in lot 3 or lot 6; note this as "r = 3 or 6." Rule 4 puts the new sedans in lot 3 or lot 6; note this. Rule 5 prohibits used trucks from being in lot 1; this can be noted above or near slot 1. The last rule says lot 2 and lot 8 have the same type of vehicle as each other; 2 and 8 aren't adjacent, so it is probably best just to write "2 = 8" next to your sketch.

$$M, m, R, r, S, s, T, t$$

```
 no T
 ___      ___      ___   =   ___      ___   ≠   ___      ___      ___
  1        2        3        4        5        6        7        8
2 = 8
r = 3 or 6
S = 3 or 6
```

Step 4: Deduction

Rules 3 and 4 should draw your attention: Both lots 3 and 6 must contain either the used roadsters or new sedans. Since these two lots are split between two vehicle types, no other type of vehicle can occupy either lot 3 or 6. Since both lots are also mentioned in other rules, it would probably be a good idea to draw out two limited options: when r is in 3 and S is in 6, and vice versa. And since lot 4 must contain the same type of vehicle as lot 3—but in different condition—lot 4 must contain either new roadsters or used sedans.

In addition, since lots 2 and 8 must contain the same vehicle type, and since lots 3, 4, and 6 must contain all or some of both the roadsters and the sedans, lots 2 and 8 cannot contain either roadsters or sedans. You've already placed most of the roadsters and sedans, so this deduction can simply be noted as "no s" or "no R" above columns 2 and 8. You now should have something like this:

M, m, R, r, S, s, T, t

2 = 8

	no t	no s		no s		no s		
			r	R		S		
Option I:	—	—	—	—	—	—	—	—
	1	2	3	4	5	6	7	8

	no t	no R			no R			no R
		S	s			r		
Option II:	—	—	—	—	—	—	—	—
	1	2	3	4	5	6	7	8

Notice that with the limited options, you were able to incorporate almost all the rules into the sketch—just remember that lots 2 and 8 have the same type of vehicle.

Step 5: Questions

1. D

For this acceptability question, test each rule against the choices. Every choice follows rule 1, but (B) violates rule 2 by placing the same type of vehicle in lots 5 and 6; (A) violates rule 3 by putting the used roadster in lot 2; (E) violates rule 5 by placing a used truck in lot 1; and (C) violates rule 6 by placing two different vehicle types in lots 2 and 8. (D) is the only acceptable display of vehicles for lots 1 through 8.

2. B

This question asks for the one choice that *could* be true; eliminate any choice that must be false. The limited options show that sedans cannot be placed in lot 2, so (A) must be false. Choice (B) is exactly what you see in option I. Since this doesn't violate any rules, (B) is correct.

From rules 3 and 4, you know that lots 3 and 6 can only contain used roadsters or new sedans, so (C) and (D) cannot be true. (E) cannot be true because if used roadsters are in lot 3, then new roadsters must be in lot 4 and new sedans must be in lot 6; since lots 5 and 6 must contain different vehicle types, lot 5 would have to contain either a moped or truck.

3. C

This "if" question stipulates that used sedans are in lot 4 and new mopeds are in lot 8; you have to find the one choice that could be true. You know you're in option II because s is in lot 4, and since M are in 8, you know that m must be in lot 2.

Option II:

	no t					no R			
	—	m	S	s	—	—	r	—	M
	1	2	3	4	5	6	7	8

You've still got T, t, and R to place. Since lots 5 and 6 must contain different vehicle types, only new trucks or used trucks could occupy lot 5. Since there are no apparent restrictions for lot 7, it could contain any of the remaining vehicles. After examining the choices, only (C) could be true.

4. B

You are looking for the one choice that must be false, so eliminate any that could be true. From the previous question, you know that new trucks could be in lot 5 and that new sedans could be in lot 3; eliminate (A) and (C). Choice (B) places new roadsters in lot 5; according to your limited options, new roadsters (R) are either in lot 4 (option I) or decidedly *not* in lot 5 (option II). So it cannot be true that new roadsters are in lot 5, and (B) is correct.

5. C

From your sketch, you know that lots 3 and 4 must contain the same vehicle type, and lots 2 and 8 must also contain the same vehicle type. You also know that lots 5 and 6 cannot contain the same vehicle type. This appears to leave lots 1 and 7 to be "free" from these types of restrictions. However, if lots 1 and 7 contained the same vehicle type, then lots 1 and 7, 2 and 8, and 3 and 4 would contain three of the four vehicle types. This would leave lots 5 and 6 to contain the last vehicle type, violating rule 2. Therefore, lots 1 and 7 must contain different vehicle types as well.

Game 5 Answers and Explanations

Step 1: Overview

Situation: Activities taking place on a cruise ship
Entities: Six activities D, G, K, S, T, and V, two groups of people a and c and three areas on a ship 1, 2, and 3
Action: Match each activity to an area and a group of people
Limitations: Three activities for adults and three for children, and each group has one activity in each area

Step 2: Sketch

Your sketch needs to include spaces for each part of the ship, and for the two different groups for whom the activities are intended. Use a grid-style sketch for this game, like this:

D, G, K, S, T, V

	1	2	3
a			
c			

Remember that area 1 is closest to the bow, or front, of the ship.

Step 3: Rules

Rule 1 tells you several things: V is offered to adults, and K is offered to children. Note this information by the respective rows for the adults and children. Also, V is offered closer to the bow/front than K; note this "V…K."

Rule 2 says G must not be offered closer to the bow/front than T. Note this is not the same as saying T is closer to the front than G. T and G could be in the same area, since there are two activities per area. "NOT G…T" works.

Rule 3 requires that S be offered in area 2; enter this rule directly into the sketch.

Step 4: Deductions

Unfortunately, there are no entities that appear in multiple rules. And since there are two activities per area, there is a lot of flexibility here. Once you've noted that D is an unrestricted entity, move to the questions. But to summarize, you have:

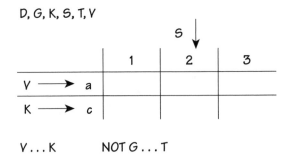

Step 5: Questions

1. C

This acceptability question allows you to eliminate incorrect choices individually using the rules. Rule 1 eliminates both (B) and (E). In (B), V is offered to children; in (E), both K and V are offered in area 1. Rule 2 allows you to eliminate choice (A), since G is in area 1, but T is in area 3. Rule 3 eliminates (D), since S is located in area 3. Therefore, (C) is correct.

2. B

This new "if" question tells you that V must be offered in area 2. Rule 1 tells you that V must be offered to adults, so you can fill in that portion of the sketch. Rule 3 tells you that S also is offered in area 2, so S must be the children's activity in area 2. You also have "V…K" from rule 1, so K (a children's activity) must be in area 3.

	1	2	3
a		V	
c		S	K

You're looking for a pair of activities that could be offered to adults. Anything with S or K is out. Eliminate (A), (C), (D), and (E), leaving (B) as the correct answer.

3. D

This "complete and accurate list" question asks you to determine which activities could be offered to adults in area 1. Dancing, a "floater," is in every choice, so that isn't any help. You know from rule 1 that K is offered to children, so you can eliminate (E). The answer to question 1 has V for adults in area 1, so eliminate (A). The remaining entities are G and T. Can they be in area 1 for adults?

Sure. Look at the partial sketch you had for question 2. We can put G and T in area 1, and D in the remaining spot in area 3:

	1	2	3
a	G/T	V	D
c	T/G	S	K

The only restriction on G and T is that G can't be closer to the bow than T. If they are both in the same area, G isn't closer to the bow, so this works. You therefore need both G and T in your complete and accurate list, so (D) is correct.

4. B

This new "if" question once again allows you to capitalize on previous work that you did for question 2. The question tells you that V is offered in area 2. Using rule 1, you once again come up with this sketch:

	1	2	3
a		V	
c		S	K

The question asks for the activity offered one area closer to the bow than G. In other words, what is right in front of G? Putting G in area 1 would make it impossible to offer an activity immediately in front of G, and both of the activities in area 2 are filled, so G must be offered in area 3. The only open slot in area 3 is with the adults, so G must be offered to the adults. V is offered to the adults in the area immediately in front of G (area 2), so (B) is correct.

5. A

This new "if" question tells you two things. First, K and T are offered to the same group. Second, K is offered immediately in front of T. Rule 1 tells you that K (and therefore T) is offered to children. Rule 1 also tells you that V must be offered closer to the front of the ship than K. If V must be closer to the front than K, but K is in front of T, then V must be offered in area 1, K must be offered in area 2, and T must be offered in area 3.

	1	2	3
a	V		
c		K	T

Next, rule 3 tells you that S goes in the remaining slot in area 2. Because T is offered in area 3, rule 2 tells you that G must be offered in area 3 as well, to ensure that G does not come before T. D goes in the last open spot—area 1, with the children. So you have:

	1	2	3
a	V	S	G
c	D	K	T

Thus, (A) is correct.

Game 6 Answers and Explanations

Step 1: Overview

Situation: Families with children

Entities: The four families (A, B, C, and D) and three children (simply labeled oldest, middle, and youngest) within each family, for a total of twelve children

Action: Matching gender to each child in each family

Limitations: Each family has 3 children, but you don't know how many girls or boys there are

Step 2: Sketch

This is a grid-type matching game; you need to keep track of the families and the age of each child, so the sketch will look something like this:

	A	B	C	D
old				
mid				
yng				

Rule 1 states each family must have at least one girl. You can make a note "each family 1+ girl." Alternatively, you can write a 'g' above each of the families, reminding you that each one needs a girl.

Rule 2 says that exactly two families have a boy as their oldest child. You can draw "b, b" next to the row for the oldest children. Since you'll want to make sure you remember that this is an exact number, you could circle these letters or highlight them in some way. You could also make a bit of a deduction—if there are exactly two boys, there must be exactly 2 girls, so you can write "b, b, g, g."

According to rule 3, at least one boy and at least one girl are the youngest children in their families. Another clue that won't fit into the sketch proper, but you can write it next to the "youngest" row: "b, g." Notice that with these three rules, you weren't given very specific information. However, with some creative techniques, you can often figure out ways to incorporate this kind of information into your sketch.

Rule 4 finally provides you with information that you can enter into the sketch: the Dwights' oldest child and the Coopers' middle child are both boys.

Rule 5 says the Arnolds' middle child is the same gender as the Dwights' middle child. The best way to represent this relationship is with an equal sign in the sketch. However, the way the sketch is currently laid out (starting with A and continuing through D) won't allow you to do that. One trick is to redraw the sketch so that columns A and D are next to each other. But if you already have data written in and feel that this could take awhile, you might just try circling the boxes that are the same. If you also write something like "A mid = D mid", the circles will be a great reminder that these boxes must be the same letter.

	g	*gg*		*g*
	A	B	C	D
old-b, b, g, g				*b*
mid	◯		*b*	◯
yng-b,g				

A mid = D mid

Rule 6 says that if the Arnolds' oldest child is a girl, then each family's oldest and youngest children are the same gender. There's no way to include this in the sketch, so make a note of this, as well as its contrapositive:

Arnolds' oldest – girl → All family oldest = youngest

Any oldest not = youngest → Arnolds' oldest – boy (i.e., not girl)

Step 4: Deductions

Despite a relatively high number of rules (six), there are no common elements among them. That's due in part to the fact that many of the rules apply to entire categories of entities, like youngest children, instead of specific entities, like the Coopers' middle boy.

There are also no big blocks of data to work with. There is one important thing to do however. Whenever you have a large and unwieldy "*if/then*" rule, you should draw it out. Not only will you undoubtedly need to do this at some point for a question, it may actually save you a lot of time (you'll see why), and it will certainly turn the vague "*if/then*" into a tangible outcome.

Here, rule 6 states that if the Arnolds' oldest is a girl, each family's oldest is the same gender as their youngest. So the Arnolds' youngest would also be a girl. The Dwights' youngest is a boy (since their oldest is a boy, from rule 4). Since each family needs at least one girl, the Dwights' middle child must be a girl, making the Arnolds' middle child a girl as well (rule 5). And since every family has at least one girl, the Coopers' oldest and youngest (which are the same, according to the "*if/then*" rule) must both be girls. If they were boys, then the Coopers would have three boys (remember rule 4—their middle child is a boy).

And what about the Bakers? You still have rule 2—among the oldest children, there are two boys (and two girls). Right now you have two girls and one boy, so the Bakers' oldest is a boy, making their youngest a boy as well. And of course, the Bakers still need a girl, so that means their middle child must be a girl.

Wow! You now have:

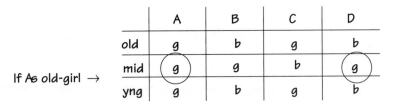

If not above sketch → **A's old – boy**

But how do you draw the contrapositive now? All you need to remember is that if *anything* is different from what is in the result, it means the trigger could not have happened; in this case, this means the Arnolds' oldest child is a boy.

Step 5: Questions

1. C

This "if" question tells you the Dwights' youngest child is a girl. This does not match up with the result you found in rule 6, meaning that you can refer to your contrapositive: The Arnolds' oldest is a boy. Based on rule 2, you now know that the other two oldest children are girls. Hence, (C) is correct. All four other answer choices could be true, but none of them must be true.

2. B

This "if" question gives you a big block of information you can insert directly into a new sketch. Rule 1 states each family must have at least one girl, so the Dwights' youngest child must be a girl. Because of the contrapositive of rule 6, you know that the Arnolds' oldest child is a boy. And then, since the Arnolds need a girl in their family, their youngest must be a girl. You now have:

	A	B	C	D
old	b	g	g	b
mid	b	b	b	b
yng	g			g

You don't know anything about the Bakers' youngest child or the Coopers' youngest child. However, one of them—it doesn't matter which one—must be a boy to avoid breaking rule 3, which says there must be at least one boy who is the youngest child in his family. Hence, (B) is correct. (C) is wrong because it must be true. (A), (D), and (E) all could be true but do not have to be.

3. B

Yet another "if" question—once you plug this new information into the sketch (which you always redraw for the individual question!) it will hopefully trigger a chain reaction of information.

First, the Coopers' oldest child must be a girl because of rule 1. Second, because of the contrapositive of rule 6, the Arnolds' oldest child must be a boy. Rule 2 tells you that the Bakers' oldest child must be a girl. Rule 1 mandates that the Arnolds' middle child is a girl, and rule 5 means the Dwights' middle child must be, too.

	A	B	C	D
old	b	g	g	b
mid	(g)		b	(g)
yng	b	b	b	g

The only slot in the game not filled in is the Bakers' middle child, and (B), the correct choice, accurately states that this child could be a girl. It also could be a boy, but that's not among the choices. Based on the information in the sketch, you know that the other four choices must be false.

4.   D

This "if" question tells you the oldest child and the youngest child in each family must be the same gender. This happens in the result of rule 6, which you have already drawn out. Let's start here—if an answer can be true (you see it in the sketch) you know it is the wrong answer. You can quickly eliminate (B) and (C). You still have three more choices, so go back to the original sketch and just work with the new "if" information that you know from this question.

Rule 1 tells you that the Dwights' middle child must be a girl (making the Arnolds' middle child a girl). It also tells you that the Coopers' youngest and oldest children must be girls. You now have:

	A	B	C	D
old			g	b
mid	(g)		b	(g)
yng			g	b

Looking at (A), (D), and (E), you see that (D) states that the Coopers' youngest is a boy. In the sketch this child is a girl, so (D) is the one that must be false, making it the correct answer.

Note that (A) and (E) cover the Arnolds and the Browns—families about which you have little or no information. This is a likely sign that a lot is possible with these families. Why did you even bother checking out the result of the *"if/then"* rule—couldn't you have just done this new sketch right from the beginning? Sure, but the sketch was already there—why not use it to help eliminate a few choices right off the bat?

5.   A

There's often no quick way to work a question like this. One tip is to see if there is any similarity among the answer choices. Notice that all of the choices here begin with information on the Arnolds' oldest child. Some choices specify that this child is a boy, others that it is a girl. Since you already have a sketch drawn out of the result when the Arnolds' oldest is a girl, you can start here. (Once again, that sketch came in handy!) Choices (A), (C), and (E) all say the Arnolds' oldest is a girl. (A) also says that the Coopers' oldest is a boy, which is not the case in the sketch you drew. Therefore, (A) creates a contradiction, and is correct. (C) and (E) are both in line with the sketch, and (B) and (D) are both possible as well.

Chapter 9: **Hybrid Games**

Finally, while any single game type may be very difficult, many games are further complicated by combining elements of sequencing, grouping, or matching in a single game.

By now, you've developed strong underlying skills, independent of one another; now see how well you can work with two or more of them at the same time.

GAME 1: THE METHOD

Don't let the fact that this is your first hybrid game, or the fact that the list of rules is fairly long, discourage or daunt you. Plan your own setup and see what you can deduce, and try each question on your own, before reading on.

Questions 1-5

A theater group is presenting seven one-act monologues—F, G, H, J, K, L, and M—over a period of seven days. The one-act monologues will be performed by three actors: Peter, Russell, and Tracy. The one-act monologues will be performed as solos, each will be performed exactly once, and no more than one monologue will be performed on any given day. The following constraints govern the seven-day program:

K must be performed earlier than H and earlier than J.

G must be performed earlier than L, but later than J.

F cannot be performed first or last.

Peter can perform only H, K, L, and M.

Russell can perform only F, H, J, and K.

Tracy can perform only F, G, H, and K.

No performer can perform on two consecutive days.

The performer who performs on the first day cannot perform on the seventh day.

Step 1: Overview

Situation: Theater group presenting one-act monologues

Entities: Monologues F, G, H, J, K, L, M; actors p, r, t

Action: Sequence the monologues, and match performers to monologues

Limitations: Each monologue is performed exactly once, one per day; only one actor performs each monologue

Step 2: Sketch

This game is a combination of sequencing and matching, with sequencing being the primary action. Your instinct might be to set up a series of seven blanks for the seven days. But if you glance at the rules, you'll notice that the sequencing rules are mostly loose sequencing. For now, listing the entities is sufficient, keeping in mind that you may need to incorporate the blanks as you go. If you need to refresh any of your sequencing or matching skills, look back at those chapters.

Step 3: Rules

You've seen all the types of issues that can be raised in the different game types, and the form that the rules can take. You'll find nothing new here.

There are eight rules governing the placement of the monologues and the matching of actors to each monologue. The first three rules all help to determine the relative sequence of several entities.

The first rule says monologue K must be performed before both H and J:

$$K \diagup^{H}_{\diagdown J}$$

The second rule requires that monologue G be performed earlier than L, but later than J. You can add this to rule 1:

$$K \diagup^{H}_{\diagdown J — G — L}$$

The third rule says monologue F cannot be performed first or last:

F—not 1 or 7

The next three rules restrict the assignment of actors to the monologues. The fourth rule says Peter can only perform monologues H, K, L, and M. The fifth rule says Russell can only perform monologues F, H, J, and K. The sixth rule says Tracy can only perform monologues F, G, H, and K. Notice that the rules are phrased in terms of what monologues a specific actor can perform. Since the monologues are the most limited entity (they can only be used once, and you need to sequence them), you should rearrange this information to get a look at which actors can perform each of the seven monologues.

Set up a chart like this:

F	G	H	J	K	L	M
r,t	t	p,r,t	r	p,r,t	p	p

The seventh rule requires that no actor perform on two consecutive days, and the last rule stipulates that no one actor can perform on the first and last days. These are more cumbersome to jot down, but something like this works:

$$p, r, t: not\ two\ consec, 1 \neq 7$$

Step 4: Deduction

Look at the sketch you made of the actors who can perform each monologue. Peter is the only actor who is able to perform monologues L and M. Therefore, Peter *must* perform monologues L and M. Also note that Russell is the only actor who can perform monologue J, and Tracy is the only actor who can perform monologue G. Therefore, Russell *must* perform J, and Tracy *must* perform G. Note this on your sketch.

M and F are the only monologues left to sequence, and F can't go first or seventh. Note that since M is performed by Peter, it can't go right before or right after L. You now have:

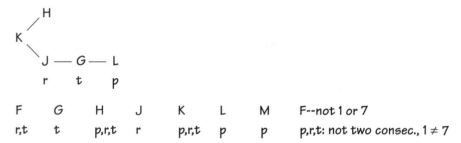

F	G	H	J	K	L	M	F--not 1 or 7
r,t	t	p,r,t	r	p,r,t	p	p	p,r,t: not two consec., 1 ≠ 7

Step 5: Questions

1. Which of the following is an acceptable schedule for the performance of the monologues, in order from first to last?

   (A) K, H, M, G, F, L, J

   (B) K, J, H, L, F, G, M

   (C) F, K, J, H, M, G, L

   (D) M, K, J, G, F, L, H

   (E) M, K, H, F, J, G, L

For this acceptability question, eliminate any answer that violates a rule. Rule 2 eliminates (A) and (B): (A) has monologues G and L performed before monologue J, and (B) has monologue L performed before monologue G. Rule 3 eliminates (C), in which monologue F is performed first. Choice (E) has monologue M performed first and monologue L performed last. Since Peter is the only actor who can perform these two monologues, this would place Peter in the first and last positions, violating the eighth rule. This leaves you with (D).

2. Which of the following must be true about the monologues?

    (A) Peter performs K.
    (B) Russell performs J.
    (C) Russell performs H.
    (D) Tracy performs H.
    (E) Tracy performs F.

Refer to the deductions you made earlier. From the sketch you made of the actors who can perform each monologue, you know that Russell must perform monologue J. Choice (B) is correct.

3. Which of the following is a complete and accurate list of the monologues, any one of which could be performed on day 7?

    (A) F, H, L
    (B) G, L, M
    (C) H, L, M
    (D) H, J, L
    (E) G, H, M

Refer back to the completed sketch. Since monologues K, J, and G must all be performed before monologue L, none of them can be performed on day 7. Therefore, eliminate (B), (D), and (E). Also remember that monologue F cannot be performed on days 1 or 7, so (A) cannot be correct. This leaves you with (C). Both monologues H and L come at the end of their respective sequences, and as long as monologue M is not performed right after L, it can be performed last as well.

4. If M is performed on day 2, which of the following must be true?

    (A) K is performed by Peter.
    (B) F is performed by Russell.
    (C) G is performed on day 4.
    (D) K is performed on day 1.
    (E) L is performed on day 7.

This new "if" question places monologue M on day 2 and asks for what must then be true. Looking over the rules, note that monologue K must be performed before everything but M and F. Since M is performed on day 2, and since F cannot be performed on day 1, this leaves only K available to perform on day 1. Therefore, (D) is correct.

5. If M is performed on day 1 and G is performed on day 4, then which of the following must be true?

    (A) Tracy performs monologue H.
    (B) Tracy performs monologue K.
    (C) Russell performs monologue F.
    (D) Peter performs monologue H.
    (E) Peter performs monologue K.

This new "if" question places monologue M on day 1 and monologue G on day 4, and then asks you for what must be true. Referring to your initial setup, you know that monologues K and J must be performed before monologue G, and since monologue K must be performed before monologue J as well, this places K on day 2 and J on day 3. Since monologue J must be performed by Russell and monologue M must be performed by Peter, monologue K must be performed by Tracy in order to satisfy the seventh rule. Therefore, (B) is correct.

1	2	3	4	5	6	7
M	K	J	G	___	___	___
p	t	r	t			

GAME 2: PRACTICE

Once again, work through the example on the following page on your own, focusing on applying Kaplan's Method and strategies, but incorporate some awareness of pacing in all your practice now. Allow yourself no more than 11 minutes for this game.

Questions 1-5

Exactly six of seven basketball players—M, N, P, R, S, T, and U—are picked for exactly one of three positions (Forward, Center, and Guard) on one of two teams: the Vipers or the Wolves. For each team, exactly one player must be assigned to each position according to the following rules:

> If either T or U or both are picked for teams, they are picked for the forward position.
>
> If picked for a team, S is picked for the center position.
>
> If picked for a team, R is picked for the Vipers.
>
> Neither P nor S is picked for the same team as N.
>
> S is not picked for the same team as M.
>
> If T is picked for the Wolves, then M is picked for the center position for the Vipers.

1. Which of the following is an acceptable list of players for the Wolves?

	Forward	Center	Guard
(A)	U	M	N
(B)	U	P	R
(C)	T	M	N
(D)	T	P	S
(E)	N	S	M

2. If T is picked for the Wolves, which of the following is an acceptable assignment of players for the Vipers?

	Forward	Center	Guard
(A)	U	S	N
(B)	U	S	M
(C)	U	M	P
(D)	R	M	N
(E)	R	M	S

3. Which of the following is an acceptable list of players assigned to the Vipers?

	Forward	Center	Guard
(A)	U	N	M
(B)	U	S	R
(C)	U	S	P
(D)	M	P	R
(E)	M	R	N

4. If U is assigned to the Vipers, which of the following is a pair of players who could also be assigned to the Vipers?

(A) M and R

(B) T and R

(C) S and R

(D) S and M

(E) M and P

5. If U is assigned to the Vipers and S is assigned to the Wolves, which one of the following must be picked as a guard for the Wolves?

(A) M

(B) N

(C) P

(D) R

(E) T

Use this space for scratchwork

Turn the page when you are ready to check your answers.

Game 2 Answers and Explanations

Step 1: Overview

Situation: Forming basketball teams

Entities: Seven basketball players M, N, P, R, S, T, U; two teams Vipers and Wolves, and three positions on each team—forward, center, and guard

Action: To select players, group them into two teams, and match the players to positions

Limitations: Select six out of seven , three per team, and one player per position; every position must be filled, and one player is not selected

Step 2: Sketch

Don't be intimidated by the number of actions here. For most hybrid games, you can often incorporate every action into one sketch. If you get stuck, think about what you would do if you were the coach making these decisions. Note that both teams will have one forward, one center, and one guard. Therefore, you can set up a table with places for each of the six selected entities. Keep in mind that one player is not selected, so make a slot for this too:

	V	W
for		
cent		
gu		

M, N, P, R, S, T, U
1 not picked: _____

Step 3: Rules

The first rule states that, if selected for a team, T or U or both must be selected for the forward position. Note this on your table next to the "forward" row. The next rule says if S is selected for a team, then S must be selected for the center position. Note this on your table next to the "center" row. The third rule restricts R to the Vipers, if R plays at all. Note this vertically on your table, above the Vipers.

The next two rules stipulate that neither P nor S can be on the same team as N, and that S cannot be on the same team as M. There are then three pairs of players who cannot be on the same team.

Finally, the last rule is a conditional: If T is picked for the Wolves (and if so, T is a forward), then M must be selected to play center on the Vipers. Also write down the contrapositive, and note that if T isn't on the Wolves, T is either on the Vipers or else does not play at all.

Step 4: Deduction

This game doesn't have a lot of deductions. Why? The biggest reason is that you don't know who is being selected for the teams. Anyone can be the non-player, so until you know more, you're operating in the land of the hypothetical. So far, there isn't a lot that *must* be true, and that is what you are looking for. Nevertheless, you have:

		If R ↓	
		V	W
If T, U →	for		
If S →	cent		
	gu		

M, N, P, R, S, T, U   No S N   If T-Wolves → M-Vipers cent
1 not picked: _____   No S M   If M not Vipers cent → T-Vipers or out
                           No P N

Step 5: Questions

1.   A

For this acceptability question, apply each rule and eliminate any choice that contradicts it. Rule 2 eliminates (D), which has S in the guard position, not the center. Choice (B) has R, and since this is a list of the Wolves, this is incorrect, according to rule 3; (E) has both S and M on the same team, a violation of the fifth rule; (C) has T placed on the Wolves, which means M must be picked for the Vipers. Since M is also listed on the team, (C) violates rule 6. Therefore, the only acceptable list of players for the Wolves is (A).

2.   D

This new "if" question says T is picked for the Wolves, and asks you to identify an acceptable list of players for the Vipers. You know from the last rule that if T is picked for the Wolves, then M must be picked for the center position on the Vipers. Therefore, eliminate (A) and (B). Rule 6 eliminates (E), because S and M cannot play on the same team. For the remaining two answer choices, you need to look at who is left to play on the Wolves. With (C), if U, M, and P are assigned to the Vipers, then R cannot be picked for either team (rule 3). The remaining players selected for the Wolves must then be N, S, and T, which violates the fourth rule by placing N and S on the same team. Therefore, only (D) is an acceptable assignment of players for the Vipers.

3.   E

This question is similar to question 1; it just asks for an acceptable list of Vipers. But this question is more difficult because at first glance, all the choices appear to conform with the rules of the game. For example, when U is listed, U is a forward. And no choice has two players that cannot be together.

In order to determine which choice is correct, you will need to see how each affects the Wolves. The most significant fact is that none of the choices has M in the center position; therefore, T cannot be selected for the Wolves. Since T is also never on the Vipers, T must be the non-player, and the remaining six players must all be selected. Therefore, R must be selected for the Vipers. This eliminates (A) and (C). (B) has U, S, and R on the Vipers, so M, N, and P must be selected for the Wolves, but this violates rule 4. (D) has M, P, and R selected for the Vipers, forcing N, S, and U to be selected for the Wolves; this also violates rule 4. Only (E) is an acceptable selection.

4. A

This new "if" question assigns U to the Vipers and asks for two other players who could also be assigned to the Vipers. Remember that, if selected, U must be selected for the forward position, which means T, who also must play forward, cannot be on the same team. Since T cannot be assigned to the Vipers, you can eliminate (B). The fifth rule, which prohibits S and M from being on the same team, eliminates (D).

Now look at how the three remaining choices affect the Wolves. In (C), if S and R are selected along with U for the Vipers, then you have M, N, P, and T left over. Since M is not on the Vipers, T cannot play on the Wolves, so the Wolves must consist of M, N, and P, violating the fourth rule. In (E), if M and P are selected for the Vipers along with U, then R could not be selected for any team, leaving N, S, and T to be selected for the Wolves; this violates the fourth rule as well, so (A) is correct.

5. C

This question assigns U to the Vipers and S to the Wolves, and asks you to find the Wolves' guard. This is a great question for a new sketch. Remember from the rules that U must be selected for the forward position, and that S must be selected for the center position. Also remember that N and M cannot be selected for the same team as S; therefore, N and M, if selected, must be selected for the Vipers. If R is selected, R must also be selected for the Vipers. M, N, and R are three players for two spots, so you have only P and T left to play for the Wolves. T must play forward (meaning that M plays center for the Vipers) and P must be selected for the guard position. The correct choice, then, is (C).

	V	W
for	U	T
cent	M	S
gu	R/N	P

Out: N/R

GAME 3: PACING

Now it's time to apply all your skills in a timed, test-like practice. Allow yourself no more than 10 minutes to complete this one.

Questions 1-6

A local museum will display six different sculptures in the park, one sculpture per week for exactly six weeks. Two sculptures will be selected from four Antiquity sculptures: F, G, H, and J; two sculptures will be selected from three Renaissance sculptures: N, O, and P; and two sculptures will be selected from three Modern sculptures: S, T, and W. The sculptures must be selected according to the following rules:

If G is selected, then P is also selected.

If H is selected, then neither F nor P is selected.

If T is selected, then neither W nor J is selected.

If F and P are selected, then F is displayed some week before P is displayed.

1. Which of the following is an acceptable selection of sculptures that the museum could display in the park for weeks 1 through 6, respectively?

   (A) F, O, G, P, N, T
   (B) H, T, N, F, O, S
   (C) H, J, S, T, O, N
   (D) J, S, O, F, W, N
   (E) J, P, W, F, S, O

2. If three sculptures chosen for the six weeks are F, N, and W, and if G is chosen to be displayed on the first week, then which of the following CANNOT be on display for the second week?

   (A) F
   (B) N
   (C) P
   (D) S
   (E) W

3. If G is scheduled for display during the third week, which of the following CANNOT be selected for the first week?

   (A) H
   (B) J
   (C) P
   (D) T
   (E) W

4. If H is selected for the first week, then which of the following sculptures must also be selected for display?

   (A) F
   (B) G
   (C) J
   (D) P
   (E) T

5. Which of the following is a sculpture that must be selected?

   (A) J
   (B) N
   (C) O
   (D) S
   (E) W

6. If G is NOT selected, which one of the following sculptures must be selected?

   (A) F
   (B) H
   (C) N
   (D) P
   (E) W

Game 3 Answers and Explanations

Step 1: Overview

Situation: Choosing sculptures for display in the park

Entities: Ten sculptures—Antiquities F, G, H, J; Renaissance N, O, P; Modern S, T, W

Action: Selection—select the sculptures to be displayed, and sequencing over six weeks

Limitations: Six sculptures out of ten, two from each category; only one sculpture per week; each sculpture is used only once

Step 2: Sketch

Your first instinct may be to draw six blanks to represent the six weeks. But hold on! You don't even know what entities will go in those six blanks. In hybrid games, you need to focus on the primary, or first, action. What action must take place first? Here, you must select the entities before you can sequence them. So for right now, A roster of entities, with two blanks under each category (denoting that two from each are selected) is sufficient.

Ant: F, G, H, J   Ren: N, O, P   Modern: S, T, W

___ ___   ___ ___   ___ ___

Step 3: Rules

Notice that in three of the four rules, sequencing isn't even an issue! This is another great sign that selection is the primary focus here. Also, all four rules are conditionals, so you may not be able to make many deductions.

The first rule says if G is selected, then P is also selected:

$$G \rightarrow P$$
$$\text{No } P \rightarrow \text{No } G$$

Rule 2 stipulates that if H is selected, then neither F nor P is selected.

$$H \rightarrow \text{No F and No P}$$
$$\text{F or P} \rightarrow \text{No H}$$

The third rule says if T is selected, then neither W nor J is selected.

$$T \rightarrow \text{No W and No J}$$
$$\text{W or J} \rightarrow \text{No T}$$

The fourth rule stipulates that if F and P are both selected, then F is displayed before P.

$$\text{F and P} \rightarrow \text{F...P}$$
$$\text{No F...P} \rightarrow \text{No F or No P}$$

Step 4: Deduction

Because you only have conditionals, it isn't likely you'll be able to deduce anything. But the number limitations might be of use. Since you must select two of each category, Renaissance and Modern are both extremely limited; by rejecting one, you will *have* to select the remaining two. And while there is no rule dealing with two Renaissance sculptures, rule 3 deals with two Moderns. If W is selected, then T is rejected, and you have W and S. Similarly, If T is selected, W is rejected, and you have T and S. Is there any way to reject S? We'd have to select both W and T, which is not allowed. So S must always be picked! This is a somewhat advanced deduction, but if you made it, you're ahead of the game.

Step 5: Questions

1. D

Apply each rule to answer this acceptability question, and eliminate choices that violate any. Nothing violates the first rule, but (B) violates the second rule: H is selected along with F. Rule 3 eliminates (C): T is selected, and so is J. Rule 4 eliminates (E): both F and P are selected, but P comes before F. You're left with (A) and (D).

But haven't you gone through all of the rules? Not quite—you need to check to see that there are two sculptures from each category. This is not the case in (A), where there are three Renaissance and only one Modern. So (A) is gone, and you're left with (D).

2. C

This question provides four selected sculptures and asks you to determine the one that cannot be on display during the second week. It sounds like rule 4 will come into play here. Since you're selecting G, you must select P, and now that you have both F and P, F must come before P. Since F is not in the first week, P can't be in the second week, and (C) is correct.

3. A

For this new "if" question, refer back to your deductions. If G is selected for the third week, then sculpture P must also be selected for display. If P is selected, then H cannot be selected at all—much less for the first week. Choice (A) is correct.

4. C

This new "if" question also requires you to combine some rules. You know from the second rule that if H is selected, then sculpture F and sculpture P cannot be selected. You also know from rule 1 that if P is not selected, then G cannot be selected. Since you must choose two of each sculpture type, you are left with only sculpture J from the Antiquity category. Therefore, (C) is correct.

5. D

This question asks you to determine which sculpture among the ten must always be selected for display. If you made the deduction that S is always selected, the answer is clear: (D) is correct.

But if you didn't see this up front, you'll have to eliminate by both using previous work and by testing each entity to see whether or not it can be rejected. Previous work doesn't help much here—the only complete list is in our answer to question 1, which doesn't eliminate anything. So you must test the choices. Can you reject J? Sure—you can select F and G. It's the same with N and O: You can select either N or O along with P, so neither one is necessarily selected. But as you saw before, it is not possible to reject S. Doing so requires selecting both T and W (to have the two required Modern sculptures) but rule 3 doesn't let you select both T and W.

6. E

If G is not selected, then you must choose two sculptures from the remaining three Antiquity sculptures (F, H, and J). The second rule says if H is selected, then F cannot be selected; therefore, if F is selected, H cannot be selected. Since you cannot select both H and F, you must select sculpture J. From the third rule, you know that if J is selected, then T is rejected. Therefore, both S and W must be selected as the two Modern sculptures, and (E) is correct.

The next practice set is your last chance to try several games without doing a full practice section; try all three in 27 minutes. Then plan on doing the practice Logic Games sections at the back of the book under full, test-like conditions.

Good luck on Test Day!

PRACTICE SETS

Directions: Each group of questions is based on a set of conditions. It may be useful to draw a rough diagram to answer some questions. Choose the response that most accurately and completely answers each question.

Game 4

Four boys—Anand, Bruce, Carlos and Dominic—and six girls—Mindy, Nancy, Olga, Penelope, Reesa and Sarah—are playing in a tennis tournament. Each match is between two participants of the same gender, and each participant plays in exactly one match. The matches take place simultaneously on five courts numbered one through five from left to right. Players are assigned to courts according to the following rules:

Players of the same gender cannot compete on adjacent courts.

Anand and Nancy do not play on adjacent courts.

If Dominic plays on court 2, then Reesa plays on court 5.

Mindy plays on a court numbered higher than the one on which Bruce plays and numbered lower than the one on which Olga plays.

Carlos and Dominic do not play on the same court.

1. Which of the following must be true?

    (A) Reesa plays on court 5.
    (B) Bruce plays on court 1.
    (C) Mindy plays on court 3.
    (D) Dominic plays on court 4.
    (E) Sarah plays on court 1.

2. If Reesa's opponent is Nancy, which one of the following CANNOT be true?

    (A) Penelope plays on court 5.
    (B) Carlos plays on court 4.
    (C) Bruce plays on court 2.
    (D) Sarah plays on court 3.
    (E) Carlos plays on court 2.

3. Each of the following statements could be false EXCEPT:

    (A) Carlos plays on court 4.
    (B) Reesa plays on court 3.
    (C) Sarah plays on court 5.
    (D) Dominic plays on court 2.
    (E) Nancy plays on court 1.

4. If Dominic plays on court 4, which one of the following could be true?

    (A) Reesa plays on court 5.
    (B) Penelope plays on court 2.
    (C) Anand plays on court 2.
    (D) Bruce plays on court 4.
    (E) Olga plays on court 3.

5. The placement of all ten participants onto tennis courts is completely determined if which one of the following is true?

    (A) Dominic plays on court 4 and Reesa plays on court 3.
    (B) Sarah plays on court 1 and Penelope plays on court 3.
    (C) Carlos plays on court 4 and Sarah plays on court 1.
    (D) Dominic plays on court 2 and Olga plays on court 5.
    (E) Mindy plays on court 3 and Penelope plays on court 5.

Game 5

At the beginning of a chess tournament, six chess players each occupy one of six positions, numbered 1 through 6 in order of rank, with 1 as the highest rank. The chess players are initially in the order of G, T, H, U, J and W, with G ranked first. Chess players change positions only when a lower positioned chess player beats a higher positioned chess player. The following rules apply:

Chess matches are played alternately in odd-position matches and even-position matches.

In an odd-position match, the chess players in positions 3 and 5 play against the chess player positioned immediately above them.

In an even-position match, the chess players in positions 2, 4, and 6 play against the chess players positioned immediately above them.

When a lower position chess player defeats a higher position chess player, the two chess players switch positions after the match.

1. Which of the following could be the order of chess players, from first to sixth, after exactly one odd-position match, if no even-position match has been played?

   (A) G, T, U, H, W, J
   (B) G, T, J, U, H, W
   (C) G, T, H, J, W, U
   (D) G, H, T, J, U, W
   (E) T, G, H, U, J, W

2. If exactly two matches have been played, beginning with an even-position match, and the lower position chess players won each match they participated in, then each of the following must be true EXCEPT:

   (A) U is one position higher than G
   (B) G is two positions higher than H
   (C) H is in the fifth position
   (D) T is in the third position
   (E) J is one position lower than H

3. If after exactly three matches the chess players, in order from first to sixth, are T, U, W, G, H, and J, then which of the following could be the order, from first to sixth, of the chess players after the second match?

   (A) U, T, W, G, H, J
   (B) G, T, U, H, W, J
   (C) G, T, W, U, H, J
   (D) T, U, G, W, H, J
   (E) U, G, W, H, T, J

4. Which of the following could be true after exactly two matches of golf have been played?

   (A) U has won two matches.
   (B) W plays against T in two matches.
   (C) W lost two matches.
   (D) G has won two matches.
   (E) J's only match was played against T.

5. After three matches, if J has won all of his matches, and the rankings of the remaining five players relative to each other remain the same, then which of the following chess players could be in the second position?

   (A) G
   (B) H
   (C) U
   (D) T
   (E) W

Game 6

In a qualifying round of a swim meet, six swimmers (Helen, Josephine, Linda, Natalie, Pam, and Roselyn) are assigned to six swim lanes. Each swimmer also represents one of six teams—U, V, W, X, Y, and Z—not necessarily in order of the names given. The assignment of lanes and teams must comply with the following:

> Each swimmer represents a different team.
>
> The swimmer representing team W is assigned to lane 5.
>
> Josephine is assigned to one of the two lanes between the lanes assigned to the swimmers representing teams V and Y.
>
> There are exactly two lanes between Roselyn's lane and the lane assigned to the swimmer representing team Y.
>
> The swimmer representing team X is in a higher numbered lane than the lane to which Josephine is assigned.

1. Which of the following is a possible assignment of swimmers' teams to lanes?

	1	2	3	4	5	6
(A)	U	V	Y	X	W	Z
(B)	V	Z	U	Y	W	X
(C)	Y	X	Z	V	W	U
(D)	W	V	U	Z	Y	X
(E)	Z	Y	X	V	W	U

2. Which of the following must be true?

   (A) Helen represents team W

   (B) Josephine represents team Z

   (C) Josephine is assigned to lane 2

   (D) Roselyn is assigned to lane 1

   (E) Roselyn represents team V

3. If Josephine is assigned to lane 3, which of the following assignments must be made?

   (A) The swimmer representing team V is in lane 1

   (B) The swimmer representing team U is in lane 3

   (C) The swimmer representing team X is in lane 4

   (D) The swimmer representing team X is in lane 6

   (E) The swimmer representing team Y is in lane 4

4. Which of the following is a complete and accurate list of the swimmers, each of whom could represent team W?

   (A) Natalie, Pam, Roselyn

   (B) Linda, Natalie, Pam

   (C) Josephine, Linda, Natalie, Pam

   (D) Josephine, Natalie, Pam, Roselyn

   (E) Helen, Linda, Natalie, Pam

5. If Pam represents team Z, it must be true that

   (A) Helen represents team X

   (B) The swimmer representing team U is in lane 6

   (C) Josephine represents team U

   (D) The swimmer representing team X is in lane 3

   (E) Linda represents team W

6. If Natalie represents team U, then which of the following could NOT be the assignment of swimmers to lanes?

	1	2	3	4	5	6
(A)	Roselyn	Linda	Josephine	Helen	Pam	Natalie
(B)	Roselyn	Natalie	Josephine	Pam	Helen	Linda
(C)	Roselyn	Josephine	Helen	Pam	Linda	Natalie
(D)	Helen	Josephine	Linda	Roselyn	Pam	Natalie
(E)	Pam	Natalie	Josephine	Roselyn	Linda	Helen

Game 4 Answers and Explanations

Step 1: Overview

Situation: A tennis tournament

Entities: The ten tennis players, four boys (Anand, Bruce, Carlos, and Dominic) and six girls (Mindy, Nancy, Olga, Penelope, Reese, and Sarah)

Action: There are two elements to this game: sequencing and distribution. The courts are numbered 1 through 5, left to right. You also may have noticed that the rules mention things being adjacent, and use the words "higher" and "lower." This tells you that sequencing is important here. But there is also an element of distribution here; the tennis players are paired up into groups. There is only one kind of entity to be placed, but this game is complicated by the two elements.

Limitations: There are five courts and ten players available. You're told that there are two players on each court and that all ten tennis players are playing, so none of them will appear more than once.

Step 2: Sketch

Since the boys and girls represent two different types of tennis players, it's helpful to distinguish them from one another visually, for example using uppercase and lowercase letters. You can create a roster of the entities, with the boys listed as a, b, c, and d, and the girls listed as M, N, O, P, R, and S.

The best way to sketch the game is to draw five courts next to each other, numbered 1 through 5, with two spaces for tennis players on each court. Also remember to list the entities next to your sketch, if you haven't already.

Boys: a, b, c, d
Girls: M, N, O, P, R, S

1	2	3	4	5

Step 3: Rules

Rule 1 says players of the same gender cannot compete on adjacent courts. You can draw this rule into the sketch by marking "does not equal" signs in between each of the courts. Alternatively, you can write down something like "no boys-boys, no girls-girls."

Rule 2 says Anand and Nancy do not play on adjacent courts. You can note this with a restricted block: how about "not |a|N|."

Rule 3 says if Dominic plays on court 2, then Reesa plays on court 5. In other words, d's behavior can trigger R's: d2 → R5 and the contrapositive, not R5 → not d2. Rule 4 is that Mindy plays on a higher-numbered court than Bruce, but a lower-numbered court than Olga. You don't yet know where in the diagram these three entities go, but you know where they are in relation to each other:

b...M...O

Rule 5 says Carlos and Dominic do not play on the same court. This also should be noted with a restricted block, but instead of placing the elements side by side, place them vertically in the sketch:

No c
d

Step 4: Deductions

This game's most significant deduction comes from combining the first rule with the fact that "Each match is between two participants of the same gender." That means there will be two matches between boys and three matches between girls. Since rule 1 says players of the same gender cannot compete on adjacent courts, the boys must play on courts 2 and 4, and the girls must play on courts 1, 3, and 5. Why look here first? This first rule covered the behavior of *every* entity; such rules are generally the most informative.

This deduction allows you to make much more concrete use of rule 4. Because Bruce must play on a lower-numbered court than Mindy, Mindy cannot play on court 1. Because Olga must play on a higher-numbered court than Mindy, Mindy cannot play on court 5. Therefore, Mindy must play on court 3, placing Bruce on court 2 and Olga on court 5.

The block of data in rule 5 also yields a pair of deductions. Carlos and Dominic cannot play against each other. There are only two courts on which boys play, so c and d must be divided between those two courts: one of them is always on court 2, and the other is always on court 4. Additionally, because Bruce must play on court 2, the only place where Anand can play is court 4. Combined with rule 2, which says Anand and Nancy must not play on adjacent courts, you can deduce that court 1 is the only place where Nancy can play.

After all those deductions, your diagram will look something like this:

Boys: all accounted for
Girls: P, R, S

1	2	3	4	5
N	b	M	A	O
	c/d		d/c	

d2 → R5
not R5 → not d2

If you make all these deductions, you'll probably spend a good bit of time just setting up the game. But you'll find that you're able to complete the questions more quickly than you would have otherwise.

One final point to note: S and P are unrestricted entities. They do not appear in any of the rules. They are also identical entities: Wherever S appears in the game, P can appear, and wherever P appears, S can appear, too. This is often significant in answering "must be true" questions, because what must be true of one also must be true of the other. It is also helpful with "could be true" questions: P and S can play on courts 1,3, and 5.

Step 5: Questions

1. C

Mindy must play on court 3, according to the second deduction. Mindy must play on a higher-numbered court than Bruce and a lower-numbered court than Olga. Court 3 is the only court that allows her to do so, so (C) is correct. (A) is wrong because Reesa can play on court 1, 3, or 5. (B) is wrong because Bruce plays on court 2. (D) is wrong because Dominic can play on court 2 or court 4. (E) is wrong because Sarah can play on court 1, 3, or 5.

2. C

If Reesa's opponent is Nancy, Reesa is playing on court 1. According to the contrapositive of rule 3, that means that Dominic must not play on court 2. That forces him to play on court 4 and Carlos to play on court 2. Choice (B) is correct. Penelope and Sarah could play on court 3 or court 5, so (A) and (D) both could be true, and (C) and (E) both must be true.

3. E

Four of these answer choices could be false, so you're looking for the one that must be true. (E) is correct because court 1 is the only place Nancy can play without being adjacent to Anand. (A) is wrong because Carlos could play on court 2. (B) is wrong because Reesa could play on court 1 or 5. (C) is wrong because Sarah could also play on court 1 or 3. (D) is wrong because Dominic could play on court 4.

4. A

If Dominic plays on court 4, then Carlos must play on court 2. Since Dominic is not on court 2, there are no constraints on where Reesa can play—she can play on any of the girls' courts, and (A) is correct. (B) is wrong because court 2 is a boys' court where Carlos and Bruce are playing. (C) is wrong because Anand always plays on court 4 to avoid being adjacent to Nancy. (D) and (E) are wrong because, according to the first deduction, Bruce always plays on court 2 and Olga always plays on court 5.

5. C

This question rewards you for noting at the beginning of the game that Sarah and Penelope are identical entities. You know that the correct response must fix the location of either S or P in the diagram so that they are no longer identical, so focus on answer choices that do so. Choice (B) is a good place to start, but it is wrong because, while it tells you where Sarah, Penelope, and Reesa play, it doesn't tell you where Dominic and Carlos play. Next up is (C), which is correct because Carlos's playing on court 4 forces Dominic to play on court 2. According to rule 3, that means Reesa plays on court 5. Since (C) tells you Sarah plays on court 1, you can place Penelope on court 3, completing the diagram. Choices (A) and (D) don't tell you where Penelope and Sarah have to play; (E) tells you Penelope plays on court 5, which, according to the contrapositive of rule 3, means Dominic must play on court 4. That places Carlos on court 2 but leaves Sarah and Reesa free to play either on court 1 or court 3.

Game 5 Answers and Explanations

Step 1: Overview

Situation: Chess tournament

Entities: The six chess players—G, T, H, U, J, and W

Action: This is what you call a "process" game. It is not the most common of game types, but it is good to practice in case you see one on Test Day. Your job is to follow the guidelines of a certain process. Here there are two processes—odd-position matches and even-position matches.

Limitations: None yet—just the 6 entities in 6 different positions

Step 2: Sketch

Notice that there are no conditions that specify any relationship among the rankings of the chess players. This is because the relationship has already been specifically detailed in the set-up. Since the game is ranking the chess players from first to sixth, sketch them vertically in descending rankings, from highest rank to lowest rank, like a sports ranking you would find in a newspaper. Leave room for the results of the next few matches, although you may well need to redraw this sketch for individual questions.

		After 1st	After 2nd
1	G		
2	T		
3	H		
4	U		
5	J		
6	W		

Step 3: Rules

Rule 1 says the matches are played alternately, with the beginning match unspecified. In other words, you can't have two odd or even matches in a row. You can jot down "odd/even alt" if this helps you remember this rule. The remaining conditions describe the "rules" of the potential match-ups between the chess players. There is an odd-position match that consists of each odd-positioned chess player playing against the chess player ranked immediately above him. Then there is the even-position match, which consists of each even-positioned chess player playing against the chess player ranked immediately above him. In a process game, you need to find easy ways of representing the different processes.

Here is one suggestion:

odd	even
1	(1)
(2)	(2)
(3)	(3)
(4)	(4)
(5)	(5)
6	(6)

The final condition specifies that if the lower-ranking chess player defeats the higher-ranking chess player, then those two chess players switch rankings after the match. From the opening paragraph, you know that this is the only time chess players change positions. Therefore, if the higher-ranking chess player wins the match, the rankings remain the same.

Take a look at the conditions again to make sure you understand the whole function of the game. You have chess players G, T, H, U, J, and W ranked vertically in that order with G ranked first. Depending on the type of match, you will either have chess players ranked 3 and 5 play against chess players ranked 2 and 4 respectively, or you will have chess players ranked 2, 4, and 6 play against chess players ranked 1, 3, and 5 respectively. Ranks will change *only* when a lower-positioned chess player defeats a higher-positioned chess player. Therefore, no chess player can advance more than one rank per match.

Step 4: Deductions

Process games are usually about the process—there isn't usually much to deduce. You don't know which round is played first, nor do you know who wins and who loses, so you can't do much else. Go on to the questions.

Step 5: Questions

1.   D

This is slightly different from the more common acceptability questions, since you cannot apply individual conditions to the answer choices. However, the question does tell you that exactly one odd-position chess match is played. This means that the third ranked player (H) must play the second ranked player (T), and the fifth ranked player (J) must play the fourth ranked player (U).

Notice that there is no one for the first or sixth ranked players to play against; therefore their positions must remain the same. An acceptable ranking of chess players must have G ranked first and W ranked sixth. Eliminate (A), (C), and (E). Since J, who is ranked fifth, is playing against U, who is ranked fourth, it would not be possible for J to obtain the third rank within one match, and therefore (B) is also incorrect. At most, J could win his match against U and thus would switch ranks with U, moving J to the fourth rank.

Notice that (B) also has H ranked fifth, which is not possible since H, initially ranked third, must play against T, initially ranked second. If H lost the match, T and H's rankings would remain the same.

2.   D

This "if" question stipulates that only two matches are played—the first one an even-position match and the second, therefore, an odd-position match. It also stipulates that the lower-positioned chess players win each match they play, so they will switch rankings with the higher-ranked chess players with whom they play. If the first match is an even-position match, then W and J switch rankings, U and H switch rankings, and T and G switch rankings. Now the rankings from first to sixth are T, G, U, H, W, J. The second match must be an odd-position match, so T and J will remain in the first and sixth positions, respectively, W and H must switch positions, and U and G must also switch positions. So the rankings from first to sixth after two matches are T, U, G, W, H, and J.

		1st round (even)	2nd round (odd)
1	G	T	T
2	T	G	U
3	H	U	G
4	U	H	W
5	J	W	H
6	W	J	J

The one choice that cannot be true is (D). T cannot be in the third position. Choice (D) is correct.

3.   D

This "if" question stipulates the chess players' rankings after three matches, and asks you to find the one choice that could be an acceptable ranking of chess players after two matches. Since you don't know the type of match, odd vs. even, don't waste valuable time recreating scenarios for the first two matches. Rather compare each choice to the rankings after the third match to see which changes in the rankings are possible.

		1st	2nd	3rd
1	G			T
2	T			U
3	H			W
4	U			G
5	J			H
6	W			J

Choices (B), (C), and (E) have G misplaced by more than one rank between the two matches and are therefore not possible; (E) also has T misplaced by more than one rank between the matches. Both (A) and (D) appear to be viable rankings—all six chess players are within one place in match 3 as compared to match 2. However, (A) has U ranked first after the second match. Since U must start the first match ranked fourth, it would not be possible for him to advance three positions in two matches. Therefore, (A) is not possible, and (D) is correct.

4.   A

You are looking for the one choice that could be true after exactly two chess matches. Refer to the initial setup to determine which statements about the rankings could be possible. U can play and win a match against H, and then play and win a match against T. Choice (A) seems possible; you should feel free to pick this if you feel confident with the game, or if you are short on time. Remember, there can only be one possible choice here. Let's look at the others for argument's sake.

Since W and T are separated by three ranks, it would not be possible for the two to play against each other for both matches, so (B) is incorrect. Since the matches alternate between odd/even-position matches, and since W is ranked sixth, he would have to win at least one match to play in both matches; therefore, he cannot lose both matches, and (C) is incorrect. Similarly, since G is ranked first, he must either lose at least one match to play in both of the matches, or else he only plays in one of the two matches. Either way, G cannot win both matches, and (D) is wrong. In order for J to play T, J must defeat U, and therefore cannot have his only match be against T. Choice (E) is incorrect. U, however, could win two matches in a row, so (A) is correct.

5.   D

This "if" question stipulates that J wins all of his matches, and that the remaining chess players' ranks relative to each other do not change. This means the order, not the ranks, from beginning to end must still be G, T, H, U, and W, with J weaving through the order with his wins.

The question does not state whether the first match is an odd-position or even-position match, so start with an odd-position match. This moves J into the fourth rank and U into the fifth rank. The remaining ranks remain relative to one another, so the resulting rankings would be G, T, H, J, U, and W.

Now the second match must be an even-position match, which means J will now defeat H and ascend to the third rank while H descends to the fourth rank. The remaining ranks remain relative to each other, so the resulting rankings are G, T, J, H, U, and W.

Now the third match must be an odd-position match, which means J will defeat T and assume the second rank, while T descends to the third rank. However, J in the second rank is not a choice. So you must begin the matches with an even-position match. This means J defeats W in the first match and the rankings remain exactly the same. The next match is then an odd-position match, which has the same result as the first odd-position match, J switching ranks with U. So now the third match will have the same result as the previous second match, J switching ranks with H, leaving T in the second position.

	1st even	2nd odd 1st odd	3rd even 2nd even	3rd odd
1	G	G	G	G
2	T	T	T	J
3	H	H	J	T
4	U	J	H	H
5	J	U	U	U
6	W	W	W	W

Choice (D) is correct.

Game 6 Answers and Explanations

Step 1: Overview

Situation: A swim meet

Entities: Six swimmers— H, J, L, N, P, R, and six teams—u, v, w, x, y, z

Action: Sequence the swimmers in lanes 1 through 6, and match each team to a swimmer

Limitations: You are given six swimmers, six lanes, and six teams. You have to assign each swimmer to a different lane. Do you have to use all six teams? The opening paragraph doesn't specify, but the fact that there are equal numbers of teams and swimmers is a clue that each team will probably be used once.

Step 2: Sketch

Since you are sequencing swimmers and then matching the teams, sketch out six columns to denote the six swim lanes. Above the columns, abbreviate your swimmers in all caps (H, J, L, N, P, R) and abbreviate your teams in lowercase (u, v, w, x, y, z)

Swimmers: H J L N P R   Teams: u v w x y z

	1	2	3	4	5	6
Swimmer:	___	___	___	___	___	___
Team:	___	___	___	___	___	___

Step 3: Rules

The first rule says each swimmer represents a different team. Now you have it in writing: Each team is used exactly once. When a rule makes a limitation concrete like this one (a loophole closer), you probably don't need to write it down.

Rule 2 says the swimmer in lane 5 represents team w; you can draw this in the sketch.

Rule 3 says Josephine is assigned to one of the two lanes in between the lanes assigned to teams v and y. You can draw this rule like this:

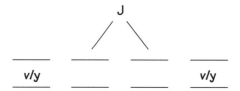

Rule 4 says there are two lanes between Roselyn's lane and team y's lane.

R _____ _____ _____ _____ _____ _____ _____ R
_____ _____ _____ y or y _____ _____ _____ _____

The last rule tells you that team x is in a higher numbered lane than the lane to which Josephine is assigned; therefore, Josephine's lane must be somewhere to the right of team x's lane. For now, just write:

J ... _____
_____ ... x

(J…x is fine too, just like R/y ___ ___ y/R is okay for rule 4. But in a hybrid game like this, where different rows belong to different kinds of entities, drawing the different rows can make deductions easier to spot.)

Note, too, that Helen is a "floater."

Step 4: Deductions

Take a closer look at the second and third rules; they both deal with team y. The second rule tells you that there are exactly two lanes between team v and team y, while the third rule tells you there are two lanes between Roselyn and team y. If Roselyn were *not* represented by team v, there would have to be a total of five lanes between Roselyn and team v, for a total of seven lanes. (The order here doesn't matter; whether R or v comes first, there will still be five lanes between them.) Since you are only dealing with six lanes, this arrangement is not possible. Therefore, you can deduce that Roselyn must be represented by team v, both of which are two lanes apart from team y. Note that this deduction does not stipulate which of these entities comes first; this new "block" could be either:

y _____ _____ Rv or Rv _____ _____ y

You just made a solid deduction using common entities and two blocks of data. You now have a new block. Note that this block takes up four of the six lanes, so its placement may have some limitations. At first glance, it might appear that this 4-lane block could begin in lane 1, 2, or 3, and end in lane 4, 5, or 6 respectively. But since w is assigned to lane 5, it would not be possible to have the block, which ends with either team v or y, end in lane 5. Therefore, the block cannot begin in lane 2. Also note that if the 4-lane block were to begin in lane 3, then Josephine (who is still somewhere in the middle of the block) would have to be in either lane 4 or 5. Since w is assigned to lane 5 and lane 6 would be assigned to team v or team y, team x would have to be placed in either lane 1, 2, or 4. This would prevent team x from being in a higher numbered lane than Josephine, violating rule 5; therefore, the 4-lane block cannot begin on lane 3. This means the 4-lane block must begin on lane 1. You don't know whether lane 1 is R v or y, but with only two options, it is best to draw both.

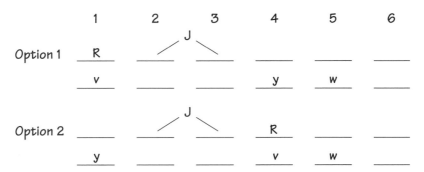

Note the power of limited options. The only rule not reflected in your sketch now is the "J…x" rule. You have no information about H, L, N, and P, nor do you know about teams u and z. But with the limited options, you're still in decent shape.

Step 5: Questions

1. **B**

This is an acceptability question dealing only with the possible arrangement of teams in the six lanes. Pay attention to what the individual rules say about the teams. Rule 2 says w is in lane 5, so eliminate (D). Rule 3 says teams v and y must be separated by two lanes, so eliminate (A) and (E). This leaves two possible answers, (B) and (C). The fourth rule says team x is in a higher numbered lane than Josephine. Choice (C) places team x in lane 2, which means Josephine would have to be in lane 1; this is not possible, since Josephine must be in one of the lanes between team v and team y. Therefore, (B) is correct.

2. **E**

From your deductions, you know that Roselyn must represent team v; therefore, (E) must be true. If Roselyn didn't represent team v, there would have to be seven lanes to separate Roselyn from team y, and team y from team v, (R __ __ y __ __ v). Since there are only six lanes, this is not possible.

3. **D**

This "if" question stipulates that Josephine is assigned to lane 3, and asks for the one lane assignment that must be made under this condition. Josephine can be assigned to lane 3 in either option, but in both options, lanes 4 and 5 are filled. Since team x must be in a higher-numbered lane than Josephine, and since lane 4 must be occupied by team v or y and lane 5 must be occupied by team w, then team x must be assigned to lane 6. Choice (D) is correct.

4.   **E**

Since team w must be in lane 5, you are looking for all the possible swimmers who could be assigned to lane 5. Since Roselyn must be represented by team v, she cannot be represented by team w; therefore, (A) and (D) are incorrect. In addition, since Josephine must be between teams v and y, she cannot be assigned to lane 5; therefore, (C) is wrong. Remaining choices (B) and (E) both contain Linda, Natalie, and Pam, but Helen is only in (E). If Helen can be assigned to lane 5, (E) is correct; if Helen cannot be assigned to lane 5, (B) is correct.

Since there is nothing preventing Helen from being represented by team w in lane 5, (E) is correct. How do you know this? Helen is a "floater"! Since she is not mentioned in any rule, she can pretty much go anywhere. This question points out the value of noting your "floaters" as you do each game.

5.   **C**

This new "if" question stipulates that Pam represents team z; it then asks you to find the one choice that must be true. When in doubt, draw what you know. If Pam represents team z, then our sketch could look something like this:

1	2	3	4	5	6
R	J	P	___	___	___
v	___	z	y	w	X

Granted, this is far from the only way to draw this sketch. J could be in lane 3, and "P z" could be in lanes 2 or 6. But sometimes drawing out one possibility will help you realize what must be true. J cannot represent team v, y, w, or x (because of the various restrictions). Furthermore, since Pam represents team z, the only team left for J is team u. Choice (C) is correct.

6.   **A**

This "if" question stipulates that Natalie represent team u, and asks you to find the one assignment of swimmers to lanes that is *not* possible. Roselyn must be in lane 1 or 4, and Josephine must be in lane 2 or 3, but this occurs in every answer choice. You also know that the swimmer who represents team x must be in a higher numbered lane than Josephine. You know from the previous five questions and your deductions that lanes 1, 4, and 5 are assigned to teams v, y, and w, though not necessarily in that order. (If this weren't already the last question, it would be a good choice to save for last.) If Josephine is in lane 2, x could be in lane 3 or 6, and if Josephine is in lane 3, x must be in lane 6. Choice (A) is not possible. Since Josephine is in lane 3 and Natalie represents team u in lane 6, there is no room for team x to come after Josephine. Since (A) cannot be true, it is the correct answer to this question.

PART THREE

Practice Logic Games Sections

Practice Logic Games Section 1

ANSWER SHEET

Remove (or photocopy) the answer sheet and use it to complete the practice test section.

Directions: Before taking each practice test section, find a quiet place where you can work uninterrupted for 35 minutes. Make sure you have a comfortable desk and several No. 2 pencils. Once you start a practice section, don't stop until you're done.

Good luck!

Start with number 1 for each section. If a section has fewer questions than answer spaces, leave the extra spaces blank.

1. Ⓐ Ⓑ Ⓒ Ⓓ Ⓔ   9. Ⓐ Ⓑ Ⓒ Ⓓ Ⓔ   17. Ⓐ Ⓑ Ⓒ Ⓓ Ⓔ   25. Ⓐ Ⓑ Ⓒ Ⓓ Ⓔ
2. Ⓐ Ⓑ Ⓒ Ⓓ Ⓔ   10. Ⓐ Ⓑ Ⓒ Ⓓ Ⓔ   18. Ⓐ Ⓑ Ⓒ Ⓓ Ⓔ   26. Ⓐ Ⓑ Ⓒ Ⓓ Ⓔ
3. Ⓐ Ⓑ Ⓒ Ⓓ Ⓔ   11. Ⓐ Ⓑ Ⓒ Ⓓ Ⓔ   19. Ⓐ Ⓑ Ⓒ Ⓓ Ⓔ   27. Ⓐ Ⓑ Ⓒ Ⓓ Ⓔ
4. Ⓐ Ⓑ Ⓒ Ⓓ Ⓔ   12. Ⓐ Ⓑ Ⓒ Ⓓ Ⓔ   20. Ⓐ Ⓑ Ⓒ Ⓓ Ⓔ   28. Ⓐ Ⓑ Ⓒ Ⓓ Ⓔ
5. Ⓐ Ⓑ Ⓒ Ⓓ Ⓔ   13. Ⓐ Ⓑ Ⓒ Ⓓ Ⓔ   21. Ⓐ Ⓑ Ⓒ Ⓓ Ⓔ   29. Ⓐ Ⓑ Ⓒ Ⓓ Ⓔ
6. Ⓐ Ⓑ Ⓒ Ⓓ Ⓔ   14. Ⓐ Ⓑ Ⓒ Ⓓ Ⓔ   22. Ⓐ Ⓑ Ⓒ Ⓓ Ⓔ   30. Ⓐ Ⓑ Ⓒ Ⓓ Ⓔ
7. Ⓐ Ⓑ Ⓒ Ⓓ Ⓔ   15. Ⓐ Ⓑ Ⓒ Ⓓ Ⓔ   23. Ⓐ Ⓑ Ⓒ Ⓓ Ⓔ
8. Ⓐ Ⓑ Ⓒ Ⓓ Ⓔ   16. Ⓐ Ⓑ Ⓒ Ⓓ Ⓔ   24. Ⓐ Ⓑ Ⓒ Ⓓ Ⓔ

Questions 1-6

Nine applicants are to be interviewed on a single day for a job position at Coffee Insurance. The applicants—Mel, Natalie, Polly, Raena, Stephanie, Tyrell, Veronica, Xavier, and Zack—are interviewed one at a time, and no one is interviewed more than once. The order in which they are interviewed is consistent with the following conditions:

Stephanie is interviewed before Natalie.

Zack is interviewed before Mel.

Raena is interviewed before Stephanie and after Mel.

Xavier is interviewed after Mel.

Polly and Veronica are interviewed after Raena.

Tyrell is interviewed before Veronica.

1. Which of the following could be the order, from first to last, in which the interviews take place?

   (A) Zack, Mel, Xavier, Raena, Veronica, Tyrell, Stephanie, Natalie, Polly

   (B) Tyrell, Zack, Mel, Xavier, Veronica, Raena, Stephanie, Polly, Natalie

   (C) Zack, Mel, Xavier, Raena, Tyrell, Veronica, Polly, Stephanie, Natalie

   (D) Tyrell, Zack, Raena, Mel, Xavier, Polly, Veronica, Stephanie, Natalie

   (E) Raena, Tyrell, Xavier, Zack, Mel, Veronica, Stephanie, Polly, Natalie

2. Which of the following could be true?

   (A) Raena is the second interview.

   (B) Polly is the third interview.

   (C) Veronica is the fourth interview.

   (D) Natalie is the fifth interview.

   (E) Mel is the sixth interview.

3. If Tyrell is interviewed eighth, then which of the following could be true?

   (A) Polly is interviewed ninth.

   (B) Veronica is interviewed sixth.

   (C) Stephanie is interviewed sixth.

   (D) Mel is interviewed third.

   (E) Zack is interviewed second.

4. If Tyrell's is the fifth interview of the day, which of the following must be true?

   (A) Stephanie is interviewed seventh.

   (B) Veronica is interviewed sixth.

   (C) Raena is interviewed fourth.

   (D) Xavier is interviewed third.

   (E) Mel is interviewed second.

5. If Xavier's is the third interview of the day, then all of the following must be false EXCEPT:

   (A) Veronica is interviewed sometime before Xavier

   (B) Tyrell is interviewed sometime before Raena

   (C) Raena is interviewed sometime before Xavier

   (D) Tyrell is interviewed sometime before Xavier

   (E) Veronica is interviewed sometime before Mel

6. If Stephanie is interviewed sometime before Tyrell, then which of the following could be true?

   (A) Zack is interviewed second.

   (B) Raena is interviewed fifth.

   (C) Tyrell is interviewed fifth.

   (D) Stephanie is interviewed seventh.

   (E) Tyrell is interviewed ninth.

Questions 7-11

A guard outfit consists of six soldiers—S, T, U, X, Y, and Z. Each soldier holds exactly one of the following ranks: sergeant, corporal, or private. No one supervises a sergeant. All other soldiers are supervised by exactly one soldier, who is either a sergeant or corporal. Each supervised soldier holds a different rank than his supervisor. The following conditions apply:

There is exactly one sergeant.

At least one of the soldiers who the sergeant supervises is a corporal.

Each corporal supervises at least one soldier.

Z does not supervise any soldiers.

Y supervises exactly two soldiers.

S supervises at least one soldier.

7. Which of the following is an acceptable assignment of soldiers to positions?

	Sergeant	Corporal	Private
(A)	X	S	T, U, Y, Z
(B)	Y	S, Z	T, U, X
(C)	Y		S, T, U, X, Z
(D)	X	Y, S	T, U, Z
(E)	S, X	U, Y	T, Z

8. Which of the following could be a complete and accurate list of the soldiers holding the rank of corporal?

(A) T, U

(B) U, X

(C) S, T

(D) S, T, U

(E) S, T, U, X, Y

9. Which one of the following could be true?

(A) There are exactly four privates.

(B) There are exactly two soldiers who supervise no one.

(C) There are no corporals.

(D) There are exactly three corporals.

(E) There is exactly one private.

10. If Y is supervised by the sergeant, and the sergeant supervises exactly two soldiers, then which of the following must be true?

(A) Z is supervised by Y.

(B) There are exactly two corporals.

(C) S is the sergeant.

(D) The sergeant supervises two privates.

(E) U is supervised by X.

11. If X supervises at least one soldier, then which of the following must be false?

(A) Y is the sergeant.

(B) Y supervises a corporal and a private.

(C) X is the sergeant.

(D) X supervises exactly two soldiers.

(E) Z is supervised by S.

GO ON TO THE NEXT PAGE

Questions 12-17

Jake is making a tape of five different songs for his brother Elwood. He can choose from nine different songs, which are each in one of three genres: four are blues (G, H, J, K), three are funk (P, Q, R), and two are soul (Y, Z). The selection of songs must meet the following criteria:

> At least two blues songs are selected.
>
> If exactly one funk song is selected, then exactly one soul song is selected.
>
> If K is selected, then neither G nor Y is selected.
>
> If P is selected, then K is selected.

12. Which of the following could be the selection of songs for the tape?

    (A) H, Q, R, Y, Z

    (B) G, H, R, Y, Z

    (C) J, K, P, Q, Y

    (D) H, J, P, R, Z

    (E) H, J, K, P, R

13. Which of the following must be true?

    (A) H is selected.

    (B) Q is selected.

    (C) R is selected.

    (D) Jake selects no songs from one of the three genres.

    (E) Jake selects no more than three blues songs.

14. If Y is selected, which of the following could be true?

    (A) Both P and R are selected.

    (B) All of the funk songs are selected.

    (C) None of the funk songs are selected.

    (D) Both Q and Z are selected.

    (E) None of the blues songs are selected.

15. If exactly one of the funk songs is selected, which one of the following must be true?

    (A) K is selected.

    (B) H is selected.

    (C) Both G and Y are selected.

    (D) Y is not selected.

    (E) Neither soul song is selected.

16. Which of the following must be true?

    (A) The selection of songs includes at least one funk song.

    (B) The selection of songs includes at least one soul song.

    (C) The selection of songs includes either P or K or both.

    (D) The selection of songs includes either G or K or both.

    (E) The selection of songs includes H or J or both.

17. If P and R are the only funk songs selected, which of the following could be true?

    (A) G and Z are selected.

    (B) H and Y are selected.

    (C) J and Q are selected.

    (D) H and J are selected.

    (E) H, J, and Z are selected.

Questions 18-23

An interior decorator has been hired to furnish three rooms in a house: the bedroom, the den, and the foyer. The decorator will place three items in each room: a chair, a rug, and a sofa. Each of those items will be grey, tan, pink, or ecru, and the house must contain at least one item in each color. The placement of items in each room adheres to the following guidelines:

> None of the items in any room is the same color.
>
> The three chairs are three different colors, as are the three rugs and the three sofas.
>
> Grey and ecru items cannot be placed in the same room.
>
> The bedroom chair is ecru.
>
> The foyer rug is pink.

18. Which one of the following could be a complete and accurate matching of items to the rooms in which they are placed?

    (A) Bedroom: ecru chair, tan rug, pink sofa
        Den: pink chair, grey rug, tan sofa
        Foyer: tan chair, pink rug, grey sofa

    (B) Bedroom: ecru chair, tan rug, pink sofa
        Den: grey chair, pink rug, tan sofa
        Foyer: tan chair, pink rug, grey sofa

    (C) Bedroom: ecru chair, tan rug, pink sofa
        Den: pink chair, grey rug, tan sofa
        Foyer: grey chair, pink rug, ecru sofa

    (D) Bedroom: ecru chair, tan rug, pink sofa
        Den: grey chair, pink rug, tan sofa
        Foyer: pink chair, pink rug, grey sofa

    (E) Bedroom: ecru chair, tan rug, pink sofa
        Den: tan chair, pink rug, grey sofa
        Foyer: pink chair, ecru rug, tan sofa

19. Which one of the following could be true?

    (A) Foyer sofa: grey, bedroom rug: pink.
    (B) Foyer chair: grey, den chair: tan.
    (C) Foyer chair: tan, foyer sofa: pink.
    (D) Den rug: ecru, foyer sofa: grey.
    (E) Den rug: grey, foyer chair: ecru.

20. Each of the following could be false EXCEPT:

    (A) The den rug is either grey or pink.
    (B) The foyer sofa is either tan or ecru.
    (C) The bedroom sofa is either grey or tan.
    (D) The den sofa is either tan or pink.
    (E) The chair in the den is either grey or ecru.

21. If the sofa in the foyer is ecru, then which one of the following must be true?

    (A) The chair in the den is grey.
    (B) The sofa in the den is grey.
    (C) The sofa in the den is ecru.
    (D) The rug in the den is ecru.
    (E) The rug in the den is grey.

22. Which of the following items must be tan?

    (A) The sofa in the foyer
    (B) The rug in the bedroom
    (C) The chair in the den
    (D) The sofa in the bedroom
    (E) The rug in the den

23. Which of the following new rules makes it impossible to furnish the house in compliance with the established guidelines?

    (A) The den chair must be grey.
    (B) The bedroom rug must be tan.
    (C) The den sofa must be tan.
    (D) The bedroom sofa must be pink.
    (E) The den rug must be ecru.

ANSWERS AND EXPLANATIONS

Game 1 (Questions 1–6)

Step 1: Overview

Situation: An interview schedule

Entities: Nine applicants: M, N, P, R, S, T, V, X, and Z

Action: The applicants must be sequenced for the interviews

Limitations: Pretty straightforward: nine applicants, interviewed one at a time; everyone must be used, and no one goes twice

Step 2: Sketch

Your first instinct might be to draw nine blanks for the nine interview slots, but take a glance at the rules. Each applicant's interview is dependent on the other applicants' interview positions; so this game is a **loose sequencing** game. Since this game depends upon how the entities relate to each other instead of how they relate to specific available slots, your sketch can be created as you move through the rules. You don't need the traditional row of blanks.

Step 3: Rules

Each rule can be sketched as a simple relationship between two or more entities. The first rule says S is interviewed before N.

$$S \text{ —— } N$$

The second rule deals with Z and M. Since there are no common entities, you can't add this in to the first sketch, so you have two choices. You can draw this rule out separately and perhaps join it later, or skip the rule and come back to it. Skip it for now.

Rule 3 says R is interviewed before S but after M. Adding this to rule 1, you have:

$$M \text{ —— } R \text{ —— } S \text{ —— } N$$

Rule 4 is that X is interviewed after M. Notice that this doesn't relate X to anything else but M: X could be right after M, or at the end of the sequence.

$$\begin{array}{c} \quad\quad X \\ \quad\nearrow \\ M \text{ —— } R \text{ —— } S \text{ —— } N \end{array}$$

The fifth rule is that P and V are interviewed after R.

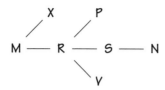

Finally, the sixth rule is that T is interviewed before V. Add in the rule you temporarily skipped; Z is before M, so the final sketch looks like this:

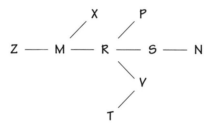

Step 4: Deductions

All nine applicants are involved in the rules; therefore, you know there can't be any unrestricted entities—every applicant's placement is dependent on at least one other applicant's.

Other than that, you can be sure that there is nothing else to glean from this information. Why? We've used every single rule in the one sketch.

With complex loose sequencing sketches like this one, pause for a second to study the sketch. Who could be first? Z for sure, but T can also be first. And who can be last? N, P, V, or X can all be the ninth person interviewed. Taking a few seconds before diving into the questions helps you focus, gather your thoughts, and avoid making unwarranted assumptions.

Step 5: Questions

1. C

This is an acceptability question. Apply each rule to eliminate any choice that violates it. The first two rules aren't much help; every choice obeys them. But rule 3 is violated in (D): R is before M. Rule 4 eliminates (E): Xavier must be after Mel. Rule 5 eliminates (B), and rule 6 eliminates (A), so (C) is the only one left and must be correct.

2. D

Go through the choices, eliminating what must be false. Both Z and M must be interviewed before R; therefore, R cannot be interviewed second, and (A) must be false. P cannot be interviewed third since P must be interviewed after Z, M, and R, so (B) is false. Both T and Z-M-R must be interviewed before V; therefore, the earliest V could be interviewed is fifth—(C) cannot be true. In (D), Natalie can certainly be fifth, as long as she comes before X, P, T, and V—that's your answer. When you have a clear, right answer, move on with confidence.

If you aren't positive, look at (E). Since M comes before X, R-S-N, *and* P and V, the latest M can be is third—(E) is certainly false.

3. C

If T is the eighth interview of the day, then V must be the ninth and last interview of the day. This eliminates (A) and (B). If T is interviewed eighth, then only Z is left to be interviewed first, with M coming second, eliminating (D) and (E). This leaves you with (C), the correct answer.

4. E

This question restates the concept tested in question 3. If T is the fifth interview of the day, then Z and M must be the first and second interviews respectively. Choice (E), M is interviewed second, is the only choice that must be true. The remaining choices could be true, but don't have to be true.

5. B

This "if" question stipulates that X is the third interview of the day and asks you to find the one choice that does not have to be false—or, in less confusing terms, the one that could be true. Since both Z and M must interview before X, Z and M must be the first and second interviews respectively.

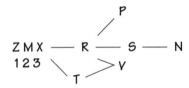

This means the fourth interview could only be R or T. Since there is no rule dictating R's position in relation to T, either one could interview fourth, and therefore (B) could be true.

6. C

This "if" question adds the additional rule that S is interviewed sometime before T, and asks for something that *could* be true. Since this question adds additional information, you should redraw your sketch. Since T now comes after S, you also need to move V, so it continues to come after T. Since T must follow S and S must follow R, you still have V after R, so rule 5 is not violated. Your revised sketch should look something like this:

We can now look at the choices. For (A), Z cannot be second (it must be first). Choice (B) is wrong, because R cannot be fifth—the latest it can be is fourth. T, however, can be fifth. Remember, even though it may look like X and P are before T in the sketch above, they need not be. In a loose sequencing sketch, pay attention to the connecting lines, and not the spatial relationships on the page. If X, P, V, and N all come after T, T will be fifth; so (C) is possible and therefore correct.

Again, in case you have doubts, (D) is wrong because S can't be seventh (at least three people come after her), and T can't be ninth (because V comes after T), so (E) is eliminated.

Game 2 (Questions 7–11)

Step 1: Overview

Situation: Military rankings

Entities: Six soldiers—S, T, U, X, Y, and Z, and the ranks: Ser, Cor, and Pri

Action: At first, this might seem like a distribution game, since you have three categories (the ranks) and you need to group the soldiers into these groups. However, you also have the issue of supervision, which is hard to reflect in a traditional distribution sketch. A loose sequencing sketch that has only 3 "levels" may allow you to reflect this issue of supervision. But the issue of distribution (the different numbers of entities in the categories) will still be important.

Limitations: There are a lot here. Except for the sergeant, all soldiers are supervised by either a sergeant or a corporal. You also know that a supervised soldier holds a different rank from their supervisor. Who can supervise a corporal? Only the sergeant can supervise a corporal; either a sergeant or a corporal can supervise a private. Who supervises a private? Either a sergeant or a corporal.

Step 2: Sketch

Once you combine all of the limitations, you see that the game requires you to divide the soldiers into a three-tier system, with the sergeant at the top who is unsupervised and can supervise both corporals and privates, corporals in the middle who can supervise only privates, and privates on the bottom who supervise no one.

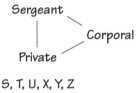

You don't have a framework with slots yet, because you don't know *how many* soldiers of each rank you have. This should be one of the first things you look for. Now go ahead and look at the conditions that apply to this game.

Step 3: Rules

The first condition says there is exactly one sergeant. "Ser = 1" works well.

The next condition is that the sergeant must supervise at least one corporal. So there is at least one corporal: "Corp = 1 +."

The next condition is that each corporal supervises at least one soldier. Since corporals can only supervise privates, you now know that any corporal must supervise at least one private. Maybe something like "All corp super 1 + pri" These first three rules may seem confusing, but we'll go back in step 4 to see what else they can yield.

The next condition tells you that Z does not supervise any soldiers: "Z super none." The next condition tells you that Y supervises exactly two soldiers: "Y super exact 2." The last condition is that S supervises at least one soldier: "S super 1 +." Note the difference between Y and S; Y must supervise EXACTLY two soldiers; S will supervise one or possibly more soldiers.

You may have noticed some deductions as you were going through the rules.

Step 4: Deductions

Notice that the first three rules deal with the number breakdowns among the three categories, while the other rules deal with specific entities. It is most important to pin down the possible numbers of the different ranks, so look at these first three rules first.

You know there is one sergeant, so the other five soldiers must be corporals and privates. They can't all be corporals, because each corporal must supervise at least one private. They also can't all be privates, because the sergeant must supervise at least one corporal. Think about the possible numbers of corporals.

If you have only one corporal, then you have four remaining soldiers, all privates. If you have two corporals, you have three privates; each corporal will be able to supervise at least one private. But if you have three corporals, you would need at least three privates, and with the one sergeant, this gives you seven soldiers. This is too many, so you can either have one or two corporals. An "either/or" situation based on the numbers is a *huge* sign that "limited options" will be useful. Draw out these two scenarios.

Option 1:

Ser: ____

Cor: ____

Pri: ____ ____ ____ ____

Option 2:

Ser: ____

Cor: ____ ____

Pri: ____ ____ ____ ____

Notice that some of the privates lack supervisors. This is only because you don't yet know who supervises them—the sergeant or a corporal. Don't assume things that may not be true; just leave this issue be.

But you have a lot more information, and you have incorporated the first three rules into the options. Remember, anytime you can make limited options based on number deductions, do so; they are some of the most powerful limited options you can set up.

Now look at the other three rules. Z can't supervise anyone, so Z must be a private. Y and S both supervise people, so they are either sergeants or corporals. Write this information down next to the rules; you can't put any of these entities into the sketch. For instance, you don't know who is supervising Z.

Step 5: Questions

7.   D

This is an acceptability question. Eliminate any choices that violate a condition. Choice (E) violates the first condition; there can be only one sergeant. Choice (C) violates rule 3; since each corporal must supervise at least one soldier, there cannot be more corporals than privates. Rules 3 and 4 eliminate (B), which has Z in the position of corporal; each corporal supervises at least one other soldier, but Z supervises no one. Choice (A) has Y in the position of private, which is not possible because Y must supervise two other soldiers and privates cannot supervise, so (D) is correct.

8.   C

This question asks you for a possible "complete and accurate list" of the corporals. But be careful—(E) is the right answer to "which of the following is a complete and accurate list of the soldiers who *could* be corporals." You want a list of soldiers that could be corporals in one scenario. Immediately rule out (D) and (E), since you've already deduced that you can have a maximum of two corporals. As for (A), (B), and (C), look at S and Y—both must be supervisors and since, other than the corporals, there is only one supervisor position left (sergeant), one of the corporals *must* be S or Y, so (A) and (B) cannot be true, which leaves (C). If S and T were corporals, then Y could be the sergeant supervising both S and T. Here's one possible way this could look:

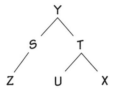

9.   A

Since this question asks what *could* be true, eliminate choices that must be false. The choices all concern the numbers of soldiers holding the different ranks; if you've thought about these numbers already, this question should be fairly easy. Look at the two limited options. Right away, you can see in option 1 that (A) is possible. Choice (B) says there are exactly two soldiers who supervise no one. Only privates supervise no one, and you either have three or four privates, so (B) is false. (C) can't be true; you must have at least one corporal. You've already seen how (D) doesn't work; you can only have one or two corporals. And rule out (E) for the same reason you ruled out (B).

10.   B

This "if" question places two additional conditions on the positions of the soldiers. Since Y now has to be supervised by the sergeant, and since Y must also supervise exactly two other soldiers, Y must be a corporal. The next "if" condition is that the sergeant supervises exactly two other soldiers. Since you already know that Y must be one of the soldiers supervised by the sergeant, the sergeant can only supervise one more soldier.

So now the question is: are you in option 1 or option 2? If you were in option 1, with only 1 corporal, you would have an unsupervised private. Therefore, you must be in option 2. The sergeant must supervise exactly two corporals: one is Y who supervises exactly two privates and the other corporal supervises one private, thus providing room for all six soldiers in the sketch.

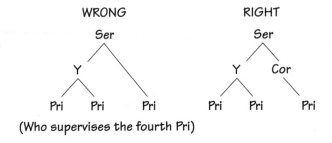

So (B) is correct. (D) could never be true since you know one of the soldiers the sergeant supervises must be Y; (A), (C), and (E) could be true, but don't have to be.

11. B

This "if" question adds the same condition to X that S has; it must supervise at least one soldier. You need to find the choice that must be false, so eliminate any that could be true. Since X must supervise at least one soldier, S, Y, and X all must supervise, so you are in option 2. T, U, and Z must be privates. S, Y, and X can all be the sergeant, so (A) and (C) are both possible. Like (A), (B) implies that Y is the sergeant (since only the sergeant can supervise a corporal). But if Y is the sergeant, Y must supervise the two corporals, and *no* privates. Therefore, (B) is correct. Y could not supervise a corporal and a private. For the record, (D) and (E) are both possible as well. X can supervise exactly two soldiers, whether X is the sergeant or a corporal, and Z could be supervised by S (or by X or Y).

Game 3 (Questions 12–17)

Step 1: Overview

Situation: Making a tape of songs

Entities: Nine songs: four blues (G, H, J, K), three funk (P, Q, R), and two soul (Y, Z)

Action: Selection

Limitations: Select five out of nine

Step 2: Sketch

In this game, you have nine entities of three different types. Three categories makes it tough to use capitals and lowercase; often, it is just as easy to write the categories:

Blues: G, H, J, K   Funk: P, Q, R   Soul: Y, Z

Below this list of songs, draw a row of five spaces to represent the five songs that must be chosen. (They do not need to be numbered, since you are not asked to put the songs in any particular order.) Whenever you have a selection game with definite numbers, blanks are a useful tool for your sketch. Alternatively, circle what is selected and cross out what is rejected. Often, the specific rules may guide you, as rule 1 does here.

Step 3: Rules

The first rule says at least two of the five songs must be blues. Designate two of your five spaces to be blues, noting that there could be more blues if needed.

The next rule is that if one funk song is selected, then exactly one soul song must be selected. Write this next to your sketch. The next rule says if K is selected, then neither G nor Y can be selected. Note this by your sketch as a conditional, with its contrapositive (if G or Y, then no K).

The final rule says if P is selected, then K is also selected; note this and its contrapositive. Your scratchwork should look something like this:

Blues: G, H, J, K   Funk: P, Q, R   Soul: Y, Z

___   ___   ___

Blues Blues

Funk = 1 → Soul = 1
Soul ≠ 1 → Funk ≠ 1

K → No G and No Y
G or Y → No K

P → K
No K → No P

Step 4: Deduction

Look over your sketch to see if you can make any deductions. Since the last three rules are "if" statements, they won't tell you what *must* be true. All you know about the numbers is what you learned from rule 1, but this still leaves the field wide open. Move on to the questions.

Step 5: Questions

12. E

For this acceptability question, test each rule against the choices. Rule 1 eliminates (A) because it only has one blues song. Rule 2 eliminates (B) because it has one funk song selected with two soul songs. (C) selects K along with Y, a violation of rule 3, and (D) has P selected without K, violating rule 4. Therefore, only (E) is an acceptable selection.

13. E

This question asks for the one choice that must be true for the entire game. The answer usually involves a deduction that can be made through the rules. Rule 3 says if K is selected G cannot be selected, and if G is selected K cannot be: You cannot have both K and G selected for the tape. Since you can't select all four blues songs, you can have at most three blues songs—so (E) is correct.

If you have doubts, (D) says one category of songs will have none selected from it. This could be true, but does not have to be. Choices (A), (B), and (C) all deal with specific entities; if needed you could rule some of these out with previous (or future) work. For example, in question 1, Q is not selected, so (B) need not be true.

14. C

This new "if" question stipulates that Y is selected for the tape, and asks for the one choice that could be true. Referring to your scratchwork, you know that if Y is selected, neither K nor P can be. Rejecting P means (A) and (B) must be false. You also know that at least two blues songs must be selected, so eliminate (E) as well. Finally, if Q and Z were selected, this would give you one funk song and two soul songs, with the remaining two spaces reserved for blues; this violates rule 2. Only (C) could be true: The tape could be G, H, J, Y, and Z.

15. B

This new "if" question says only one funk song is selected, and asks for the one choice that must be true. You know from rule 2 that if one funk song is selected, then only one soul song is selected. This leaves the remaining three spaces available for blues songs only. Since G and K can never be selected together, H and J must be two of the blues selections; the third can be either G or K. So (B) must be true.

16. E

This question asks for the one choice that must be true. In question 4 you saw that G and K can never be selected together; you also know that at least two songs must be blues. So the two blues songs can never be G and K—therefore at least one of the blues songs must be H or J or both, and (E) is correct.

17. D

This new "if" question stipulates that P and R are the only funk songs selected, and you have to find the one choice that could be true. If P and R are the only funk songs, then Q is not selected. Rule 4 says if P is selected, K is selected as well; if K is selected, neither G nor Y can be selected (rule 3). Since you already have three songs selected (P, R, and K), there's only room for two more songs. You must select two from H, J, and Z. Choice (D) is correct; (A), (B), and (C) select G, Y, and Q—the three entities that are definitely rejected—and (E) would create a tape with six songs instead of five:

K	H/J	___	P	R
Blues	Blues	B/S	Funk	Funk

Game 4 (Questions 18–23)

Step 1: Overview

Situation: Decorating a house

Entities: Nine pieces of furniture: three chairs, three rugs and three sofas; each can be one of four colors: grey, tan, pink, or ecru

Action: To match a color to each piece of furniture in each room

Limitations: Exactly one chair, one rug, and one sofa per room; all colors must be used at least once

Step 2: Sketch

Use a grid-style sketch for this game, something like this:

	Bed	Den	Foy
C			
R			
S			

Step 3: Rules

Rule 1 says none of the items within a room are the same color. It might seem hard to sketch this, so notate it somehow. "All rooms different" is one way. Rule 2 is similar—it says all three chairs are different colors, as are the three rugs and the three sofas. Again, something like "All chairs/rugs/sofas different" could work. Remember, with rules like these, it is better to pause a second and think through what they really mean. If you truly understand the rule, you won't be in danger of misinterpreting your notations.

Rule 3 stipulates that g and e items cannot be placed in the same room. Note this next to the sketch: "No g and e in room." Rule 4 says the chair in the bedroom is ecru, and rule 5 says the rug in the foyer is pink. These two rules can be entered directly into the sketch.

	Bed	Den	Foy
C	e		
R			p
S			

Step 4: Deduction

This game supports numerous deductions. But before you go rushing to fill in "not e" in the rest of the bedroom and for the other two couches, remember that your goal is to focus on what *must* be true, and not what *can't* happen. Rule 3 is the key here. Since a room must have three different colors, and grey and ecru can't be in the same room, you can deduce that each room *must* have one pink item, one tan item, and one grey or ecru item.

Look at the bedroom first. You have a ecru chair, so you still need a "p" and an "m." Since the foyer rug is pink, and you can't have two rugs of the same color, the pink bedroom item must be the sofa, which leaves the bedroom rug to be tan.

	Bed	Den	Foy
C	e		
R	t		p
S	p		

Each room must have a pink item, and since you already have a pink rug and a pink sofa, the pink item in the den must be the chair. The den also needs a tan item. It can't be the chair, because the den's chair is pink, and it can't be the rug, because the tan rug is in the bedroom, so the den's tan item must be the sofa. With tan items now in the bedroom and den, you know that the tan item in the foyer must be the chair. You only have two pieces of furniture left—the rug in the den and the sofa in the foyer. Each of these can be either grey or ecru. You now have:

	Bed	Den	Foy
C	e	p	t
R	t	g/e	p
S	p	t	g/e

When you have a sketch that is almost complete, as in this game, you may want to compare it *en masse* to the answer choices in an acceptability question. But this can sometimes be more trouble than it is worth, because in doing so, you concentrate on a lot more than just the entities that violate the rules. Better to use the failsafe method of using the rules one by one to eliminate answer choices. Rule 1 eliminates (D), as both the chair and the rug in the foyer are pink. Rule 2 eliminates (B), since the rugs in both the den and the foyer are pink. Rule 3 eliminates (C), since the chair in the foyer is grey and the sofa is ecru. Rule 5 eliminates (E), as the rug in the foyer is ecru. By process of elimination, (A) is correct.

Step 5: Questions

19. D

Four of the choices are false, and the correct answer is possible. Use your sketch to eliminate everything but (D). It is possible for there to be a ecru rug in the den and a grey sofa in the foyer, so (D) is correct.

20. D

This question may seem confusing, but it really just asks for the answer that must be true. Choice (A) could be false, because the den rug could be ecru. Likewise, the foyer sofa could be grey, so (B) does not have to be true, and (C) and (E) must be false: The bedroom sofa is pink, as is the chair in the den. Choice (D), however, must be true. Don't be thrown off by the "either/or" construction. Since the sofa in the den is tan, it must be true that the sofa in the den is either tan or pink.

21. E

This new "if" question stipulates that the sofa in the foyer is ecru. What else must be true? If you noticed that all of the choices concern ecru and grey items, you may have gotten the answer quickly. Remember from the setup that each color must be used at least once. If the foyer sofa is ecru, you still need a grey item. Since the rug in the den is the only item left, it must be grey, and (E) is correct.

22. B

This question asks you to draw on the rules and deductions to determine which item must be tan. From the sketch, you know the answer must be either the bedroom rug, the sofa in the den, or the chair in the foyer. The bedroom rug is (B), so it is correct.

23. A

This question asks you to find the choice that, if true, makes it impossible for you to complete the game. Don't let the question's strange structure fool you—this is really just another way of asking which choice must be false, and (A), with its grey chair in the den, contradicts your sketch. (A) must be false and is correct.

Practice Logic Games Section 2

ANSWER SHEET

Remove (or photocopy) the answer sheet and use it to complete the practice test section.

<u>Directions:</u> Before taking each practice test section, find a quiet place where you can work uninterrupted for 35 minutes. Make sure you have a comfortable desk and several No. 2 pencils. Once you start a practice section, don't stop until you're done.

Good luck!

Start with number 1 for each section. If a section has fewer questions than answer spaces, leave the extra spaces blank.

1. Ⓐ Ⓑ Ⓒ Ⓓ Ⓔ	9. Ⓐ Ⓑ Ⓒ Ⓓ Ⓔ	17. Ⓐ Ⓑ Ⓒ Ⓓ Ⓔ	25. Ⓐ Ⓑ Ⓒ Ⓓ Ⓔ
2. Ⓐ Ⓑ Ⓒ Ⓓ Ⓔ	10. Ⓐ Ⓑ Ⓒ Ⓓ Ⓔ	18. Ⓐ Ⓑ Ⓒ Ⓓ Ⓔ	26. Ⓐ Ⓑ Ⓒ Ⓓ Ⓔ
3. Ⓐ Ⓑ Ⓒ Ⓓ Ⓔ	11. Ⓐ Ⓑ Ⓒ Ⓓ Ⓔ	19. Ⓐ Ⓑ Ⓒ Ⓓ Ⓔ	27. Ⓐ Ⓑ Ⓒ Ⓓ Ⓔ
4. Ⓐ Ⓑ Ⓒ Ⓓ Ⓔ	12. Ⓐ Ⓑ Ⓒ Ⓓ Ⓔ	20. Ⓐ Ⓑ Ⓒ Ⓓ Ⓔ	28. Ⓐ Ⓑ Ⓒ Ⓓ Ⓔ
5. Ⓐ Ⓑ Ⓒ Ⓓ Ⓔ	13. Ⓐ Ⓑ Ⓒ Ⓓ Ⓔ	21. Ⓐ Ⓑ Ⓒ Ⓓ Ⓔ	29. Ⓐ Ⓑ Ⓒ Ⓓ Ⓔ
6. Ⓐ Ⓑ Ⓒ Ⓓ Ⓔ	14. Ⓐ Ⓑ Ⓒ Ⓓ Ⓔ	22. Ⓐ Ⓑ Ⓒ Ⓓ Ⓔ	30. Ⓐ Ⓑ Ⓒ Ⓓ Ⓔ
7. Ⓐ Ⓑ Ⓒ Ⓓ Ⓔ	15. Ⓐ Ⓑ Ⓒ Ⓓ Ⓔ	23. Ⓐ Ⓑ Ⓒ Ⓓ Ⓔ	
8. Ⓐ Ⓑ Ⓒ Ⓓ Ⓔ	16. Ⓐ Ⓑ Ⓒ Ⓓ Ⓔ	24. Ⓐ Ⓑ Ⓒ Ⓓ Ⓔ	

Questions 1-6

Four dental hygienists—Carol, Eddie, Fiona, and Greg—and three dentists—Joe, Lea, and Max—will attend a series of five professional development seminars, each held in a different one of five classrooms numbered 1 through 5 from left to right. The following conditions determine attendance at each seminar by the seven dental professionals:

> Each seminar will either be a one-person or two-person seminar, and each person must attend exactly one seminar.
>
> Each two-person seminar must be attended by one dental hygienist and one dentist.
>
> Greg must attend a two-person seminar, and Joe must attend a one-person seminar.
>
> Max and Lea cannot attend seminars in adjacent classrooms.
>
> Eddie must attend the seminar in classroom 3.

1. If the seminars in classrooms 1 and 2 are each attended by one dental hygienist and are not two-person seminars, then which one of the following is a complete and accurate list of people who must attend the seminar in classroom 4?

   (A) Greg
   (B) Carol and Lea
   (C) Greg and Max
   (D) Joe
   (E) Fiona

2. Which one of the following is a complete and accurate list of the people who must be among those who attend a two-person seminar?

   (A) Eddie, Greg
   (B) Greg, Fiona
   (C) Greg, Max, Lea
   (D) Greg, Carol, Lea
   (E) Greg, Carol, Fiona

3. If the seminars in the first three classrooms are attended by dentists, which of the following must be true?

   (A) Greg attends the same seminar as Lea.
   (B) Fiona attends the same seminar as Lea.
   (C) Lea attends the seminar in classroom 1.
   (D) Greg attends the seminar in classroom 1.
   (E) Max attends the seminar in classroom 2.

4. Once Joe has been assigned to a seminar, what is the maximum number of different classrooms, each of which could be the classroom in which Greg attends a seminar?

   (A) one
   (B) two
   (C) three
   (D) four
   (E) five

5. If the four dental hygienists are assigned to seminars in consecutively numbered classrooms and Greg is assigned to the seminar in classroom 5, then which of the following is a complete and accurate list of classrooms each of which CANNOT host a two-person seminar?

   (A) classroom 4
   (B) classroom 2
   (C) classroom 1, classroom 2
   (D) classroom 2, classroom 4
   (E) classroom 1, classroom 4

6. If Lea attends the seminar in classroom 3 and Carol alone attends the seminar in classroom 1, then which one of the following must be true?

   (A) Joe attends the seminar in classroom 5.
   (B) Greg attends the seminar in classroom 5.
   (C) Joe attends the seminar in classroom 2.
   (D) Fiona attends the seminar in classroom 2.
   (E) Greg attends the seminar in classroom 4.

Questions 7-12

A motel is made up of five buildings, numbered 1 through 5 from left to right. Each building consists of a single top-floor room and a single bottom-floor room. Eight people—Bianca, Chuy, Galena, Karl, Manjari, Royce, Steffi and Tony—have checked into the hotel and been assigned to a room; two rooms remain empty. The guests are assigned to rooms in accordance with these conditions:

The room above Bianca's is not empty.

Chuy is assigned to a room in the building immediately to the right of the building to which Steffi is assigned.

The top floor room in building 2 is empty.

Karl is assigned to the room above Manjari.

Royce and Tony are not assigned to the same building.

The room above Galena is empty.

Tony is not assigned to building 1 or building 2.

7. Which one of the following must be true?

(A) Tony is assigned to building 3.
(B) Tony is assigned to building 5.
(C) Galena is not assigned to building 4.
(D) Manjari is not assigned to building 2.
(E) Bianca is assigned to building 1.

8. Which one of the following CANNOT be true?

(A) Chuy is assigned to building 2.
(B) Karl is assigned to building 1.
(C) Manjari is assigned to building 4.
(D) Royce is assigned to building 3.
(E) Steffi is assigned to building 5.

9. If Bianca and Chuy are assigned to buildings 4 and 5, respectively, which one of the following can be true?

(A) Royce is assigned to building 1.
(B) Tony is assigned to building 4.
(C) Manjari is assigned to building 5.
(D) Galena is assigned to building 4.
(E) Steffi is assigned to building 3.

10. If Karl is assigned to building 4, which of the following must be false?

(A) Royce is assigned to building 5.
(B) Bianca is assigned to building 1.
(C) Galena is assigned to building 2.
(D) Tony is assigned to building 3.
(E) Steffi is assigned to building 1.

11. Which one of the following must be true?

(A) If Bianca is assigned to building 4, then Tony is not assigned to building 5.
(B) If Royce is assigned to building 2, then Galena is not assigned to building 4.
(C) If Manjari is assigned to building 4, then Chuy is not assigned to building 2.
(D) If Chuy is assigned to building 3, then Royce is not assigned to building 5.
(E) If Steffi is assigned to building 4, then Karl is not assigned to building 3.

12. If Royce is assigned to building 4, and Steffi is assigned to building 2, which one of the following must be true?

(A) Galena is assigned to building 1.
(B) Karl is assigned to building 3
(C) Tony is assigned to building 3.
(D) Manjari is assigned to building 5.
(E) Tony is assigned to building 5.

GO ON TO THE NEXT PAGE

<u>Questions 13-17</u>

Each of five nurses at a hospital—Akiko, Brent, Chloe, Damon and Eleora—is to complete exactly one of three jobs: paperwork, rounds, or supervision. One of the jobs takes one hour to complete, another takes two hours to complete, and the third takes three hours to complete. Each of the jobs is completed by at least one of the nurses. The nurses complete the jobs in a manner consistent with the following:

Damon completes the job that takes three hours.

Paperwork takes longer than supervision.

Chloe's job takes longer to complete than Eleora's.

More nurses complete supervision than complete paperwork.

13. Which one of the following could be a complete and accurate assignment of nurses to the jobs they complete?

(A) Akiko-rounds, Brent-supervision, Chloe-paperwork, Damon-rounds, Eleora-supervision

(B) Akiko-rounds, Brent-supervision, Chloe-supervision, Damon-rounds, Eleora-paperwork

(C) Akiko-supervision, Brent-supervision, Chloe-paperwork, Damon-paperwork, Eleora-rounds

(D) Akiko-supervision, Brent-supervision, Chloe-paperwork, Damon-paperwork, Eleora-supervision

(E) Akiko-supervision, Brent-supervision, Chloe-paperwork, Damon-supervision, Eleora-rounds

14. Which one of the following nurses CANNOT complete the three-hour job?

(A) Akiko
(B) Brent
(C) Chloe
(D) Damon
(E) Eleora

15. If supervision is the job that takes two hours to complete, then which one of the following nurses must complete rounds?

(A) Akiko
(B) Brent
(C) Chloe
(D) Damon
(E) Eleora

16. Which one of the following nurses CANNOT complete supervision?

(A) Akiko
(B) Brent
(C) Chloe
(D) Damon
(E) Eleora

17. Which one of the following could be a complete and accurate list of the nurses who complete the job that takes one hour?

(A) Akiko
(B) Brent
(C) Akiko, Brent
(D) Akiko, Chloe
(E) Akiko, Damon

Questions 18-23

During a period of seven consecutive days, numbered 1 through 7, seven movies—L, M, N, O, P, Q, and R—will be screened at the Paramount Theatre. Exactly one movie will be screened on each day. The movies must be screened in accordance with the following conditions:

M is screened on either day 2 or day 4.

P is not screened on day 3 or on day 5.

If N is screened on day 1, then Q is screened on day 2.

If R is screened on day 3, then P is screened on day 4.

L is screened the day after Q is screened.

18. Which of the following could be the order in which the films are screened from day 1 through day 7?

   (A) N, Q, R, P, M, L, O
   (B) N, Q, L, M, P, O, R
   (C) Q, L, M, P, O, N, R
   (D) P, M, R, Q, L, N, O
   (E) P, Q, L, M, N, O, R

19. If N is screened on day 1, which one of the following movies could be screened on day 5?

   (A) L
   (B) M
   (C) P
   (D) Q
   (E) R

20. If R is screened on day 4 and N is screened sometime after Q is screened, which of the following must be true?

   (A) Q is screened on day 1
   (B) Q is screened on day 6
   (C) L is screened on day 7
   (D) O is screened on day 3
   (E) O is screened on day 5

21. If Q is screened on day 1, which of the following is a complete and accurate list of movies, any one of which could be viewed on day 3?

   (A) N
   (B) O
   (C) N, O
   (D) O, R
   (E) N, O, R

22. If Q is screened on the day after R is screened, and if M is screened on the day after P is screened, then R could be screened on

   (A) day 1
   (B) day 2
   (C) day 3
   (D) day 5
   (E) day 6

23. If L and P are screened before the day on which M is screened, then which movie is screened on day 2?

   (A) P
   (B) L
   (C) Q
   (D) O
   (E) N

ANSWERS AND EXPLANATIONS

Game 1 (Questions 1–6)

Step 1: Overview

Situation: Seminars for dental professionals

Entities: The seven attendees—four dental hygienists (D, E, F, and G) and three dentists (j, l and m)

Action: You need to distribute the seven professionals among the five classrooms

Limitations: Not a lot—there is nothing that says that each classroom must have an attendee. With just the opening paragraph, it isn't clear how many people can be placed in a room—this is one of the first things you need to look for.

Step 2: Sketch

Your sketch should show five different classrooms, arranged horizontally and numbered from 1 to 5. Your sketch must also allow for multiple attendees in each classroom (although some of the spaces will be left blank).

Step 3: Rules

Rule 1 is that you can have a maximum of two people per seminar. Each of the seven people must go to exactly one seminar, and they go either by themselves or with exactly one other person. Write something like "1 or 2 per." Rule 2 says that all two-person seminars are to include one dentist and one dental hygienist. Something like "2—one of each" will work (if you did something else, that's fine, as long as you understand it and it reflects the meaning of the rule). Rule 3 is that Greg must attend a two-person seminar, and Joe must attend a one-person seminar. Write down exactly what this says:

$$\frac{G\,j}{\underline{\quad}}\ X$$

Rule 4 is that Max and Lea must not be in adjacent classrooms. Draw this as a restrictive block: "No l m or m l." Rule 5 says that Eddie must be in classroom 3; put this in your sketch. You now have:

Hygienists: C, E, F, G
Dentists: j, l, m

1	2	3	4	5
		E		

1 or 2 per
2—one of each
G j
___ X
No l m or m l

Step 4: Deductions

You have a lot of information about the numbers here (one- or two-person seminars, etc.). Think through the implications.

You know that at most two people can go into a classroom, and since you must use everyone, you have one of two situations: 2:2:2:1, or 2:2:1:1:1 (i.e., there will be either two or three two-person classrooms). You also know that you only have three dentists, and each two-person seminar must have a dentist. So are both number breakdowns allowed? Not quite: Joe is always by himself, so there are only two dentists available for the two-person seminars. Based on your work with the numbers, you know that the remaining two dentists *must* be in two separate two-person seminars—otherwise, we'd run out of classrooms! Furthermore, one of these dentists must be in the same seminar as Greg. You now have:

Hygienists: C, E, F, G
Dentists: j, l, m

1	2	3	4	5
		E		

5 groups: G m/l j ____ ____

l/m ____

No l m or m l

Once again, you have two identical, unrestricted elements: Carol and Fiona. Unless an "if" question tells you otherwise, C can appear anywhere in the sketch that F can, and vice-versa.

Step 5: Questions

1. D

Based on information in this "if" question, you know that two dental hygienists are in classrooms 1 and 2, and they are alone. These hygienists can't be Eddie (who is in room 3) or Greg (who is with a dentist), so they must be Carol and Fiona. So you have:

1	2	3	4	5
C/F	F/C	E		
X	X			

Now you have the two two-person seminars, which can never be adjacent, since Lea and Max can't be next to each other. So they are split between classrooms 3 and 5, leaving Joe as the remaining person for classroom 4. Therefore, (D) is correct.

2.   C

See how great deductions are? You've already done this work, while another test taker is just starting to think this through. Look at the groupings: Both Leo and Max need to be in two-person seminars. Of course, there's also Greg—mandated by rule 3 (but notice that Greg is in every choice). Choice (C) is correct.

Another strategy, especially helpful if you haven't made the important deductions, is to skip a question like this and save it for last (and use previous work), or at least to use work you've already done. For example, the sketch in question 1 shows Carol and Fiona attending one-person seminars. This allows you to eliminate (B), (D), and (E).

3.   D

This "if" question says classrooms 1, 2, and 3 must be occupied by the dentists, Joe, Lea, and Max. Rule 4 stipulates that Max and Lea must not be in adjacent classrooms, so one of them must be in classroom 1 and the other in classroom 3, leaving 2 to Joe.

1	2	3	4	5
l/m	j	E		
	X	m/l		

And since Eddie is already in room 3, Greg (the other two-person attendee) must be in 1—as (D) states.

Choice (A) is wrong because Greg could attend the seminar with Lea or Max; (B) is wrong because Lea attends a seminar with either Greg or Eddie; (C) is wrong because Lea also could attend the seminar in classroom 3; (E) is wrong because Joe must attend the seminar in classroom 2 by himself.

4.   C

Eliminate (E) and (D) immediately: Greg can never attend a seminar with Joe, who always attends one-person seminars, or with Eddie, who is also a dental hygienist. (And since Joe and Eddie are always at separate seminars, there are only three left to which Greg could be assigned.)

There are no shortcuts for the rest of this question. To choose between the remaining choices, plug Joe into the sketch somewhere and see how many different options you can come up with without breaking any rules: Greg has to be in a two-person seminar, and Lea and Max must not be in adjacent rooms. It doesn't matter which classroom Joe is in, so use classroom 1:

1	2	3	4	5
j	G	E	C/F	F/C
X	l/m	X	m/l	X

1	2	3	4	5
j	F/C	E	G	F/C
X	l/m	X	m/l	X

1	2	3	4	5
j	C/F	E	F/C	G
X	X	m/l	X	l/m

With the three sketches, you can see that Greg can go in any one of the remaining three classrooms, and (C) is correct.

5. E

For this "complete and accurate list" question, the correct choice must include any and all possibilities. Since Greg is in room 5, the four dental hygienists are assigned to 2, 3, 4, and 5. There is only one classroom left where Joe can attend a one-person seminar: classroom 1. You also know that Greg must attend a two-person seminar in classroom 5 with either Lea or Max.

1	2	3	4	5
j	C/F	E	F/C	G
X				l/m

Eliminate (A), (B), and (D) because they don't include classroom 1. The choice between (C) and (E) requires you to figure out if it's 2 or 4 that cannot host a two-person seminar. There's no reason 2 can't host a two-person seminar, so (C) is eliminated. A two-person seminar in 4, however, would require Max and Lea to attend seminars in adjacent rooms, breaking rule 4, so (E) is correct.

6.   B

With Lea attending a seminar in classroom 3, rule 4 tells you that Max cannot be in room 2 or 4. That leaves 1 or 5, and with the question telling you that Carol is alone in classroom 1, you know that Max must be in 5.

1	2	3	4	5
C		E		
X		I		m

Rule 3 requires Greg to attend a two-person seminar with one of the dentists. Since Joe always attends a one-person seminar, Greg must be in room 5 with Max, and (B) is correct. As for the other choices, Joe and Fiona attend one-person seminars in either 2 or 4. Therefore, (C) and (D) could be true, but neither must be. Choice (A) is false because Joe and Max cannot attend a seminar together. Choice (E) is false because placing Greg in classroom 4 also would force Max to be in room 4, adjacent to Lea.

Game 2 (Questions 7–12)

Step 1: Overview

Situation: Guests checking into a motel

Entities: Eight guests: B, C, G, K, M, R, S, and T

Action: To match each guest to his or her motel room; there are some sequencing and distribution elements

Limitations: One person is assigned to each room, and two rooms remain empty. To represent the two empty rooms, we'll add x and x to our roster of entities.

Step 2: Sketch

The sketch for this game will look like a standard matching sketch, but with two rows instead of one to represent the top and bottom floors of the motel:

B, C, G, K, M, R, S, T, x, x

	1	2	3	4	5
top					
bot					

Step 3: Rules

Rule 1 tells you that the room above B is not empty. You can infer several things. For one, B is on the bottom floor. Second, B and another person make up a small "block" which you might draw like this:

Rule 2 says C is assigned to the building immediately to the right of S. However, you don't know the floor to which either of them is assigned. Be careful to represent that in the sketch of this rule:

Remember, either of these buildings could be the same building that B (or any other letter) is in.

Rule 3 says the top floor in building 2 is empty; use an "x" to incorporate this directly into the sketch. Rule 4 is that K is assigned to the room directly above M; render this with a standard block:

Rule 5 provides you with the material for another restricted block clue:

Rule 6 tells you that G is on the bottom floor and that the room above hers must be empty, which you can note with a block. Note that this block *could* be building 2, but it does not have to be, since there are two empty rooms.

Rule 7 says T must not be in building 1 or 2. So T is in building 3, 4, or 5. Enter that information directly above your sketch.

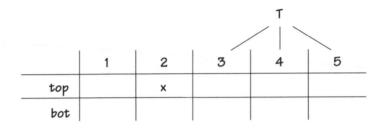

Step 4: Deductions

You have many blocks, but unfortunately, they are all too small to be placed definitively. All of the entities are mentioned in the rules, so there are no "floaters." Despite the large number of rules in this game, only one entity, T, appears in more than one rule. You can't determine anything concrete about T by combining rules 5 and 7, so move directly to the questions.

Step 5: Questions

7.   D

Because this question provides you with no new information, you know that you must find the answer using only your rules and deductions. Rule 4 tells you that M must be assigned to the room directly below K, but rule 3 specifies that the top floor of building 2 is empty. Therefore, it must be true that M is not assigned to building 2; the correct answer is (D).

8.   E

Again you're faced with a question that provides no additional information, so we'll turn to the rules. Because C must be assigned to the building directly to the right of S, S must not be assigned to building 5; (E) is correct.

9.   A

This "if" question states that B is assigned to building 4 and that C is assigned to building 5. Rule 1 tells you that B must be on the bottom floor, and rule 2 tells you that S must be in the building that is directly to the left of C's building, so your sketch looks like this:

	1	2	3	4	5
top		x		S	C
bot				B	

Eliminate (E), because you know S must be in building 4. Eliminate (B) and (D), since B and S must occupy the two rooms in building 4. Finally, eliminate (C), which must be in building 5, and since M and K must always be in the same building, M cannot be in building 5. As a result, (A) is correct.

10. C

This "if" question assigns K to building 4, so you can place your K M block. Can you place any other blocks? Our two other vertical blocks (with B and G) can apparently go anywhere, but what about the horizontal S C block? Since building 4 is full, the S C block must go in buildings 1 and 2 or 2 and 3. So either S or C must be in building 2. And since the top floor of building 2 is empty, either S or C must be on the bottom floor.

	1	2	3	4	5
top		x		K	
bot		S/C		M	

This means that choice (C), which puts Galena in building 2, must be false.

R can be in building 5, placing T in building 3, so (A) and (D) are possible:

	1	2	3	4	5
top	x	x	T	K	R
bot	G	S	C	M	B

And both B and S can be in building 1, ruling out (B) and (E):

	1	2	3	4	5
top	R	x	T	K	x
bot	B	S	C	M	G

	1	2	3	4	5
top	R	x	x	K	T
bot	S	C	G	M	B

11. B

The wording of the answer choices makes this question *five* new "if" questions. For each choice, plug in the new information, and determine the validity of the second half of the choice. (B) is correct for the same reason that (C) was correct in question 10. If R is assigned to building 2, it occupies the bottom floor while the top floor, according to rule 3, is empty. If G is assigned to building 4, rule 6 requires that the top-floor room be empty. As a result, it would be impossible to assign C to a building to the immediate right of the building where S is assigned.

12. C

This new "if" question assigns R to building 4 and S to building 2. Rule 2 tells you that C must be assigned to building 3. That means that at least one room is occupied in 2, 3, and 4. Rule 4 tells you that K and M require an entire building to themselves, and rule 6 says G also needs an entire building (with an empty room on the top floor). As a result, you know buildings 1 and 5 are fully occupied; one by K and M, one by G and x. You have B and T left. T can't go in building 4 with R (rule 5), so the only open building is building 3. B must therefore be in building 4, with R. Here's one way the motel could be arranged:

	1	2	3	4	5
top	K	x	T	R	x
bot	M	S	C	B	G

Only (C) must be true; (A) and (D) are possible, but this sketch shows that they need not be true. And choices (B) and (E) must be false.

Game 3 (Questions 13–17)

Step 1: Overview

Situation: Nurses working in a hospital

Entities: Nurses A, B, C, D, and E; jobs Paperwork, Rounds, Supervision; Time 1, 2, 3

Action: Hybrid: distribution of the nurses to the different jobs, and matching the three different time lengths to each job

Limitations: Each nurse completes one job, and each of the jobs is completed by at least one nurse

Step 2: Sketch

Use a standard distribution sketch, leaving spaces for the time each job takes. Since you know that each job is completed by at least one nurse, start by putting one blank in each group. You may find it helpful to write out the beginning of each group name, although P, R, and S works too.

Paper t =	Rounds t =	Super t =
____	____	____

Step 3: Rules

Rule 1 tells you that D's job takes 3 hours to complete; note "D = 3." Rule 2 says paperwork takes longer than supervision; note this next to your sketch: "Paper longer than Super." Rule 3 is that C's job takes longer than E's to complete; note "C longer than E." Notice how these first three rules all concern the length of time required to complete different jobs. You may be able to come back to these to make some deductions later.

Rule 4 says that more nurses complete supervision than paperwork; note "more Super than Paper."

Step 4: Deductions

Rule 4 concerns the *number* of nurses completing the different jobs, so start there. Since every job is done by at least one nurse, you already have three nurses accounted for. If more nurses do supervision than paperwork, one of our remaining two nurses *must* supervise. The fifth nurse can do either rounds or supervision (but not paperwork, because then paperwork and supervision would be completed by two nurses each).

Now let's turn to the time each job takes. Based on rule 2, you can deduce that paperwork does not take 1 hour to complete, and that supervision does not take 3 hours to complete. If supervision doesn't take 3 hours, then Damon can't supervise. After all those deductions, your sketch looks like this:

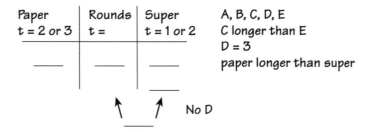

Before moving to the questions, make a note that A and B are identical, unrestricted entities.

Step 5: Questions

13. A

This partial acceptability does not specify the time each job takes. Since most of our rules deal with this information, you may not be able to use the rules one by one as you would normally. Start with the rules that concern the assignment of people to jobs. The game tells you that each job must be assigned to at least one person. In (D), no one does the rounds, so (D) can be eliminated. And rule 4 tells you that more people complete paperwork than supervision, which is not the case in (C). That leaves (A), (B), and (E).

You deduced that D cannot supervise, because D does the 3-hour job and paperwork is longer than supervision—so (E) cannot work. You also know that C's job takes longer than E's job. In (B), C does supervision while E does paperwork (the longer job), which is not allowed, and (B) can be eliminated. Therefore, (A) is correct.

14. E

This question provides you with no additional information, so you will be able to answer using only the rules and deductions. Rule 3 is that C's job takes longer to complete than E's. That makes it impossible for E's job to take 3 hours to complete, so (E) is correct.

15. E

This new "if" question tells you that supervision is the 2-hour job. Rule 2 tells you that paperwork takes longer than supervision, so paperwork must be the 3-hour job, and, consequently, rounds must be the 1-hour job. Rule 1 tells you that D completes the job that takes 3 hours, so D must do paperwork:

Paper $t = 3$	Rounds $t = 1$	Super $t = 2$
D	___	___
		___

↑   ↑
___

Rule 3 is that C's job takes longer than E's job. Since no one else can do paperwork, C must complete supervision, and E must do rounds. (E) is correct.

16. D

This question provides no additional information, so look to the rules and deductions to point the way to the answer. You deduced that D cannot supervise (because D does the 3-hour job and supervision must take less time than paperwork), so (D) is correct.

17. C

This "complete and accurate list" question asks for the choice that includes a selection of nurses who could, in a given scenario, be the only ones to perform the 1-hour job. Right away you can eliminate (E), as rule 1 specifies that D completes the 3-hour job. Eliminate (D): Since C's job must be longer than E's, C cannot complete the 1-hour job.

That leaves (A), (B), and (C). Since nothing differentiates Akiko from Brent, it is not likely that (A) would be right and (B) wrong, or vice versa. So (C) would be a good guess. But let's see why (C) is correct.

Since neither C nor E is included in remaining choices (A), (B), and (C), you know that in this scenario, neither of their jobs will be the 1-hour job. Rule 3 allows you to conclude that E completes the 2-hour job and C completes the 3-hour job. Since D also completes the 3-hour job, that makes a total of two people completing the 3-hour job. Since only one person does paperwork, and supervision does not take 3 hours, the 3-hour job, completed by C and D, must be rounds. Paperwork must therefore be the 2-hour job, and supervision must take 1 hour (rule 2). Since E does the 2-hour job, E fills up the one slot in paperwork. So you have:

Paper $t = 2$	Rounds $t = 3$	Super $t = 1$
E	C	___
	D	___

Since at least two people supervise, and everyone else is assigned already, both Akiko and Brent *must* supervise. It is not possible for only one of them to supervise. So (A) and (B) can't work, and choice (C) is correct.

Game 4 (Questions 18–23)

Step 1: Overview

Situation: Movie screenings

Entities: Seven movies (L, M, N, O, P, Q and R)

Action: Sequencing—the movies are screened over seven consecutive days

Limitations: 7 movies, 7 days, one per day

Step 2: Sketch

Since the game deals with a calendar-type sequencing of events, the easiest diagram would include seven boxes side by side, numbered 1 through 7 from left to right. Remember also to list the seven entities for easy reference.

The first rule is that M is screened on day 2 or on day 4. Jot this down next to your sketch, something like "M—2 or 4." The second rule is that P cannot be screened on days 3 or 5. Note this in your sketch. The third rule says that if N is screened on day 1, then Q is screened on day 2. Note this *if/then* next to your sketch, and write down the contrapositive as well. The fourth rule is that if R is screened on day 3, then P is screened on day 4. Another conditional, which you should handle the same way as the last one: write down the *if/then* and the contrapositive. The last rule states that L must be screened on the day following the screening of Q. Note that Q and L now form a movie block occupying two consecutive days. Your sketch and rules look something like this:

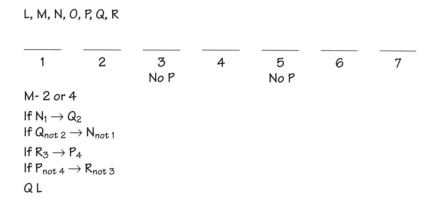

Step 4: Deductions

There are a lot of rules here, so it might seem like there should be some major deductions. However, two of your rules are conditionals—you won't be getting much from them. You know that M is either on day 2 or 4; you *could* sketch out both of these options, but there aren't any other rules that deal with M. Sure, you might see that if M is on day 2, then N can't be on day 1 (because of rule 3). But remember, when making deductions, concentrate on what *must* be true. There isn't a lot of that here, so move on to the questions.

Step 5: Questions

18. E

This is an acceptability question; apply each rule to the choices and eliminate those that violate any. Starting with the first rule, (A) does not have M on day 2 or day 4. Neither does (C), so both (A) and (C) are wrong. Choice (B) has P on day 5, violating rule 2. Rule 3 doesn't help much, but rule 4 says that when R is on day 3, P must be on day 4; (D) has R on day 3, but does not have P on day 4, so it is wrong. This leaves (E). Without even looking at it, you know (E) is the only acceptable distribution.

19. E

This "if" question places N on day 1 and then asks you to find the one choice that could be screened on day 5. Sketch out all new "ifs." If N is screened on day 1, then Q must be screened on day 2 (according to the third rule). Since Q is screened on day 2, M must be screened on day 4 to satisfy the first rule. Also, if Q is screened on day 2, then L must be screened on day 3 to satisfy rule 5.

K	Q	L	M	O/R		
1	2	3	4	5	6	7

Now you know the days on which L, M, and Q must be screened, and since none of these is day 5, eliminate (A), (B), and (D). According to the second rule, P cannot be screened on day 5, so eliminate (C) as well. The only remaining choice, (E), is correct.

20. D

This "if" question places R on day 4 and stipulates that N is screened after Q, which means that N is screened sometime after the QL block. Since R is screened on day 4, M must be screened on day 2 according to the first rule. Also, since QL makes up a block of two consecutive days, and N is screened after this block, then Q, L, and N have no other place to go except days 5, 6, and 7 respectively. This leaves P and O to be screened on the remaining days, 1 and 3.

QL ... N

P	M	O	R	Q	L	N
1	2	3	4	5	6	7

Since P cannot be screened on day 3, P must be screened on day 1 and O must be screened on day 3. Therefore, (D) must be true.

21. C

This "if" question places Q in day 1 and asks for a list of all the potential movies that could be viewed on day 3. Since Q is screened on day 1, L must be screened on day 2. This means M must be screened on day 4. Now you are left with four movies (N, O, P, and R) to be screened on the remaining days. However, P cannot be screened on day 3. According to the contrapositive of rule 4, if P is not on day 4, then R cannot be on day 3. So neither P nor R can be screened on day 3.

Q	L	N/O	M			
1	2	3	4	5	6	7
		No P, R		No P		

Only two movies remain: N and O. (C), therefore, is a complete and accurate list of all the movies that can be screened on day 3.

22. D

This "if" question creates two additional blocks that need to fit into the week's schedule. The first block is that Q is screened on the day after R is screened. This creates a three-day block of RQL. The second block places M immediately after P, creating a two-day PM block. Since P cannot be screened on day 3, the PM block must go on days 1 and 2. This appears to leave five remaining days in which to place the RQL block; it looks like the block could begin on day 3, 4, or 5. However, if R is screened on day 3, then P must be screened on day 4, which cannot happen, since P is already being screened on day 1. Therefore the RQL block will either occupy days 4, 5, and 6, or days 5, 6, and 7, with R occupying either day 4 or day 5.

Two blocks: RQL and PM

P	M	N/O	R	Q	L	O/N
1	2	3	4	5	6	7

or

P	M	N/O	O/N	R	Q	L
1	2	3	4	5	6	7

R could be screened on day 5, so (D) is correct.

23. C

This "if" question positions L and P to be screened before M. Remember that Q and L must be screened consecutively, so there are really three movies to be screened before M. This forces M to be screened on day 4. Since Q and L form a two-day block, they will either occupy days 1-2 or days 2-3 (you weren't directly told the relative order of L and P). However, if the QL block occupies days 1 and 2, this would force P to be screened on day 3, violating the second rule. Therefore, the QL block must fall on days 2 and 3.

$$QL \searrow$$
$$\qquad M$$
$$P \nearrow$$

P	Q	L	M	___	___	___
1	2	3	4	5	6	7

Q is the movie screened on day 2, and (C) is correct.